Action Learning, Leadership and Organizational Development in Public Services

Unprecedented investment is being made in leadership development across the public sector in the hope of raising organization capacity, and delivering modernization and improvement of public services. Leadership programmes and courses are mushrooming and leadership development is a core theme of organizational capacity-building initiatives. Within this activity action learning has been attracting increasing interest as an approach that can simultaneously address individual and organizational development, where learning is embedded in participants' real complex problems, as well as being social in that they interact with others from diverse contexts.

Action Learning, Leadership and Organizational Development in Public Services collates examples of this extensive action learning activity and considers the evidence for its effectiveness as an approach to public leadership development. With a rich collection of accounts drawn from across different public services, including health, local government, civil service, police and probation services, it is particularly unique in focusing on developing organizational capacity and on the wider public service system, as well as on individual development, including examples from both intra- and inter-agency contexts. The book contextualizes the growing interest in action learning, outlining the policy environment for placing emphasis on leadership for enhancing the capacity of public service organizations to address public service issues. Learning theory and theories of organization are drawn on to help explain the potency of action learning for individuals' development as well as for connecting individual and organization change.

The book draws insights from across all the contributions to raise new questions, concerning the role of the facilitator, the value of a 'bilingual' ability with both public service issues as well as with facilitation, comparisons with coaching and mentoring, and implications for employing action learning in a politicized or hierarchical environment and on a consultancy basis.

Clare Rigg is Senior Lecturer in the School of Business and Social Studies at the Institute of Technology, Tralee, Ireland. She previously worked at the University of Birmingham's School of Public Policy and has used action learning and action research on a variety of organization development, leadership and management development programmes.

Sue Richards is Director of the Centre for Strategic Leadership at the National School of Government, London. She has performed a number of advisory and governance roles in relation to public service, having been a special advisor to various parliamentary select committees, an Audit Commissioner and a member of the Advisory Board of the Office of Public Services Reform.

Routledge Studies in Human Resource Development
Edited by Monica Lee, Lancaster University, UK

HRD theory is changing rapidly. Recent advances in theory and practice, how we conceive of organizations and of the world of knowledge, have led to the need to reinterpret the field. This series aims to reflect and foster the development of HRD as an emergent discipline.

Encompassing a range of different international, organizational, methodological and theoretical perspectives, the series promotes theoretical controversy and reflective practice.

Action Learning, Leadership and Organizational Development in Public Services

Edited by Clare Rigg with
Sue Richards

Routledge
Taylor & Francis Group

LONDON AND NEW YORK

First published 2006
by Routledge
2 Park Square, Milton Park, Abingdon, Oxon OX14 4RN

Simultaneously published in the USA and Canada
by Routledge
270 Madison Ave, New York, NY 10016

Routledge is an imprint of the Taylor & Francis Group, an informa business

Typeset in Garamond by
Book Now Ltd
Printed and bound in Great Britain by
Biddles Ltd, King's Lynn

British Library Cataloguing in Publication Data
A catalogue record for this book is available from the British Library

Library of Congress Cataloging in Publication Data
Action learning, leadership, and organizational development in public
services/edited by Clare Rigg with Sue Richards.
    p. cm.
    Includes bibliographical references.
    1. Great Britain–Officials and employees–In-service training. 2. Local
officials and employees–Inservice training–Great Britain. 3. Active
learning–Great Britain. 4. Leadership–Study and teaching–Great Britain.
5. Organizational learning–Great Britain. 6. Organizational change–Great
Britain. I. Rigg, Clare. II. Richards, Sue.

JN450.I5A55 2006
352.23'6–dc22   2005037230

ISBN10: 0–415–37270–4

ISBN13: 978–0–415–37270–1

Contents

Illustrations

Figures

Tables

Acknowledgements

There are many people whose ideas have contributed to this book, through their comments and conversations, experiences they have discussed with us, and writings that have stimulated us. In particular, we acknowledge those action learning participants who have been so generous and open in contributing their views. We thank the reviewers of our original proposal for their thoughtful and valuable feedback. Others who provided sharp commentary along the way particularly include Kiran Trehan and Simon Warren. Fay Wilson, Amanda Williams and Caroline Rance provided invaluable transcription and administrative support. Finally our thanks to our Routledge editor, Terry Clague, for his support in seeing this project through.

Contributors

Frank Blackler is Professor of Organizational Behaviour at Lancaster University and Director of the University's Centre for Collaborative Intervention in the Public Sector. He is concerned with the applicability of social science theories and concepts. His current work centres on the development of theories of practice and action research methodologies.

David Coghlan is a member of the School of Business Studies at the University of Dublin, Trinity College, Ireland. His research and teaching interests lie in the areas of organization development, action research, action learning, clinical inquiry, practitioner research and doing action research in one's own organization. His most recent books include *Doing Action Research in Your Own Organization* (co-authored with Teresa Brannick, Sage, 2001), *Changing Healthcare Organizations* (co-authored with Eilish McAuliffe, Blackhall, 2003) and *Managers Learning in Action* (co-edited with T. Dromgoole, P. Joynt and P. Sorensen, Routledge, 2004).

Paul Coughlan is Associate Professor of Operations Management at the University of Dublin, School of Business Studies, Trinity College, Ireland, where, since 1993, he has researched and taught in the areas of operations management and product development. His active research interests relate to the continuous improvement of practices and performance in product development and manufacturing operations. He is president of the Board of the European Institute for Advanced Studies in Management, and a member of the board of the European Operations Management Association.

Pam Fox has for the last seven years been working nationally on local government modernization and improvement, including three years as a member of the Local Government Modernisation Team at the Office of the Deputy Prime Minister where she was the leading adviser on new political management arrangements. She has carried out a number of national studies and published extensively on leadership, diversity, political management arrangements and member/officer relations. For the past two years a significant proportion of her work has been in supporting authorities carrying out research on comprehensive performance assessment and improvement planning. Prior to this she had worked for twelve years as a senior manager for a variety of local authorities (three London boroughs, a district council and a new unitary authority). Her last post in local government was as Deputy Chief Executive of Portsmouth City Council.

Andy Kennedy is Director of Lysis Consulting, a specialist consulting firm working with healthcare organizations. He was formerly a senior fellow of the King's Fund, Honorary Professorial Fellow at the Lancaster University Management School, and Executive Director of the Winterthur Health Initiative, Switzerland.

Michael Lyons is Deputy Chairman of the Audit Commission, Chairman of the English Cities Fund and Professor of Public Policy at the University of Birmingham. He has recently undertaken independent reviews of relocation and asset management on behalf of the government and is currently exploring the future of council tax. He was formerly Chief Executive of three major local authorities – Birmingham City Council (1994–2001), Nottinghamshire County Council (1990–4) and Wolverhampton Borough Council (1985–90). He spent a short period as an elected councillor between 1980 and 1983.

Michael Marquardt is Professor of Human Resource Development at George Washington University and Executive Director of the Global Institute of Action Learning. He is author of 80 articles as well as 15 books including *Action Learning in Action* (Davies-Black, 1999), *Building the Learning Organization* (Davies-Black, 2002) and *Optimizing the Power of Action Learning* (Davies-Black, 2004). He has introduced action learning to nearly 100 organizations such as Nokia, Caterpillar, Alcoa, Boeing, Constellation, Samsung, Singapore Airlines and the United Nations Development Programme. He has held senior management positions within the Overseas Education Fund, Tradetec, Grolier and the American Society for Training and Development.

Geoff Mead is a Visiting Research Fellow in the School of Management, University of Bath, UK. Having combined a 30-year career as a public service professional with a passionate interest in education and development, he now works as a freelance educator and organizational consultant whilst continuing to develop his interests as a writer and storyteller. The theme of his Ph.D., which he completed in 2002 at the Centre for Action Research in Professional Practice, University of Bath, is realizing a scholarship of living inquiry – bringing lived experience into the realms of conscious inquiry, research and scholarship. His current interests include experimenting with artistic and creative forms of representation to enliven research writing, and exploring the role of storytelling in sense-making and community-building.

Sue Richards is Professor of Public Management at the School of Public Policy, University of Birmingham, currently seconded to the National

School of Government in London as Director of the Centre for Strategic Leadership. She has wide experience as an academic analyst and consultant in public policy and management, particularly on cross-cutting issues in public service. She has been a member of the Audit Commission for England and Wales, and has held a number of government advisory positions. She has led and taught on many public leadership and top management programmes.

Clare Rigg is Senior Lecturer in the School of Business and Social Studies at the Institute of Technology, Tralee, Ireland. Her early work was in local government and the voluntary sector working on urban regeneration. For many years she has worked with practitioners from all sectors, integrating action learning and action research to issues of organization development, leadership and management development and improving inter-agency working. She has researched and written on action learning, critical action learning, management learning and human resource development.

Deborah Waddill has provided instructional and curriculum design consultation services for the past 27 years in the capacity of manager, educator and designer. As a manager of an instructional design group, Deborah has earned awards and letters of commendation from the Global Institute of Action Learning, AT&T, the Federal Deposit Insurance Corporation, the International Society for Performance Improvement and elsewhere, for the design and delivery of high-quality learning products. Deborah earned her doctorate in education through the George Washington University's Executive Leadership Program, and a masters degree in educational technology leadership. She has published on the topics of action learning and e-learning design.

Martin Willis is a Senior Lecturer in the Institute of Local Government Studies at the University of Birmingham. He has previous experience in local government both in social care and as an elected councillor. His current work includes research on user-centred outcomes and user-led evaluation of service delivery. He facilitates a range of learning sets and leadership programmes for public service managers.

Carol Yapp has 15 years' experience in local government as a manager of training and development services and providing internal organizational development consultancy. She has extensive experience of group facilitation, coaching, mentoring and action learning. As an internal consultant her roles have included member development, performance management, learning strategy, employee development planning and corporate planning. Since 2003 she has worked at the Institute of Local Government Studies at the University of Birmingham. Her research interest is in managers and organizational models of management in 'excellent' and 'recovering' authorities.

1 Developing public service leadership

The context for action learning

Clare Rigg

Introduction

Leadership, civic leadership, distributed leadership, community leadership, leadership capacity-building – is there a clue here? Great faith is being placed in leadership to deliver the modernization and improvement of public services. In the hope of raising organization capacity, unprecedented investment is being made in management and leadership development across the public sector, particularly in health, local government, education and civil service organizations. Leadership programmes and courses are mushrooming; investment is growing, and leadership development is a core theme of organizational capacity-building programmes. Within this activity are a broad array of approaches to learning and development, including a growing interest in action learning as an approach that can simultaneously address individual and organizational development.

But how confident can we be that this investment in individuals' leadership capacity will translate into improved organizational capacity? And how optimistic can we be that it will help that other fundamental of modernization – partnership – and aid the joined-up multi-agency approaches that it is so widely agreed are required if inroads are to be made into the complex systemic public policy issues that face us? Whilst increasing sums are being invested in leadership development, there remains a significant gap in practical understanding of how individual learning and development can best translate into changed organization or systemic practice.

This book focuses specifically on the role of action learning in developing organization and leadership capacity in public services. It comprises an edited collection of chapters on a range of themes that draw from across different public services, including approaches to individual and organizational development, with examples from both intra- and inter-agency contexts. In this way it includes illustrations from internal organization development as well as partnership working across the public service system.

The book has three main aims, which are to:

1   present accounts of different ways in which action learning is currently

being deployed in leadership and organization development in public
service organizations;

2   provide an evaluative critique of the outcomes, lessons and issues in terms
    of capabilities developed, resources, opportunities and constraints for
    action learning approaches;

3   explore implications for future approaches to the development of public
    service leaders and organizations.

Fundamental to these issues are questions of what is meant by 'leadership' so
that it might be developed, and what is action learning, so that it attracts
the hopes of delivering enhanced leadership? This introductory chapter sets
the scene by introducing key ideas of action learning, outlining public
sector interest in leadership development, and exploring different ways in
which 'action learning' is being deployed in leadership and management
development in a range of countries. These main themes are expanded in
ensuing chapters and the final role of this introductory chapter is to provide a
signpost to the structure of the book overall and the content of each individual
chapter.

What is meant by 'action learning'?

The second question above asked what there is about action learning that
might promise enhanced leadership. This section looks at early and more
recent uses of what is termed action learning, with a view to clarifying core
ideas.

Reg Revans is generally described as the father of action learning, starting
with his work in the 1940s in the UK coal industry and the Belgian Inter-
University Programme (Revans, 1983). When pit managers had problems, he
encouraged them to meet together in small groups, on site, and ask one another
questions about what they saw in order to find their own solutions, rather than
bring in 'experts' to solve their problems for them. Revans' key idea was that
'there can be no learning without action and no (sober and deliberate) action
without learning'. In current times there are many and varied interpretations
of action learning across the world. Raelin, in his introduction to the *Management Learning* special issue on 'The Action Dimension in Management' (1999:
115), draws from Brooks and Watkins (1994) and categorizes action learning as
one of six forms of action-focused approaches to management and organization
development, along with action research, participatory research, action science,
developmental action inquiry and co-operative inquiry.[1]

To these six could easily be added other action methods, such as appreciative
inquiry (Cooperrider, 1995), and transformative action research (Bonnet *et al.*,
2001), as well as earlier experiential learning approaches such as Freire's
advocation of dialogue, praxis, working with others and conscientization
(Freire and Shor, 1987) and more recent ideas such as situated learning (Lave

and Wenger, 1991). Raelin (1999) argued that, despite the variety, the six action methods as he categorized them had in common two key features. One was that they tended to be more long-term and with multiple aims linked to the development of useful new knowledge and learning in specific contextual situations. The second was an emphasis on relationships between action and concurrent feedback, for the purposes of both improving knowledge and developing more effective action.

Recent research at the Revans Institute (Pedler, Burgoyne and Brook, 2005: 10) concluded that action learning is more an ethos than a definable method, but that there are certain key original principles, what they term RCP (Revans' classical principles), namely:

- the requirement for action as the basis for learning;
- profound personal development resulting from reflection upon action;
- working with problems (that have no right answers) not puzzles (which are susceptible to expert knowledge);
- problems are sponsored and aimed at organizational as well as personal development;
- action learners work in sets of peers to support and challenge each other ('comrades in adversity' as Revans (1982) termed them);
- the search for fresh questions and 'q' (questioning insight) takes primacy over access to expert knowledge or 'p'.

Pedler, Burgoyne and Brook also found other features that are commonly employed even though not advocated by Revans (Pedler *et al.*, 2005: 5), such as sets of about six people; the use of facilitators; and tasks or problems that are chosen independently by individuals rather than given to them, and worked on by them individually rather than collectively.

Interestingly Pedler, Burgoyne and Brook (2005: 12) report a number of instances where people use the terminology of action learning, but in contexts that others would dispute because of the extent to which they depart from the classical Revans principles. Examples include:

- **critical action learning** which 'engages participants in a process of drawing from critical perspectives to make connections between their learning and work experiences, to understand and change interpersonal and organizational practices' (Rigg and Trehan, 2004: 1);
- **auto-action learning**, where an individual works alone through cycles of action, reflection and learning, systematically and regularly using a set of questions to structure a review;
- **action mentoring or coaching**, in which one-to-one relations of mentor–mentee or between peers employ learning through cycles of action and reflection;
- **on-line/remote action learning**, through which questions designed to promote reflection are posed on-line or through tele-conferencing;

- **self-managed action learning**, in which a group facilitates themselves;
- **business-driven action learning** (Boshyk, 2002: 99) which emphasizes organization tasks and downplays personal development.

Pedler, Burgoyne and Brook's study makes clear that within the widely employed terminology of action learning the meaning for practitioners and the experience of participants vary considerably. These ideas on the variety and objectives of action learning will be used at various points in this book as a framework for reflecting on the nature of action learning being used in the chapter accounts of practice, and will be revisited in the final chapter. In the next section we examine the UK public services context in which action learning is thriving as a route to expanding leadership potential and enhancing organization performance.

Leadership – essential ingredient of public services improvement

Leadership has been positioned as central to the modernization of local government (DTLR, 2002), and links between management and leadership development and improved performance are increasingly made (CEML, 2002a; DfES/DTI, 2002; Alimo-Metcalfe and Nyfield, 2002). In the past few years Britain has seen a multitude of public service leadership colleges and academies springing up, including the NHS (National Health Service) Leadership Centre (recently subsumed within the Institute for Innovation and Improvement), the National Police Leadership Centre (part of Centrex, the central Police Training and Development Authority), the National College for School Leadership, the Defence Leadership Centre (part of the Defence Academy of the United Kingdom), the Local Government Leadership Centre, the National School of Government for the Civil Service, as well as a Leadership Foundation for Higher Education and a Centre for Excellence in Leadership for the learning and skills sector (further education, adult learning). Additionally, the Improvement and Development Agency (IDeA) for local government runs a virtual Leadership Academy with the aim of developing political leadership amongst elected members. In Wales and Scotland, there is some increased cross-sectoral development, such as the Scottish Leadership Foundation, but sector-specific institutions still prevail, such as the Welsh National Leadership and Innovation Agency for Healthcare or the Scottish Head Teacher Leadership Academy. In the voluntary or third sector, there is no equivalent sector-wide college or academy for voluntary sector leadership, but there are several new initiatives designed to develop good leadership, such as the National Council for Voluntary Organizations' (NCVO) leadership programme for Chief Executives and Chairs, and work by ACEVO (the Association of Chief Executives of Voluntary Organizations) and the Directory for Social Change.

It is clear there has been a recent upsurge in enthusiasm for and investment in public management and leadership development. Following somewhat behind, in most cases, has been exploration of the kinds of leadership capabilities public organizations might require, whether or not they are distinctive, and what approaches to leadership development might be most appropriate. In terms of desirable leadership capabilities, it has long been a contentious issue as to whether generic management competences can be prescribed across all sectors and types of organization. Work by Perren and Burgoyne (2002) which presented a framework of management and leadership capabilities, tentatively extended earlier profiling of generic management standards. However, no particular attention is paid in their research to public organization managers. Gold (2002) incidentally offers a little more insight in his study of management and leadership within professions, in that many professionals are central to public services (such as nursing, other medical professions and librarians). He found a general rejection of generic management standards, though an interest in building on what he calls 'an irreducible core' of management capabilities (Gold, 2002: 6). The Council for Excellence in Management and Leadership (CEML, 2002a) investigated both public and private sector organizations, but said little that specifically enhanced our understanding of public leadership development requirements.

The various public service leadership colleges and centres have expressed their thinking on leadership more recently, in the development of competency or capability frameworks. Interestingly, and in conflict with any one system approach, there is little convergence on definitions or frameworks, with each of the above sectors developing their own. For example, for UK local government a Leadership Development Commission (LDC) published a strategy for leadership development in local government, that both presents a framework of leadership capacities and offers definitions that differentiate between management and leadership as follows: 'Management is the effective handling of complex situations and demands to deliver what should be happening, be it a service or an initiative' whilst 'leadership is creating and "making happen what wouldn't otherwise happen". Above all it is getting significant new things done and improvements made' (LDC, 2004: 14).

The National College for School Leadership has a leadership development framework derived from ten key propositions about school leadership, 'which focus on values, creating an active learning community and on the importance of distributed leadership' (National College for School Leadership, 2005). The Defence Leadership Centre differs again, with a definition that: 'leadership is visionary, it is the projection of personality and character to inspire the team to achieve the desired outcome. There is no prescription for leadership and no prescribed style of leadership' (Defence Leadership Centre, 2005).

The National Health Service Leadership Centre developed a NHS Leadership Qualities Framework. However, in July 2005 the centre's work became integrated into the NHS Institute for Innovation and Improvement. This is an interesting, more integrated approach, with the aim of supporting the rapid adoption of new ideas and guidance on change. Leadership capacity-building is combined with developing capability for service transformation, technology and product innovation and learning (National Health Service Institute for Innovation and Improvement, 2005).

In summary, the UK presents a picture of increasing investment in public leadership development and a growing infrastructure in the form of sector-specific colleges, centres and academies. However, we see little deliberate convergence in their thinking on the nature of leadership capabilities required. Some lone but significant views advocate development of leadership as a route for enhancing the capacity of organizations to facilitate the kinds of inter-agency collaboration which now characterizes responses to many complex cross-cutting issues (Chesterman and Horne, 2002; SEU, 2000). Indeed there are some voices that argue that joined-up government would be better served by a one-system approach that viewed 'all those who contribute to public policy and the delivery of public services as a single set' (Lyons, 2003/4: 9). The implication of this view is for shared leadership development – shared across public sector organizations if not alongside private sector as well. An exemplar of such cross-sectoral development is Leaders UK, a joint venture between the UK Cabinet Office, the CBI, the NHS, local government, the criminal justice and education sectors, the Association of Chief Executives in Voluntary Organizations and the Association of Chief Police Officers (Leaders UK, 2005). However, such integrative development is rare.

This chapter has argued so far that 'leadership' is seen as essential to improving and modernizing public services, although there is little consensus across different parts of the UK public services on the definition of the leadership capabilities required. Despite this, action learning as an approach to development is experiencing a resurgence of interest within public bodies, for example being specified within tender documentation for leadership and organization development programmes. In the next section we look at examples of the deployment of action learning within leadership development, both within the UK and internationally, and in particular the rationales for expecting this to impact on organizational capacity.

Approaches to leadership development

There is a pressing need to extend our knowledge of the relative effectiveness of different approaches to the development of leadership capabilities required for public organizations. There remains a significant gap in terms of applying learning theory to developing a practical understanding of how people learn and therefore might develop leadership capabilities. In leadership and organization development policy this is either neglected entirely or left implicit. Of the various leadership centres and academies described above, only one, the National College for School Leadership, refers explicitly to principles of learning in developing leadership. The UK Council for Excellence in Management and Leadership (CEML) refers to this with their concern to see 'that there is better understanding of the relationship between teaching, learning and management practice' (CEML, 2002a: 13). Although uptake of management qualifications may increase, this does not necessarily equate to capacity-building. In particular, doubts have been cast over whether MBAs have been a good preparation for leadership, particularly in abilities to translate theory into practice and in developing inter-personal skills (CEML, 2002b; Deutschman, 1991). The CEML report goes on to say that the 1990s saw a shift away from 'teaching in the traditional classroom sense' and 'Action learning and facilitative support to individuals and groups have become the aspirational models for management development' (CEML, 2002b: 24).

Within some initiatives action learning or action inquiry has been embraced as a way of supporting leadership development, where learning is embedded in participants' real complex problems, as well as being social in that participants interact with different people from varying contexts (see Pedler, 1997; Revans, 1980; and Weil and McGill, 1989, for example). This is potentially encouraging in the light of theory that suggests people learn more deeply, and with more integration between the development of their practical capability and their conceptual understanding, than when their management/leadership education is primarily an individual theoretical experience (Argyris *et al.*, 1985; Bateson, 1973; Belenky *et al.*, 1986; Kolb, 1984; Vince, 1996).

However, even with action-orientated approaches to individual development the link to organizational impact is more hoped for than strongly established. Some evaluations have followed Kirkpatrick's model (1975) and have also addressed the value of development for participants in terms of organization benefits. But the latter is more easily said than done. Recent thinking suggests that the most effective organizational interventions are with intra-organizational teams, rather than decanting individuals out of the workplace into mixed organizational groups (Hawkins and Chesterman, 2004). In a similar vein, Vince (2004a) also argues that action learning should not be seen as a group process for individual problem-solving, but as a collective process in a specific context for inquiring into actual organizational projects and practices.

Internationally, there is a wealth of examples of the use of action learning approaches in public as well as private and voluntary/community sector development. In Australia, action learning has been used in the Australian Flexible Learning Framework which funds a range of professional development activities focused on managers and practitioners (Australian Flexible Learning Framework, 2001). The Ireland Trainers Network used action learning to develop trainers in partnership groups across the country (Ireland Trainers Network, 2003). Denmark has some interesting applications to continuing and in-service training for vocational college teachers (Training Village, 2003). Canada's School of Public Service includes an Accelerated Executive Development Program for aspiring senior managers, a core component of which is action learning 'defined as a process of collaborative inquiry among a group of committed and competent people who . . . reflect on and address real work situations or challenges that are important to them and their organization'. They use the process of questioning and reflection to help each other learn from their experiences, to challenge their beliefs and their assumptions, and to open up new possibilities for action. The development of listening and questioning skills are critical to the group's success as well as to individuals' competence as public service leaders (Canada School of Public Management, 2005).

The World Bank Participation and Civic Engagement Group promotes methods and approaches, incorporating action learning, that encourage stakeholders, including service users, to influence and share control over priority-setting, policy-making, resource allocations and access to public goods and services (World Bank, 2005).

It is timely to take stock of this extensive recent action learning activity to review the evidence for its effectiveness as an approach to public leadership development. The level of investment of time, money and hope make the following questions deeply pertinent:

- When different programmes and initiatives claim to use action learning, what do they mean, and do they mean the same, similar or very different things?
- What value does action learning add to public leadership development?
- What does action learning offer in terms of public service capacity-building that not only develops the individual but also tackles other objectives such as organization capacity-building, partnership-building, networking, working with diversity, and collective problem-solving?
- How can we know? What is the evidence that investment in individuals' leadership capacity will translate into improved organizational capacity?

These are questions that the chapters in this book provide insights into, and that will ultimately be revisited in more integrated depth in the concluding chapter.

The shape of the book

This book draws together a collection of chapters from across different public services, including health, local government, the civil service, the police and the probation services. Each recounts experiences of using action learning in diverse contexts, including as an approach to individual, organizational and systemic development, and providing examples of both intra- and inter-agency work. In Reason and Bradbury's (2001) terms, this can be expressed as work with first-person inquiry, changing individual practice; second-person inquiry, two or more people exploring mutual concerns; and third-person inquiry, seeking wider systemic change with others outside the learning/inquiry group. As a result, this book is a rich collection of accounts of different ways in which action learning is currently being deployed in leadership development, from internal organization development as well as partnership working across the wider public service system.

Each account is written reflexively by the facilitator of the action learning process, so is from their perspective, although in most chapters participants also contributed, either through commenting on a draft or providing their voice on the experience. The concluding chapter presents an evaluative critique of the outcomes, lessons and issues in terms of capabilities developed, resources, opportunities and constraints for action learning approaches to development of public service leaders and organizations.

Following this introductory chapter the book is structured into five further sections. The first section, 'Context', contains three chapters that together contextualize the growing interest in action learning for leadership and organization development. In Chapter 2 Sue Richards outlines the policy environment for placing emphasis on leadership in the UK government's modernization and improvement agenda of enhancing the capacity of public service organizations to address public service issues. She situates the expectations of leadership in the context of twentieth-century paradigm changes in the purpose and accountability of public services and the role of professionals within them. In Chapter 3 Mike Marquardt and Deborah Waddill navigate learning theory to show how an understanding of ways individuals learn helps us appreciate why action learning might be so potent for individuals' development. Clare Rigg extends this theme in Chapter 4 to question what the grounds are for hoping that engaging individuals in action learning might deliver organizational developments. She explores how applications of action learning are not only rooted in different philosophies of learning and change, but also in different theories of organization which, in turn, help explain its potential impact on connecting individual and organization change.

The second part of the book contains nine accounts of action learning employed in practice. These are presented in three sections: 'Practice – developing leaders', 'Practice – developing organizations' and 'Practice – networks and partnerships: developing the public policy system'. Chapters 5–7 are examples of action learning employed with leaders in three different parts of the public sector. In Chapter 5, Michael Lyons, a three-times local authority chief executive himself, reflects in interview with Clare Rigg on the experience of convening three learning groups specifically set up for new local authority chief executives. He traces the diverse and common issues which emerged in all three groups. He reviews differences in the dynamics of the groups and the perceived benefits identified by participants, and reflects on his own role as experienced practitioner/novice facilitator, drawing parallels between facilitating and coaching/mentoring. Chapter 6, by Sue Richards, is an account of a ten-year-old action learning set of chief probation officers, which explores the value of action learning to them as new and maturing leaders. She explores the rationale and implications of the original choice of facilitator as public policy expert to help members navigate their changing professional territory. A key theme she ends with is the implication of trying to make action learning work when hierarchy entered the group. Working with experienced leaders, Frank Blackler and Andy Kennedy in Chapter 7 describe an action learning programme designed to 'renew and refresh' long-serving chief executives in the English National Health Service who were facing considerable performance pressures. They present the theoretical underpinning of the programme, based on activity theory, and explore how they used this to inform a design that could help participants re-engage with their objectives and operate with resilience in the face of the conflicts and tensions in their organizations.

Whilst investment in individual leadership implicitly hopes for organization-wide benefits, Chapters 8–10 are accounts of action learning interventions where the primary objective was to achieve organization development. In Chapter 8 Carol Yapp draws from her work in local government, and reiterates the themes of hierarchy and in-organization context in an experience of introducing a local authority divisional management team to action learning. With reference to deepening levels of action learning, she considers the challenges presented both to the facilitator and the participants in their particular context, and reflects self-critically on her interventions in the face of discomfort, tension and flight. Chapter 9 has further echoes of the tensions of working with action learning approaches in a hierarchical context, with Geoff Mead's account of developing police leaders. As an insider-facilitator his experience conveys a mixture of reception and rejection by an organization culture unfamiliar with many of the collaborative principles he tried to work with. This is followed in Chapter 10 by a different kind of organization-wide intervention that used action learning sets with senior officers from local authorities deemed poorly performing by the UK government's Comprehensive Performance Assessment (CPA) framework. Here the agenda prioritized development of the organizations over that of individual participants, and there are some interesting insights into the interconnection and at times tensions between the individual and organizational levels.

Chapters 11–13 turn to systemic interventions, with examples of action learning used with the primary aim of developing the public service system more broadly. In Chapter 11 Geoff Mead describes the UK Cabinet Office-established Public Service Leaders Scheme for rising leaders across the sector, drawn from central and local government, health, police and voluntary organizations. This was a rolling three-year programme with an annual intake of 70–100 participants, in which action inquiry was integral to the scheme, with participants coming together regularly in facilitated action inquiry groups. Under the umbrella question 'How can we improve our practice as public service leaders?', the groups pursued a wide range of self-generated inquiries. Reflecting on how and why the process did not take the form originally intended, the chapter draws on the concept of communicative space to offer valuable insights into the tensions between differing perspectives of the various stakeholders involved in such a complex, systemic programme. Chapter 12, by Martin Willis, adds a different angle with an account of four partnership action learning sets designed to develop collaborative relationships across health and social care, as part of the Department of Health-funded Social Care Leadership Development Initiative (SCLDI). Reviewing their different trajectories, he highlights tensions between processes of individual learning and addressing organizational tasks. Critical reflections on his own facilitation role lead to some interesting observations about the pull to structure, control and avoid conflict. In Chapter 13 David Coghlan and Paul Coughlan explore how action learning can also perform a role in contributing to inter-organizational learning and change. They present two case studies, one of a public sector organization moving into the private sector and the other a cross-organizational action learning set combining a contractor and their suppliers. This chapter offers different insights which are particularly pertinent to a world of more fluid boundaries between sectors in the provision of public services, in which public service managers are increasingly confronted with private–public partnerships and supplier relationships.

In the final section, 'Conclusion', the editors draw from these three themes of practice to illustrate relations between individual, organizational and systemic levels of public leadership, and to draw together overarching themes and outstanding questions. The final chapter draws from all the contributors to provide an evaluative critique of the outcomes, lessons and issues in terms of capabilities developed, resources, opportunities and constraints for action learning approaches. It ends with an exploration of implications for future action learning-based approaches to the development of public service leaders and organizations.

Note

1 Action research is a process wherein researchers participate in studies both as participants and observers, with the explicit intention of addressing deep-rooted organizational issues through recurring cycles of action and reflection. Participatory research is when ordinary people play a key role in undertaking research, for the purpose of knowledge creation and with a wider social change agenda. Action science is an approach using reflection-in-action, i.e. based on the principle that people can improve their interpersonal and organizational effectiveness by exploring the beliefs that underlie their actions. Developmental action inquiry, described by Torbert (1999), interweaves first-person inquiry, second-person inquiry and third-person inquiry with the aim of becoming aware of transformations between intuition, thinking, communicative practices and effects on others. Co-operative inquiry is a radically participative form of inquiry in which all those involved are both co-researchers and co-subjects, participating in the context that is being researched.

Section I

Context

2 New public policy paradigm – new leadership

Sue Richards

Introduction

Joined-up government has become the fashionable solution to many of the problems of co-ordination and control in government. It raises issues of organizational and system design which are inherent in any complex situation. All governments wish to use public policy to achieve change in the real world, and require joined-up government and public service in order to do so. They have to decide how to define their problem and what the best policy is for solving it, how best to mobilize support for these changes, what policy instruments are likely to lead to the right results, how to allocate resources to incentivize and enable people to deliver those results, how to deploy organizational responsibilities and accountabilities for delivery, and how to evaluate and learn from the experience in order to do better next time. How this is done in any given circumstance is likely to reflect the core strategic purposes a particular government sets itself. What are the key themes by which they will be judged? The approach to organizational and system design also reflects the key drivers and enablers of change in the wider political, economic, social and technological environment, all of which will impact on a government's capacity to achieve its purpose.

This chapter argues that an older paradigm of public policy and public service, in place in the three decades following the Second World War, was characterized by government joined up through policy consensus and the community of professional practice. As the conditions for this paradigm decayed, it was replaced by another paradigm, which was designed to achieve increased economy and efficiency in public spending, but, in achieving these, fragmented the system for delivering service outputs. This paradigm too ran its course, achieving part of the core purpose of increased economic competitiveness, until being replaced, as seems to be happening now, by a new paradigm, which focuses on the effectiveness of the outcomes of public policy and service. All governments have to deal with issues of co-ordination, but this chapter argues that these have been made particularly problematic at the present time by the legacy of past paradigms of public policy and public service, which perpetuates fragmentation. In this context one of the key enablers of modernization and improvement is seen as being enhanced leadership capability, of individuals generally as well as distributed across organizations. The chapter concludes by exploring the implications of the public policy context for leadership.

Paradigm change in public policy

In order to understand the nature of the current situation, it is important to explore more of its origins. There appear to be three fundamental paradigms of public policy and public service in the UK's post-war history, each relating to the 'core project' of governments at the time, involving mission and strategy which for much of the time came to dominate the policy agenda. These are summarized in Table 2.1.

The first paradigm had its peak in the wartime and post-war creation of a welfare state providing planned security from cradle to grave, with a protected economy to maintain full employment and powerful professionals to ration resources according to their judgements about need. This paradigm itself grew out of a reaction to a previous paradigm characterized by ad hoc and uncertain provision of welfare, provided by local boards, friendly societies and charitable bodies, and from laissez-faire economic management, which led to periods of high unemployment. Planning and co-ordination at the top combined with a pluralist distribution of power between central and local government, and between elected politicians and key groups of public service professionals. This distributed system of decision-making ensured that many different perspectives contributed. Changes in the nature of services delivered required the development of a consensus amongst the key players. Change did happen but it took time to happen.

The characteristic organizational form was the large bureaucracy, ideally suited to the delivery of planned outputs to a standard level in conditions of environmental stability. Mintzberg (1993) divides bureaucracy into two forms – machine bureaucracy and professional bureaucracy – and both were characteristic of this time. In some cases the task to be undertaken by the organization was straightforward enough to be turned into a set of simple rules and procedures requiring little front-line discretion – as for instance in the case of

Table 2.1 Paradigm change in public policy and public service

	Public expenditure	Structural form	Public	Centralization	Fatal flaw
1 Input (1945)	High tax, high spend	'Functional', bureaucratic	Client	Power sharing	Not cost conscious
2 Throughput (late 1970s)	More for less – efficiency	Purchaser/ provider	Consumer	Centralized	Wicked issues
3 Outcome (1997?)	Effectiveness	Matrix/ partnership	Citizen	Tight/loose	Yet to emerge

delivering non-discretionary social security benefits. Machine bureaucracies like this deliver standard outputs by having a standardized process. Where the task is not so easily simplified, as for instance in the application of complex medical sciences to observable symptoms in the human body, the more appropriate model is the professional bureaucracy, where standardization is through the skills and knowledge of the front-line practitioners, acquired through initial training and then through continuing professional development. This description has been elaborated in order to remind us what in this first post-war paradigm were the characteristic modes of co-ordination – joined-up government through planning and professional consensus.

There were characteristic flaws in this paradigm – the paternalism of dominant professionals who decided things for us, not with us, and the relatively weak levers for keeping down costs. But no one talked about 'joined-up government' because they were actually doing it, in a form appropriate for the paradigm. In the end, this paradigm lost legitimacy and the way was opened by the end of the 1970s for a wholly different recipe. The second paradigm was born out of the decay of the social and economic conditions which had earlier applied, the rise of individualism, and the fiscal crisis that accompanied it. The core project of this new paradigm was global competitiveness: a reaction against the perceived failure of protectionism in economic policy.

For public services the significance of this change was massively increased attention to unit costs and their reduction, as the state 'overhead' was cut back, and increases in the opportunity for the private sector as public services were opened up to market forces. Local government and public service professionals were subject to measures which reduced their scope for autonomous action, and powers were concentrated in Whitehall – perhaps necessary to break the old paradigm. The pressure to reduce costs led to new organizational design principles coming into play. Simplified structures, focused on delivery of cost – and in some cases quality improvement within narrow boundaries – became the order of the day. The key change was a belief in the necessity of separating out the strategic commissioning of services from their provision, thus avoiding 'producer capture' by public service professionals. Executive agencies in central government, the purchaser–provider split in health, and the divide into client and contractor functions in local government – these were all structures designed to improve performance by narrowing the focus and injecting competition. These developments in the United Kingdom were mirrored in many other countries as they responded to the same international pressures – although the response in each case was conditioned by its own internal factors.

For the United Kingdom there were many improvements in productivity, overcoming the underlying flaw in the 'welfare state' paradigm – lack of cost consciousness. But all such institutional arrangements have their flaws, and the flaw in this 'efficiency' paradigm was that power was centralized into a Whitehall structure and a culture built on silo principles. In the past, the presence of corporate planning mechanisms, with collective responsibility in the cabinet at the centre, and the more distributed nature of power – in local government and amongst professionals – had counterbalanced this tendency. Now, however, these checks and balances were reduced in importance.

One effect of this was the emergence of 'wicked problems' (Clarke and Stewart, 1997; Jervis and Richards, 1997). The term 'wicked problems' was identified as a product of the silo structures, occurring because rational efficient behaviour – narrowly defined – had consequences for other policy and service areas, creating irrationality and inefficiency at an overall system level. The classic example is the difficult pupil, excluded from school by a head teacher who needs to improve his or her school's performance measurement and thus position on league tables of measured outputs. The young person then frequently becomes a charge on the criminal justice budget in the first instance, and then later on the social security budget as they face adult life ill-equipped for modern employment conditions.

That kind of problem is obviously the product of the perverse incentives created by a narrowly defined, output-driven performance management system, and the term 'wicked problem' has been used to refer to this. But the term had a slightly different meaning originally. It was used in the operational research field to denote an intractable problem that we do not know how to solve (Nelson, 1968). The emergence of a raft of such wicked problems in this paradigm seems to have undermined its legitimacy with the general public, just as the flaws in the previous paradigm had. The wicked problems were interlocking and deep-seated social problems relating to lack of work, low skills, poor health, drug abuse, the rise in crime, the fear of crime, the desertion of public spaces and the consequent reduction in informal social control of disaffected young people.

The two paradigms outlined here represent archetypal positions in the continuing dilemmas about the state and the market, each bringing characteristic benefits and disbenefits in its wake. So a new paradigm, aimed at achieving both 'economic dynamism' and 'social justice', seems to be emerging: a form of social democratic politics, which seeks to maintain the momentum of competitiveness but also to intervene heavily on the supply side to solve these social problems. These interventions are not merely compensatory, to ease the pain of change, but are designed to enhance competitiveness by solving the wicked problems, focusing on developing skills and employability in individuals, and by addressing social and community conditions which might harm employability and thus competitiveness. This paradigm, too, will have its flaws, since all paradigms do. Perhaps a key one will be the transaction costs of partnership-working, or a muddying of lines of accountability, resulting as new structures add to the problems of complexity expressed in the term 'congested state' (Sullivan and Skelcher, 2002).

It is clear that the problems to which joined-up government is an answer are quite diverse in nature, and the next section explores the different types of problem and the issues for joining up.

Intractable problems, tamable problems and seamless service

The first set of policy problems are intractable. Typical is a focus on issues of social exclusion and social capital. The argument is that a vicious circle prevails. Having lost their traditional economic base, and the disciplines and self-respect that go with employment, some communities which did not have access to the new prosperity – for reasons of geography, ethnicity, culture or other excluding factors – seem to have suffered a steep decline in social order, with people hiding behind their front doors, reluctant to take on the role of active citizen and community member. The full impact of this emerged as the last paradigm matured. Health inequalities between the top and bottom strata of society had grown; while educational standards achieved in the mainstream began to rise, for sink schools on sink estates they remained firmly at the bottom, and crime rose, with the fear of crime coming out as the top issue in studies of public opinion.

This is the situation for which the term 'wicked problem' was originally coined in the United States. In the United Kingdom wicked problems were less racially differentiated, but this did not make the problems any less intractable. Certainly public services do not seem to have helped. The pattern of provision in services like education and health has been based on values of universalism, where special need was, and probably still is, under-recognized in the policy planning process. The need to retain the support of the mainstream for public services has ensured that they have not been as redistributive as they might have been. While improved public services for these communities are part of the answer, there is more to it than that. What is needed is, in effect, the redevelopment or strengthening of community capacity, networks between people that become the means for ensuring community safety, mutual support for well-being, better health and quality of life, and all of this resulting in the re-establishing of social control that keeps down anti-social behaviour, a task which is impossible for the police without public support and assistance.

For these intractable problems, it is necessary to recognize the fundamentally situational character of both the problems and the solutions. In driving public services to achieve better results, government ministers frequently have in mind 'average' service users, and require service deliverers to work to this norm. If by doing that they remove the scope and the drive for responding in a situationally distinctive way to the intractable problems outlined above, they will have diminished rather than enhanced joined-up government. While no one knows how to solve these problems in a general way, hence the term 'intractable', because there are many examples of success it is possible and indeed desirable for local leadership and entrepreneurial energy to emerge and flourish (Leadbeater, 1997).

It is possible that careful learning from these many situations will provide us with more generalizable knowledge of what works. In which case, by definition, the problems would stop being intractable and be defined as tame instead.

While they remain intractable, a strategy of decentralized policy and service development, integrated into structures that focus on locality or community, seems to be the key to appropriate joining up. The central drive should be on facilitating local players to achieve outcomes. Forcing them to try to achieve outputs defined at the centre will not work.

Tame problems are those where solutions are known, or where there is a chance through investment in research and evaluation of finding an answer. Looking at the rise in many social indicators which occurred during the post-war years, it is evident that this was a time when intractable problems were tamed, and solutions embedded in the professional practice and policies of the welfare state. There does appear to be a new class of problems, tame rather than intractable, which lie on the boundaries between different jurisdictions, and which have remained relatively unaddressed in the recent past. One example would be in the rehabilitation of offenders, as it becomes clear that a large proportion of the population of offenders suffer severe educational disadvantages, lacking the skills that might enable them to build a stake in society. In the modern economy, those without life and work skills will go to the wall. A proportion will be drawn into crime as their own personal salvation. Working across the boundaries of prisons, probation and the employment service allows a focus on the particular needs of this special group, with the development of programmes which address their offending behaviour and also their educational disadvantage.

These problems are individual to the service user or client rather than situational in the 'community' sense outlined above. They are therefore susceptible to the 'what works' approach, and to a top-down strategy which requires partnership working across the silo structures. Whereas in the case of intractable problems it is right to let a 'thousand flowers bloom', each plant within its own unique habitat, in this case, joining up through a programmatic design may be the best way of achieving desired outcomes.

The final category of problems to which joined-up government is the answer relates to a wide range of services which have been established in the past, using the technology of the time, and which technological change may now allow to be delivered differently and seamlessly. In the past, users have taken for granted inconvenience and high transaction costs as they deal with different parts of the public sector. Advances in customer service in the private sector, supported by the information and communications technology revolution, have had the effect of ratcheting up expectations of public service. Users increasingly expect services to meet their needs, at the time that suits them, giving them choice.

Seamless service is now feasible, since systems can be redesigned so that they link up a range of currently separate services around user needs, whether it be life episodes such as birth, starting school, starting work, retirement or particular client needs, such as the multiple needs of disabled children. The joining up of services around principles other than function, principles such as 'life episode' which make a great deal more sense to service users and clients, has raised expectations resulting from private sector advances in this capacity. Electronic links are one answer to overcoming the propensity of different organizations within a service delivery network not to communicate with each other.

In summary, joined-up public services hide a multitude of different sorts of problems, some intractable, some tame, and with diverse solutions. The next section explores issues of accountability, which lie at the heart of the question of whom public service employees see themselves working to and for, and of the very purpose of public service organizations.

Joined-up government and accountability

An implication of the paradigm changes outlined above is that the processes through which accountability is exercised are no longer necessarily fit for purpose, with implications for leadership roles. Indeed, as quasi-constitutional features of the public policy system they are likely to have changed less than the rest of the system. Earlier, it was suggested that development of the public sector after 1945 reveals three substantial step changes in its organizing principles. The first of these paradigms, with its focus on planned, universalistic provision of welfare and economic protection, was dominated by bureaucratic organizational forms, machine bureaucracy and professional bureaucracy.

Public accountability systems were rather well aligned with machine bureaucracy. The notion that one figurehead at the top of the pyramid could decide on policy, which would then be delivered through a carefully designed cascade, fitted well with constitutional notions of ministerial responsibility. For professional bureaucracies, accountability was primarily to self-regulating professional bodies, such as the Royal Colleges in health, and to local government structured into committees, which in turn mirrored local government professionals. Self-regulation fitted the culture of paternalism and deference that still prevailed.

The paradigm change that began in the late 1970s brought greater challenges to existing processes of accountability. The bureaucratic forms which aligned so well with old processes of accountability lost legitimacy and public support, because a more demanding set of service users were no longer content with the quality of service received. Structural and cultural changes designed to enhance service quality and value for money moved public bodies out of alignment with traditional accountability processes. Machine bureaucracies, such as the system for delivering social security benefits, were substantially altered in becoming executive agencies in order to improve their performance. Perhaps the most significant change was the appointment of a chief executive, to act as the managerial leader of the organization, rather than as a mere functionary who would report up the line to the Secretary of State. Taking the strategic direction set by ministers, as expressed in the policy and resources framework, chief executives were to work within that framework in leading change.

The place of public accountability in the story of public management reform in the United Kingdom reveals the system's characteristic difficulty in addressing constitutional issues directly. No change was made in the formal process of ministerial responsibility and accountability, thus ensuring one of two outcomes. Either the significance of the processes of accountability would be diminished, as they were seen to be out of touch with the modern world, or the reforms would be undermined because the dimension of accountability had not been addressed. In fact, the picture which emerged was mixed. Some holders of the office of chief executive took that to mean that they were just civil servants like any others, and under-performed in leading service improvements. Others managed a careful balance, and one at least came to grief through acting as he thought a chief executive should act, being sacked by his Secretary of State for not behaving like a civil servant. Over time, however, new conventions on value for money have taken root to legitimate a more modern approach to public management.

Professional bureaucracies were subject to changes in formal accountability. The purchaser/provider split in health placed decisions about how best to meet the health needs of a particular local population, and the assurance of quality in health service, in the hands of health authorities, rather than with senior doctors, who in turn were to be held to account through contracts for the delivery of the service. But this was a plan that failed. Doctors were able to claim greater legitimacy than the ministerially appointed small businessman who was the typical non-executive appointee to local health boards. The provider side of the NHS was in fact able to retain the initiative, and before the internal market was abolished it had stopped functioning as a full market, still incurring the transaction costs of the market, but without its benefits.

Rather more successful was the introduction of new forms of accountability in school education. The new inspectoral regime established under Ofsted was focused on providing parents and the wider public with information about comparative school performance, rather than on helping teachers improve, as the previous HMI had been – holding the profession to account rather than being part of the professional community. Teachers were unable to retain the initiative in the same way as doctors, and found themselves accountable for performance to others, particularly boards of governors, outside the profession for the first time. The key difference between the two cases seems to be the involvement of consumers, the parents. While no quasi-market for state schooling ever materialized, Ofsted's practice involved treating parents as customers who needed information in order to make a choice of school. In mimicking the practice of the market, Ofsted was able to invest itself with the legitimacy of market-like behaviour.

The case also raises the significance of what Professor John Stewart refers to as twin aspects of accountability: being held to account for your stewardship by a superior body, and rendering account to consumers and citizens about how you are serving their needs. Codes of stewardship require that those who act as agents of the public be held to account for their stewardship. The principle is a deeply embedded feature of the processes for legitimization of collective action in the United Kingdom. It cannot be substituted by rendering an account to the public about performance, but it is not the only source of legitimacy, and wise public servants will seek to expand their influence by opening up channels of communication with consumers of the service and the wider public. What this suggests is that there was no smooth adjustment in the processes of accountability to enable them to cope with the new patterns of public service activity developing in that second paradigm. The nature of the way that public bodies were directed and managed changed, and the institutions of accountability ceased to be as fit for purpose as they had previously been. Nonetheless there was a process of adaptation, characterized by a renewed focus on value for money, evident in the work of elected chambers and the public audit bodies.

As a new outcomes-focused paradigm develops, new challenges to old accountability systems will emerge, and many of these will focus on joined-up government. Each of the types of joined-up government will present its own accountability challenges. The three categories of joined-up government discussed above, dealing with intractable problems, tame problems and developing seamless service, will each need different accountability treatments. In the model described in Table 2.1, it was indicated that in order to address these issues a decentralized approach is needed, driven by outcome-based performance targets recognizing the situational nature of the problem and its solution, with community-based partnership as the key structure. Accountability mechanisms will need to be developed which are congruent with these principles, empowering local people to be responsible and accountable for their actions. The major challenge will be to ensure that the national accountability of many of the public services, which will be important in those local situations, does not override their local contribution. There have been indications, for example, of police forces too busy meeting nationally set targets to give proper attention to their crime and disorder partnership work; of schools so busy meeting individualized targets that they play the performance management game and dump the youngsters who need them most; of GP practices unwilling to provide care for homeless people because it would interfere with their capacity to deliver nationally set targets on vaccination and screening, on which part of their remuneration is based. Public officials, schooled under the second paradigm, assume that their national accountability requires them to impose this centralized framework. In order clearly to legitimate a more appropriate set of behaviours, innovation is needed in the accountability processes involved.

Summary

This chapter has presented an argument that the public policy system is undergoing one of its periodic step changes, and that the issues of joined-up government are intimately connected with these changes. The last major step change, in focusing effort on efficient performance, actually created or made worse the problems of integration and joined-up working. While there was increased efficiency in a narrowly defined sense as a result of this, the wider impact on the public policy system was to reduce effectiveness for some services and some clients. When faced with the challenges of a globalized economy, a revolution in the working technology of public service and the social malaise resulting from a period of rapid economic change, this was enough to propel us into seeking a new way, the Third Way, which would achieve both economic dynamism and social justice, ensuring effective outcomes in solving difficult social and economic policy problems.

This chapter suggests that such policy and service problems can be differentiated. 'Wicked problems' consist of two types – intractable problems that are situationally dependent, and tame problems that can only be solved by working across organizational boundaries. In addition, ICT creates the potential for reconfiguring a vast array of services better to meet the needs of users, following the lead of the fundamental changes in private sector service management. All of these issues have been labelled as requiring 'joined-up government' solutions, although they present different leadership challenges.

Third paradigm leadership

What is the implication of this paradigm change for leadership? What are the key leadership tasks; what skills and competences do we need?

A key problem is that during the last 20 years the policy priorities, and the structures, processes, cultures and competencies that went with them, have diverged from those solutions that might have worked in the past. The extent to which practitioners know how to achieve better outcomes in public policy should not be underestimated. However, the knowledge and skill base required to solve policy problems is distributed across a number of service structures; hence design which gives access to the required knowledge and skill is essential. This also requires cross-sector leadership capacity.

Bringing about sustainable transformations to the organization of public services can only be done with and through the people engaged in the delivery of those services. Performance management systems are good for monitoring the achievement of objectives and targets. But they do not energize people to feel they can make a difference through their front-end delivery. This requires a leadership style that enables people to envisage how they make a difference, one that creates a framework in which innovation and creative contribution to performance improvement is balanced against the need for control and accountability. Providing a vision, energizing people and enabling them to take action requires a new approach to the leadership, management and development of people.

Achieving the modernization agenda cannot come about by incentives and sanctions alone. While a certain level of incentive to achieve results can be built into this process via comparative evaluation, a key component in joining up this type of problem is leadership which focuses attention on results. Where there are well-established ways of delivering outcomes through known outputs, the job will be to continue to drive down costs, delivering more for less. Where outcomes can only be achieved through new outputs, which require partnership working for their production, leadership will be needed to create and maintain this capacity. These two quite different tasks demand a mix of transformational and transactional leadership competences from public service leaders (Alimo-Metcalfe, 1998; Newman, 2001). In addition, better joined-up responses to non-routine, intractable wicked issues will benefit from a heavy emphasis on experimentation, evaluation and learning.

In terms of desirable leadership capabilities, it has long been a contentious issue as to whether generic management competences can be prescribed across all sectors and types of organization. Work by Perren and Burgoyne (2002), which presented a framework of management and leadership capabilities, cautiously extends earlier profiling of generic management standards. The Council for Excellence in Management and Leadership (CEML, 2002a) investigated both public and private sector organizations, but said little that specifically enhanced our understanding of public leadership development requirements. As outlined in Chapter 1, the various public service leadership colleges and centres have gone their own ways in developing diverse competency or capability frameworks, in which, contradicting any one system approach, there is little convergence on definitions or frameworks. An alternative perspective on the attempt to refine competency models is advocated by Briscoe and Hall (1999) who propose 'meta-competencies' of adaptability and identity as essential for self-directed ongoing learning and development. Adaptability encompasses attributes such as flexibility, openness to novelty and diversity, exploration and openness to challenge, which would facilitate continued learning. Identity refers to the ability to reflect on self, to gather and respond to personal feedback, and to explore personal values, which are so central to leading purposefully in the right domain.

With this perspective on leadership, development of capability is not about simply becoming more effective within unchallenged frames of assumptions. Fisher and Rooke (2000) suggest a framework of leadership development, where the highest expectations are typically that someone aspires to be an expert/achiever. Strategic leaders have an increased understanding of the complexity of the wider system and are willing and able to step outside their existing frames. To become a strategic leader requires a personal transformation in understanding and behaviour, a transformation that cannot be achieved solely by propositional learning, but also requires challenging experiences that take learners to their 'learning edge'.

3 Optimizing the power of learning within action learning

Michael Marquardt and Deborah Waddill

Action learning has proven to be a powerful tool, which generates significant, relevant, and long-lasting learning in relatively short periods of time (Revans, 1980, 1982; Marsick, 1992). The uniqueness of action learning is its wide-ranging application to both learning and action for individuals, teams and organizations (Dilworth and Willis, 2003; Marquardt, 1998, 2003; Pedler, 1997). Practitioners and theorists from diverse disciplines such as management science, psychology, sociology, engineering, political science, sociology, anthropology, and higher education embrace its practical effectiveness (Marquardt, 2004; Marquardt and Berger, 2000). Action learning has been used for numerous purposes including strategic development, curriculum design, knowledge management, organizational development, human resources, executive coaching, and team dynamics (Dilworth and Willis, 2003; Marquardt, 2004; Pedler, 1997; Yorks *et al.*, 1999). It has been applied both in a face-to-face mode and online (Waddill, 2005).

Adult learning, andragogy, is concerned with how adults learn. Andragogy recognizes and acknowledges that a number of factors influence how adults learn differently from children (pedagogy). Knowles (1970, 1984; Knowles *et al.*, 1998) identified the following six factors that distinguish andragogy from pedagogy: (1) the adult learner is self-directing; (2) adults' experiences make them rich resources for one another; (3) their readiness to learn can be triggered by effective role models; (4) adults enter an educational activity with a life-centered, task-centered, or problem-centered orientation to learning; (5) adults need to know why they are learning something before learning it; and (6) the more potent motivators for adults are internal such as self-esteem, recognition, better quality of life, self-confidence, and self-actualization. Since Knowles first delineated the features of andragogy, theoretical schools have developed around adult learning.

In this chapter we will illustrate ways in which the five adult learning schools underpin action learning and contribute to its success. Some adult learning theories are more relevant than others in the analysis and description of action learning. These limitations appear as one analyzes the distinct elements of action learning. However, it is our purpose to highlight the potency of action learning due to the theoretical schools which support it. Because action learning utilizes theories, principles and practices of each of the five major adult learning orientations, it bridges these meta-theories and offers a compelling argument for its applicability in a variety of environments including the public sector (Marquardt, 2004; Waddill and Marquardt, 2003). The authors contend that the high level and quality of learning in action learning is explained by its impressive ability to employ and apply a diverse array of learning theories.

Action learning

Since Reg Revans first introduced action learning in the coal mines of Wales and England in the 1940s, there have been multiple variations of the concept. However, all forms of action learning share the elements of real people resolving and taking action on real problems in real time, and learning through questioning and reflection while doing so. The attraction of action learning is its power to simultaneously and resourcefully solve difficult challenges and develop people and organizations at minimal costs to the institutions. Revans never operationalized action learning into a standard approach (Marsick and O'Neil, 1999), but over the years a number of individuals have developed approaches and models that capture the essence and critical elements that make action learning successful (Dilworth, 1998; Dotlich and Noel, 1998; Marquardt, 1999, 2004; Mumford, 1991; Pedler, 1997; Weinstein, 1995). We selected the Marquardt approach because it captures the essential components of the process originally proposed by Revans, has been effectively implemented worldwide in public and private sector organizations including Siemens, Fairfax Public Schools, Samsung, Baxter, Novartis, Hong Kong Mass Transit, Constellation Energy, American University, Deutsche Bank, the US Department of Agriculture, Mauritius Business School, and Sodexho (Lenderman *et al.*, 2004; Marquardt, 2003, 2004), and has been frequently cited as a key approach for understanding action learning (Bannan-Ritland, 2003; Coughlan *et al.*, 2002; Dotlich and Noel, 1998; Salopek, 1999; Yorks *et al.*, 1999).

Marquardt's approach to action learning is built around six components: (1) a problem or challenge that is urgent and important to the group or an individual within the group; (2) a set or group of four to eight members, ideally from diverse backgrounds and/or parts of the organization; (3) a process that emphasizes questions and reflection; (4) the power and authority to take action on strategies developed; (5) a commitment to learning at the individual, team, and organizational levels; and (6) an action learning coach who focuses on and ensures that time and energy are devoted to capturing the learning and improving the skill level of the group (Marquardt, 1999, 2004).

Schools or orientations of adult learning

Over the past century a number of adult learning schools, also called orientations or meta-theories, have emerged (Ormond, 1999). Merriam and Caffarella (1999) categorized the theories into five schools, each with distinctive, although sometimes overlapping, perspectives and approaches to learning.

Other categorizations of adult education (Charters and Hilton, 1989) and learning theories exist (Hergenhahn, 1988), but we relied upon Merriam and Caffarella's approach because of its broad scope, inclusiveness, positive review (McKenna, 1992) and the concurrence of other scholars (Ormond, 1999; Swanson and Holton, 2001). The five schools/orientations can be described as follows:

Cognitivist – Cognitivists focus on how humans learn and understand using internal processes of acquiring, understanding, and retaining knowledge. Cognitivists believe that humans are capable of insight, perception, and attributing meaning. Learning occurs when humans reorganize experiences, thereby making sense of input from the environment.

Behaviorist – Behaviorists concentrate on learning through control of the external environment. The emphasis is on changing behavior through processes such as operant conditioning. Behaviorists believe that learning is built on three assumptions: (1) changed behavior indicates learning; (2) learning is determined by elements in the environment; (3) repetition and re-enforcement of learning behaviors assist in the learning process (Merriam and Caffarella, 1999).

Humanist – Humanists emphasize the development of the whole person and place emphasis on the affective domain. This orientation views individuals as seeking self-actualization through learning, and being capable of determining their own learning. Self-directed learning is embraced by members of this school.

Social learning – Social learning theory (also referred to as social cognitive theory) focuses on the social context in which people learn; i.e. how they learn through interacting with and observing other people. People can learn from imitating others (thus the importance of role models and mentoring). Social learning, for example, occurs when the culture of the organization is passed on to new employees teaching them how to be effective in that organization.

Constructivist – Constructivists stress that all knowledge is context-bound and that individuals make personal meaning of their learning experiences through internal construction of reality. This school emphasizes the importance of changing oneself and the environment.

Action learning utilizes all the schools of adult learning

The pursuit of relevant and potent learning drives practitioners and theoreticians to search continuously for new and better learning methodologies. Action learning, because of its strength and successes, has generated widespread interest about its inherent learning elements. Although action learning has been primarily linked with adult learning theories such as action/reflection approach (Marsick *et al.*, 1992; Yorks *et al.*, 1999), work-based or situated learning (Gregory, 1994), and problem-based learning (Dotlich and Noel,

1998), it has not been examined by other authors regarding the five learning schools. In this chapter, we have sought to answer two questions:

1   What do theorists from the five learning schools say about learning relative to the six components of action learning?
2   How does action learning utilize the principles and theories from the five schools of adult learning?

Figure 3.1 depicts the universality of the action learning approach as each element satisfies features in the adult learning schools. In order to illustrate

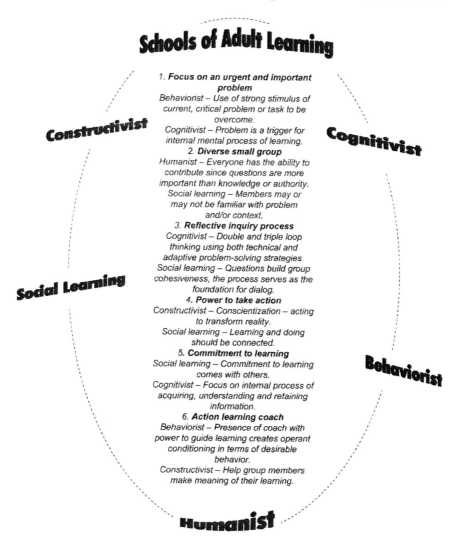

Figure 3.1 Action learning elements with examples from the schools of adult learning.

how action learning incorporates and bridges the various schools of action learning, the text is accompanied by case examples from the public and corporate sectors demonstrating how the adult learning orientations were present in each of the six components of action learning. We used the strongest links for examples.

Action learning elements and the five schools of adult learning

The connections between action learning elements and the schools of adult learning are readily apparent. The strength of those connections adds credence to the broad-based application of action learning. In this section, we will delineate specific theoretical features of the schools and link them to the action learning elements. We begin with the fundamental element of action learning which is the existence of an urgent and critical problem.

A problem, project, or challenge

Action learning is built around an urgent problem, project, or challenge, the resolution of which is of high importance to an individual, team, and/or organization. The problem should be significant, be within the responsibility of the team or individual to resolve, and provide opportunity for learning (Revans, 1982). As Revans (1980: 292) notes:

> Thus, the conundrums of action learning are to be problems, to excite the interest of the participants in what they cannot see rather than enhance their skill in elaborating what they can see already. The project task must therefore be open-ended . . . inter-departmental and of serious concern to those who offer it.

It is one of the fundamental beliefs of action learning that the problem or project gives the group meaningful, relevant work, and creates a hook for experimentation using stored knowledge.

Each of the schools of adult learning acknowledges the value of learning from the presented problem or challenge. To highlight two: for the behaviorists, the problem may serve as the external stimulus that begins the learning process. The cognitivists perceive the problem as the trigger for the internal mental process of learning. As Argyris (1991: 107) notes, "the key to any educational experience . . . is to connect the program to real business problems."

Problems and action learning at Deutsche Bank

In the late 1990s, Deutsche Bank faced tremendous changes in its business and staff structure, with critical implications for corporate culture. Organizational change was critical and the following steps were considered:

- Reconfiguration along divisional product lines.
- Shift from regional to global operational structure.
- Shift from multinational to global leadership structure.
- Acquisition of several US entities and their leadership model.
- Change in corporate language from German to English.

Key business challenges were identified and a six-month action learning program was begun. The CEO, program director, and/or program manager selected the problems best suited for Deutsche Bank and for the action learning participants. Each problem had to meet four criteria to qualify for consideration. It had to be:

- of strategic importance to the bank;
- a potential source of significant organizational change;
- strategic – not tactical – in nature, to "stretch" participants;
- broad in scope, offering rich learning opportunities.

Twenty participants were selected. Following a two-day introduction to action learning, the four groups met over a period of six to eight weeks on a part-time basis working on their problem. The final two days of the program included the presentation of actions taken, as well as capturing the learning that could be applied throughout Deutsche Bank. The program was considered a great success, having attained innovative and cost-effective actions for each of the company's problems.

A diverse small group (also referred to as an "action learning set")

To optimally solve the problem and create as much learning as possible, action learning occurs within a group, or set, which is composed of four to eight individuals. When possible, the membership of the group should be diverse so as to maximize various perspectives and to obtain fresh viewpoints (Dilworth and Willis, 2003). Groups may be composed of individuals from across functions or departments, or even suppliers or customers. Revans (1980: 16) describes the set as follows: "The central idea of this approach . . . is that of the set, or small group of comrades in adversity, striving to learn with and from each other as they confess their failures and expand upon their victories." Revans (1988: 8) states that "the ultimate power of a successful [group] lies not in the brilliance of its individual members, but in the cross-fertilisation of its collective abilities."

All of the five schools of adult learning recognize the importance of the group and its members in the learning process. However, for the humanist, the small group plays a critical role. The interaction within a small group can increase the participant's value and self-esteem as he contributes to the actions and learning of the group. The caring and support for group members empha- sizes the "human" element of the learning process (Rogers and Freiberg, 1994). As there is freedom, openness, and strong support for each person to ask fresh questions, members quickly acquire greater self-confidence and develop a strong rapport with fellow group members.

Social learning theorists recognize that learning thrives in the milieu of a group working together on a problem. The members bring varying levels of familiarity to the problem or context of the problem which generates social learning. Learning requires social interaction, collaboration, and participation. Individuals model the reflective inquiry process for each other. The literature regarding communities-of-practice and learning communities incorporate many of the principles of action learning (Lave and Wenger, 1991; Wenger *et al.*, 2002). Communities-of-practice, like action learning groups, are "often more fluid and interpenetrative than bounded, often crossing the restrictive boundaries of the organization to incorporate people from the outside" (Brown and Duguid, 1991: 49).

Action learning with service employees at Fairfax County public schools

As part of Fairfax County's leadership program for support employees, an action learning group composed of a maintenance supervisor, two finance assistants, a customer service supervisor and an administrative assistant was given the challenge of developing a comprehensive orientation program for individuals new to support services. The initial action taken was to survey the various offices in the human resources department to determine the pertinent information needed for new employees. Also, a survey of support employees was taken to determine what information they would like to receive as new employees.

The action learning group developed and submitted to the school district's top leadership a comprehensive orientation program that would be beneficial to all employees, both support and instructional.

With great enthusiasm, FCPS has now incorporated the group's recommendations into what is now the school district's New Employee Orientation program.

Some of the thoughts of participants in the groups are:

Action learning is one of the best tools for solving problems. Different people, ideas, backgrounds, experiences, careers, coming together for one purpose . . . what power (custodial supervisor).

What an outstanding concept. I had fun ironing out team ideas as well as confrontations. I thoroughly enjoyed the experience (maintenance supervisor).

What a great approach to team building and working as a team. My usual impulse was to get things done and cut off input, thereby reducing ownership of projects (administrative assistant).

Reflective inquiry process

Action learning tackles problems through a process of first asking questions to clarify the exact nature of the problem, which is followed by reflecting on and identifying possible solutions, and only then taking action. By focusing on the right questions rather than the right answers, action learning focuses on what one does not know as well as what one does know (Mumford, 1995). Action learning employs the formula: $L = P + Q + R$; i.e. Learning = *Programmed* knowledge (i.e. knowledge in current use, in books, in one's mind, in an organization's memory, lectures, case studies, etc.) + *Questioning* (fresh insights into what is not yet known) + *Reflection* (recalling, thinking about, pulling apart, making sense, trying to understand) (Marquardt, 1999: 29). Questions help to create a common goal, strengthen listening, coalesce groups, increase the learning, and ensure dialogue.

Revans (1980) describes how his work with the National Coal Board caused him to recognize the critical importance of the reflective inquiry approach. He suggested sidestepping learned experts in favor of having workers and management resolve their own problems. Part of the well-documented success of this effort came from his thesis that "action learning shows its strength, not in finding the answers to questions that have already been posed, but in finding the questions that need to be answered" (1980: 118).

Cognitivists emphasize locus of control (which is within the individual) and focus on the learner's mental processes. Questions become a primary way for acquiring knowledge. Argyris and Schön (1978) illuminate the value of questioning and reflection in the learning process when examining the contradictions between espoused theories and theories-in-use. Double-loop learning occurs when one questions one's own premises (espoused theories) and triple-loop is questioning one's learning process (theories-in-use), both processes resulting in successively deeper levels of learning. The greatest value occurs to the learners when they are reflecting and looking for patterns in behavior, knowledge or process. The reflection process includes relating new information to previously learned knowledge. This can occur when the learner questions his/her structural or fundamental assumptions. The reflective process can take place both during action and after the action has taken place (Schön, 1983).

The social learning school embraces two features of reflective thinking. First, reflective thinking involves a state of doubt, hesitation, perplexity, and mental difficulty. Rather than threatening self-efficacy, these force the learner to generate creative alternatives that preserve self-efficacy. Self-efficacy is maintained because the person being questioned is simply encouraged to look at different possibilities. Second, reflective thinking involves an act of searching, hunting, and inquiring to find material that will resolve the doubt as well as settle and dispose the perplexity (Rotter, 1992). Dewey (1933), whom Merriam and Caffarella (1999) identify as a social learning theorist, describes the general features of a reflective experience as including feelings of perplexity, confusion and doubt (i.e. recognition of a problem), making a conjectural anticipation (i.e. establishment of a tentative hypothesis), and performing a careful survey (which occurs through examination, inspection, exploration, and analysis). Questions build a foundation for dialogue, a process which is basic to social learning and action learning.

Questions with Mass Transit Railway Corporation – Hong Kong

Serving over 2.3 million passengers daily, Mass Transit Railway Corporation (MTR) is one of the most intensively utilized mass transit railway systems in the world, transporting one in three of Hong Kong's population every day. MTR has been recognized by recent benchmarking studies as one of the world's finest railways for reliability, customer service and cost-efficiency. Action learning has become an important HRD methodology utilized by MTR for developing leaders, building teams, solving problems and changing the company into a learning organization. Reflective inquiry is seen as critical in the success of MTR's action learning programs. Questions are carefully considered at the problem reframing, goal setting, strategy development, and action implementation stages of the action learning process.

Power to take action

At least one member of the action learning group must have the power and authority to take the action or be assured that their recommendations will be implemented by the organization or sponsoring individual presenting the problem. In action learning, the most valuable learning occurs when action is taken, for one is never sure the idea or plan will be effective until it has been implemented (Pedler, 1997). Revans (1988: 11) states, "responsible experience alone is the true motivator, the impartial witness, and the final judge of meritorious learning." Action enhances learning because it provides experience which serves as the critical dimension for reflection. Most importantly, one action is worth many hours of discussion (Revans, 1980). Mezirow (1991), as a constructivist, identifies two levels of reflective action – lower and higher. The lower or less critical level of reflective action focuses on content (what) and process (how). Premise reflection, which is the higher form of reflective action, enables a perspective transformation and is concerned with why we perceive, think, feel or act as we do. Weick (1995) uses the term *enactment* to imply taking action to change the environment. Freire (1973) introduced the idea of "conscientization." This is where, through acting on what one has learned, there is a deepening awareness on the part of the individual of his or her capacity to transform reality.

Social learning theorists emphasize the relevance of learning through experience and the application of knowledge gained in a new situation. Lindeman (1926: 89) writes "Active participation in interesting affairs furnishes proper stimulations for intellectual growth." Dewey (1916) notes the need for adults to have learning connected to doing. Kolb (1984) explains that testing concepts in new environments through concrete experiences is important in the cycle of learning.

Cutting the costs of moving at a Malaysian business college

A budget of $100,000 had been established to move all the equipment and other furnishings from the current site to new buildings across the city of Kuala Lumpur. An action learning group composed of teachers, students, and administrative personnel explored a variety of options, and eventually decided that they could do much of the moving themselves. A careful, item-by-item plan was developed. Over a weekend, the entire move was completed for under $40,000, in a much more rapid time period, and with new, cross-functional teams and greater collegiality among all the people of the college.

A commitment to learning

Action learning places the same emphasis on the learning/development of individuals, teams, and organizations as it does on the action. The greater longer-term strategic, multiplier benefits of action learning are gained from the learning. As the individuals and the group master the reflective inquiry process, they are better able to identify innovative solutions and strategies. Action learning is a science in which the group members (all "scientists" in an objective search for the truth) learn about everything that is connected to the problem and that can help solve it. The learning is acquired through questions asked by the coach as well as by individual group members requesting feedback from each other. Significant learning occurs through the process of the group discovering together new insights and ideas.

There is the resulting application of the group's learning on a system-wide basis throughout the organization. Revans (1980: 108) pointed this out in his own experience with the British Coal Board:

> Any organization ought to be able to learn from its own everyday experience, simply by asking itself what it thinks it is trying to do, what is preventing it from doing it and what measures it might take to overcome its problems and to move nearer to its goals.

All five schools of adult learning endorse a commitment to learning, but social learning theorists and cognitivists highlight that commitment. Social learning theorists believe that significant learning can only come from reflection on deep experiences, and thus are pleased to see how action learning groups transform existing knowledge into new knowledge within the social setting of the group and their influence on one another. Rotter (1992) explains that change occurs only when one has a sense of personal control over one's life. In the action learning process, the learner has control of his/her course of action on the problem. Expectancy of a positive outcome (Bandura, 1986) can create greater learning. Learners in the action learning set take control over the problem they present, and that commitment generates the expectancy of a positive outcome.

The cognitivists view learning as the process whereby knowledge is created through the transformation of experience. For them, the commitment to learning is a commitment also to learning "how" to learn – also called deutero-learning or metacognition (Argyris *et al.*, 1985; Schön, 1983). In the learning process, the cognitivist focuses on the internal process of acquiring, understanding, and retaining information. This form of learning involves use of mental associations where the learner actively relates incoming information to a previously acquired psychological frame of reference or schema. The mental associations are then reflected in overt behavior changes. Cognitivists see knowledge acquisition as an active process (Bruner, 1965) and believe that reflection and dialogue are critical in developing the learner (Schön, 1983). As action learning groups search for solutions, detect and correct strategies, and reflect on the learning experience, they fulfill the cognitivists' expectations relative to the active internal processes critical to knowledge acquisition and skill development.

Harvesting learning at the US Department of Agriculture (USDA)

Developing individual, team and organizational learning is a key focus of action learning programs at the US Department of Agriculture. At the beginning of each action learning program, participants identify the three leadership skills that they would like to develop during the four-month set which meets one day a month. At the end of each day, members identify how they have attempted to practice their leadership competencies. Other members provide supportive feedback and suggestions. Based upon pre- and post-test scores, USDA reports that action learning has significantly improved the leadership skills of all action learning participants (Raudenbush *et al.*, 2003). At the end of each action learning session, individual learning and group learning is captured and diligently applied throughout USDA.

Action learning coach

It is important that the action learning group regularly pause from working on the task to reflect on their experience and to capture their learning and apply it. Marquardt (2004) has discovered that if one of the group members (referred to as an action learning coach) focuses solely on the group's learning and not on the problem, the group will more quickly become effective both in problem-solving abilities and in group interactions. Revans (1998), it is important to note, was very wary of action learning groups becoming dependent on facilitators or professional educators, feeling that their presence could hinder the group's growth. To offset this potential negative impact, the action learning coach *only* asks questions, and focuses on questions that are related to the learnings (a) of the *group* (e.g. What are our strengths as a group thus far? What could we do better? What is the quality of our questions?); (b) of the *individual* (What have we learned about ourselves? What leadership skills have been demonstrated?); and (c) of the *organization* (What have we learned that we could apply to our organizations? What elements of the organization's culture cause these obstacles?).

The person serving as the action learning coach may be a working group member or an external participant. Through her questions, she helps group members reflect on how they listen, how they may have reframed the problem, how they give each other feedback, how they are planning and working, and what assumptions may be shaping their beliefs and actions. The coach also helps participants focus on what they are achieving, what they are finding difficult, what processes they are employing, and the implications of these processes (Marquardt, 2004; O'Neil, 1999). The action learning coach must have the wisdom and self-restraint to let the participants learn for themselves and from each other. Revans (1980: 9) noted the value of this approach when he stated: "The clever man will tell you what he knows; he may even try to explain it to you. The wise man encourages you to discover it for yourself." The action learning coach must behave like a wise man.

The presence of the learning coach touches on issues that are central to both theoretical ends of the spectrum so to speak in terms of the level of facilitator/instructor control in a learning situation. Knowles *et al.* (1998) point out in their chapter entitled "Theories of Teaching" that behaviorists and cognitivists view teaching as a directive position whereas constructivists and humanists interpret the role of instructor as a non-directive facilitator. These apparently antithetical descriptions blend in the role of action learning coach. While directive on matters regarding the action learning process, the learning coach is non-directive in leading the set members to a solution (O'Neil, 1999). Marquardt's approach balances these opposites.

The presence of a coach with the power to intervene with questions related to the group's learning aligns with the behaviorists' belief in operant conditioning (Skinner, 1976). The coach enforces behavior conducive to learning. For example, he ensures that statements are made rather than questions, and he periodically intervenes in order to focus on norms and learning. Set members recognize that the coach will be asking for what they have learned so they will be subconsciously thinking about how to respond to such a question.

Constructivists, on the other hand, interpret the role of the instructor as one who "facilitates and negotiates meaning with the learner" (Merriam and Caffarella, 1999). Constructivists prefer to yield control of the learning to the learner himself. In the action learning set, the learning coach acts as facilitator when she enables the group members to make sense of their learning by helping the participants both with the process (asking questions, reframing, providing feedback) and by challenging assumptions. The coach's actions are collaborative and provocative of thought rather than directive (Mezirow, 1991). The coach ensures that the members individually and the group as a whole identify how they will be able to apply their new values and learning in the workplace and in the community.

Constellation Energy

Constellation Energy, headquartered in Baltimore, Maryland, recognizes the importance of having trained action learning coaches available at every one of its numerous sites across the United States. Nearly 100 employees have been trained to serve as action learning coaches. Thus, when site managers encounter projects such as safety issues, work scheduling, pricing fuel resources, or developing leadership programs, they can access an action learning coach and immediately begin the action learning process.

Contributions to public leadership and organization development

The potency of the action learning process can be attributed to the fact that it satisfies a variety of theories of learning. In so doing, action learning maintains its robust and far-reaching application. Theories of learning are developed with the learner in mind. Theories of learning deal with adults at different life stages and with different skill sets and learning styles. When examined through the lens of each adult learning theory, action learning satisfies the full range of adult learning needs. Just as a music student can play piano without knowing music theory, action learning can be implemented by those who do not know about its theoretical underpinnings. However, music composed with an understanding of music theory reaches a broader audience. Likewise, action learning celebrates a wide application in both the public and private arena and in a never-ending number of environments because of its broad theoretical base.

American University masters degree in public administration

American University's award winning masters degree in public administration has made action learning the cornerstone of its academic success. The theories, principles, and practices of action learning are introduced at the first class. Then each senior public official selects an important and urgent project within their public agency, forms an action learning team to work on the project, and develops and implements an action plan. The final examination in the MPA program involves the student presenting the results and learning from his/her action learning project to the MPA faculty.

Action learning is such a powerful learning tool because its six components interweave and incorporate so many of the principles and theories of each of the five schools of adult learning. Action learning stimulates learning at the individual, team, and organizational levels. Action learning principles, such as questioning/reflection, can be applied at an interpersonal, within-group, between-groups, and/or at an organizational level. Rather than highlighting the differences between the schools of learning, action learning accents the basic commonalities. Action learning, because of its flexibility in learning, can be applied in a variety of ways and settings in both the public and the private sectors.

Each of the schools of adult learning theory is represented in the elements of action learning. Although some of the components may be more aligned to one school than another, taken in their entirety, action learning has the amazing capacity to utilize and synergize a wide array of diverging as well as complementary forces. Action learning demonstrates how one methodology and approach can satisfy the key conditions necessary for learning established by each of the different schools.

4 Understanding the organizational potential of action learning

Clare Rigg

Marquardt and Waddill have shown in Chapter 3 how an understanding of ways individuals learn helps us appreciate why action learning might be so potent for individual development. The further challenge is to comprehend why action learning might be beneficial for extending organizational and collaborative capacity or, put in other words, for engaging second- and third-person level enquiry (Reason and Bradbury, 2001). This is not simply a question of the sum of parts, in the sense of the greater the number of qualified people the greater an organization's capacity. We have also to look to two further questions: first, where is the individual, organization, and system in the intent of the action learning intervention?; and, second, what is 'an' organization that 'its' capacity might be increased?

The purpose of this chapter is twofold. It will draw from organization theory, particularly non-structuralist ideas of organization as a process of social interaction to explore how this elucidates the potential of action learning to link individual and organizational development. However, the chapter starts by exploring the intentions with which action learning has been deployed and implicit theories of change underlying the practice.

Action learning intent

Chapter 1 outlined different forms of action learning and the ways in which they variously engage individual participation. To understand the potential for organization impact it is useful to recognize that the diverse applications of action learning are, as Marsick and O'Neil (1999) illustrate, rooted in different philosophies of learning and change, which in turn influence the design of applications and the practice of learning set facilitators. They maintain that action learning in general is rooted in fundamental assumptions that 'human beings can shape their environment' and 'in the value of scientific method in ... improving the human condition' (Marsick and O'Neil, 1999: 170). They argue that all action learning has roots in John Dewey's progressive educational theories and Kurt Lewin's social psychology, both combining assumptions 'that individuals learn as individuals, but that their experience is shaped and understood in social contexts' (Marsick and O'Neil, 1999: 170). However, their thesis is that action learning in practice has evolved in discrete directions, eclectically drawing on other theories, either implicitly or explicitly. These directions they defined as three idealized types of action learning practice: scientific, experiential and critical reflection.

Practitioners of the scientific school base their approach on Revans' (1982) problem-solving model comprising Systems Alpha, Beta and Gamma. Problems are addressed and learning occurs through the interaction of the three systems. In System Alpha, participants collect data to analyse the problem context, examining the value system of the person and of the wider organization, the external system affecting decisions on the problem, and the internal system in which the problem-holder operates. In System Beta the participant tries out a solution, systematically deploying stages of survey, hypothesis, experimentation, audit and review (Revans, 1982). System Gamma is the participant's cognitive framework: their assumptions and prior understanding. Revans (1982) argued that learning occurs when changes to this cognition result from the process of working through the actions of System Beta, asking questions, collecting data and bringing in appropriate 'programmed' knowledge from expertise or literature.

What Marsick and O'Neil (1999) describe as the experiential learning school of action learning is practice allied to Kolb's cycle of experiential learning (1984). They argue that theoretical roots here include humanistic psychology, with implicit assumptions that learning is a cognitive process deriving from reflection on action, conceptualization leading to plans for new action, implementation, reflection and so on. Key to experiential action learning is the review process, the opportunity to reflect on action by the individual, within the set and within the wider organization or system. There is also an implicit assumption of rationalism in the learning process: that people learn to change their behaviours in response to external stimuli.

The critical reflection approach to action learning is informed by critical theory. Assumptions are that learning is prompted by deep reflection on underlying assumptions, beliefs and values which leads to more penetrating insights into the personal and systemic causes of organization problems (Rigg and Trehan, 2004). Critical reflection can transform perspectives (Mezirow, 1991) as people recognize the disjuncture between their previous beliefs and their current experience, and come to radically new understandings.

Marsick and O'Neil's framework is useful in presenting an idealized typology of approaches and their theoretical underpinnings on change. However, they argue that the intent of action learning is always primarily instrumental, in that it is focused on solving problems and concerned with developing 'the capacity of individuals and systems to learn how to learn' (1999: 170). A contrasting view is offered by Pedler *et al.* (2005), who, drawing on Lyotard, suggest that the rationale for action learning in different contexts varies between three purposes: speculative, emancipatory and performative. Their argument is that for some practitioners the intent is speculative in the sense of generating knowledge for its own sake. There is no pre-set outcome and no instrumental concern. For others, the intent in using action learning is emancipatory for the purpose of eliminating oppression, either by individuals removing mental shackles through the process of learning, or through tackling material problems. Performative intent is the use of action learning to improve practice of some kind. Here is the instrumental rationale for deploying action learning: the search for improved individual practice or the quest for organizational improvements.

In order to further our understanding of organizational impacts of action learning, I want to draw from these ideas of intent and to differentiate between individual and organizational focus. This is captured in Figure 4.1, a heuristic model of intent designed to capture two major spectrums of priority. One is whether the emphasis of learning intervention is on individual transformation

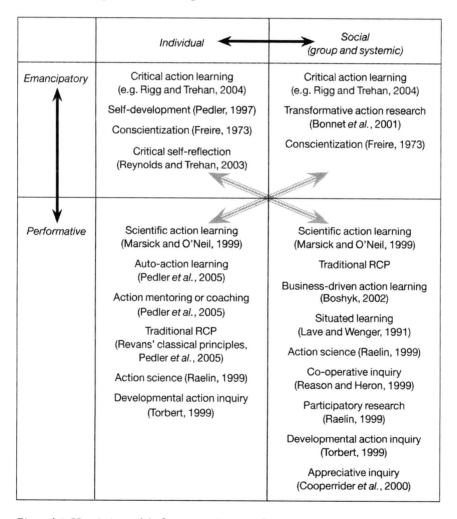

	Individual ←——→	Social (group and systemic)
Emancipatory	Critical action learning (e.g. Rigg and Trehan, 2004)	Critical action learning (e.g. Rigg and Trehan, 2004)
	Self-development (Pedler, 1997)	Transformative action research (Bonnet *et al.*, 2001)
	Conscientization (Freire, 1973)	Conscientization (Freire, 1973)
	Critical self-reflection (Reynolds and Trehan, 2003)	
Performative	Scientific action learning (Marsick and O'Neil, 1999)	Scientific action learning (Marsick and O'Neil, 1999)
	Auto-action learning (Pedler *et al.*, 2005)	Traditional RCP
	Action mentoring or coaching (Pedler *et al.*, 2005)	Business-driven action learning (Boshyk, 2002)
	Traditional RCP (Revans' classical principles, Pedler *et al.*, 2005)	Situated learning (Lave and Wenger, 1991)
	Action science (Raelin, 1999)	Action science (Raelin, 1999)
	Developmental action inquiry (Torbert, 1999)	Co-operative inquiry (Reason and Heron, 1999)
		Participatory research (Raelin, 1999)
		Developmental action inquiry (Torbert, 1999)
		Appreciative inquiry (Cooperrider *et al.*, 2000)

Figure 4.1 Heuristic model of intent in the uses of action learning.

or social transformation, and here the term 'social' is intended to mean organizational and/or systemic. The second spectrum is whether the desired outcome of learning is primarily performative or emancipatory. The intention of the arrows in the figure is to indicate an interplay between the individual and the social, in the sense that they are inevitably interconnected.

Ideas about action learning that emphasize individual emancipatory change include critical self-reflection (Reynolds and Trehan, 2003) as well as many traditions of self-development (Pedler, 1997) and adult education (Brookfield, 1994; hooks, 1993, 1994; Lather, 1991; Omolade, 1987). Other approaches are concerned with interconnections between individual and social levels of emancipatory change, including critical action learning (e.g. Rigg and Trehan, 2004), and conscientization (Freire, 1973). As Marsick and O'Neil (1999) indicate, this is action learning as the first step of a journey toward greater self-insight, especially the capacity to learn from experience and obtain greater awareness of the political and cultural dimensions of organizational life. Herein lies the potential for emancipatory learning. For organizations, they say that it is perhaps the first step toward linking individual learning with systemic learning and change. One approach in this tradition, which prioritizes radical organizational or systemic change, is transformative action research (Bonnet *et al.*, 2001).

Approaches where the intent is individual performance improvement include auto action learning (Pedler *et al.*, 2005) and action mentoring or coaching (Pedler *et al.*, 2005). In contrast situated learning, co-operative inquiry, appreciative inquiry (Cooperrider, 1995) and business-driven action learning (Boshyk, 2002) focus on performance at the organizational and/or systemic levels. A number of approaches interweave levels: for example, action science, based on the principle that people can improve their interpersonal and organizational effectiveness by exploring the beliefs that underlie their actions; developmental action inquiry (Torbert, 1999) linking first-person inquiry; second-person inquiry; and third-person inquiry to help people to become aware of transformations between intuition, thinking, communicative practices, and their effects on others. Traditional RCP (Revans Classical Principles: Pedler *et al.*, 2005) and scientific action learning (Marsick and O'Neil, 1999), also integrate their emphasis on individual and organization performance.

The intention of Figure 4.1 is not to ignore the fact that many action learning practitioners and advocates integrate the individual and social, or to suggest that the actual impacts do not traverse the two. For example, Rigg (2005) has argued in respect of critical management learning that focus on emancipatory ideals is not incompatible with improved performance. Rather the figure is a heuristic device to clarify where, when action learning interventions are designed, the priority is placed in the intended impact. The heuristic model helps to clarify how the intent of action learning varies in its emphasis, such that for many uses the primary intended outcome is some measure of organizational change. However, intent alone does not explain why, as an approach to leadership development, action learning has such potential for organizational transformation. The next section will draw from organization theory to explore this question.

Links between individual learning and organizational development – not simply the sum of the parts

Evidence of potential connections between individual learning and development of organization capacity is hindered partly by a lack of empirical evaluation, but also by a paucity of theorizing the links between individual learning and organizational practice. If there is little commonality in understandings of what leadership is within public service bodies, there has been even less apparent attention to questions of how people learn or develop leadership capability, and even less explicit theorizing on what 'an' organization is that 'it' might develop as a result of individual leadership.

Understanding how individual development might translate into organizational transformations is hindered not least because of the poverty of theory in the evaluation of learning and development interventions. Many evaluations have followed Kirkpatrick's model (1975) and addressed the value of development for the organization as well as for participants. But this is more easily said than done, and a model like Kirkpatrick's, whilst a valuable framework, offers no guide to methodology. Evaluation frameworks have frequently failed to encompass the difficulties faced by individuals who have engaged in action learning away from their workplace, in making radical challenges to their bosses and colleagues. Weinstein's work illustrates a typical complaint:

> Despite the positive results at an individual level, Weinstein's participants doubted that their newly acquired learning skills would be sufficient in themselves to transform their organizations into learning organizations. They doubted whether they would be able to affect their wider work environments so that these skills would become recognized and valued.
>
> (cited in Easterby-Smith et al., 1997: 353)

Easterby-Smith *et al.* (1997: 351) suggest that impacts on organization are 'more readily apparent as outcomes from specific projects and programmes and less easily apparent in terms of building a "learning organization"'. Several writers have illustrated the complexity of linking individual learning and development into organization practice (e.g. Lewis, 1994).

Bramley (1991: 4) points out 'the logic of [the] approach that, as organizations are made up of individuals, it must be possible to change the organization by changing the members ... is a great simplification'. Katz and Kahn (1978: 658) described this kind of approach as having 'a long history of theoretical inadequacy and practical failure'. Bramley (1991) offers an alternative framework, described as an 'increased effectiveness' model, that works to collect evidence against pre-set criteria, such as specified behaviours, that would indicate improved effectiveness in a particular organizational context.

Nevertheless, this model still does not explicitly theorize what 'an' organization is that it might improve, and it treats the concepts of 'data-gathering' as well as that of evaluation as unproblematic.

So what is 'an' organization that there might be transformation as a result of action learning?

Organizations – the real thing

The word 'organization' is a noun not only in the sense of a structure or arrangement, but also in the sense of an act or process of organizing. Yet most writing about organizations and capacity building is dominated by *representationalist thinking*' (Chia, 1996: vii): the attempt to capture and describe an external reality, or some 'thing' that exists outside the individuals that inhabit the organization or system. Illustrations of such thinking abound in official documents, with realist language of construction, structures and organizations as entities. The UK National Health Service (NHS) Modernization Agency (2004: 7), for example, talks of the importance of leadership to '*build* partnerships' and expresses the ubiquitous intention of enhancing the 'organization's ability to deliver *its* goals'. And the NHS is by no means alone. The significance is that realist language is likely to reflect structuralist thinking with concomitant actions.

However, despite the pervasiveness of policy language that suggests underlying representationalist thinking about organization, there is also evidence of policy thinking informed by newer organization theory. In contrast to structural perspectives is a more processual perspective of organizations: 'negotiated orders', in which the organization is conceived as 'the temporary product of interactional processes' (Reed, 1992: 84). Whilst there is still some sense of reification, there is a stronger sense that an organization cannot exist without people. Weick (1979) has argued that:

> most 'things' in an organization are actually relationships, variables tied together in a systematic fashion. Events, therefore, depend on the strength of these ties, the direction of influence, the time it takes for information in the form of differences to move around the circuit.

Organizations as patterns of social interaction

Grant *et al.* suggest (1998: 12): '"organization" can be seen as a continuous process of social accomplishment which, in both senses of the term, is *articulated* by and through the deployment of discursive resources'. This way of thinking encompasses both discursive resources (language, frameworks of thinking, concepts, assumptions) and discursive practices (patterns of interaction, the multiple acts of everyday communication). Woodilla also emphasizes the role of talk: 'Socially constructed meaning is created in language-based interactions with "conversation" as the most common taken-for-granted practice' (1998: 31).

Ideas of organizations as *interactions* differentiate between an organization as an individual conception, a constructivist conception, which sees the organization as in the mind of the individual, and a social constructionist perspective, where an organization is a collective framework of shared meanings (Fletcher, 2002).

The idea of an organization combining shared meanings, yet having some sense of realism, is found in conceptions such as Clegg and Hardy's, in which they are

> sites of *situated social action* more or less open both to explicitly organized and formal disciplinary knowledges such as marketing, production, and so on, and also to conversational practices embedded in the broad social fabric, such as gender, ethnic and other culturally defined social relations.
>
> (Clegg and Hardy, 1999: 3)

This notion that an organization is more than just the sum of the people is also articulated by Barbara Czarniawska, in her conception of 'an institutionalized action-net ... interconnecting acts of organizing' (1998: 26). This perspective suggests an organization is a community of meaning rather than a community of life (or people). As such 'an' organization can be understood as 'a network of interactively shared meanings' (Fletcher, 1997: 94), where a network is: 'the social relations in which every individual is embedded' (1997: 49). 'Collective meanings become institutionalized within the organization through social relational patterns and the development of a common language' (1997: 94). 'The mix of social relational processes are continuously being aligned and negotiated as organizational members attempt to achieve their daily work tasks and personal goals' (1997: 4).

Such processual conceptions of organization would seem highly pertinent to the complex, multi-stakeholder contexts of public services, where direction and priorities have to come from the collaboration of people with multifarious perspectives, values, worldviews and experiences. And there is evidence of some such thinking in the language of public policy bodies. For example, taking the NHS Modernization Agency again, they say in describing partnership working (2004: 6): 'they [members of the group] have found that creating a forum for talking about ambition for the system builds a shared understanding and trust between their organization'.

Power, politics and emotion in organization dynamics – the brew of action learning

One final area of organization thinking that offers insights into understanding the potential of action learning for organization development is insights into power, politics and emotion in organization dynamics. Morgan (1990) offers the view of an organization as the product of people's unconscious minds: 'Organizations ... are rich in symbolic significance, and many organizational events and activities are to be understood as manifestations of deep psychic processes.' Vince (2004a, b) argues that individual capacity to act is constrained by dominant organization routines and power relations and that organizing processes develop around organization members' emotions and power dynamics. From this perspective, increased capacity is not the result of adding up the numbers of those with particular qualifications and competency certificates, but is the effect of organizational processes and systems that have improved, and dysfunctional ones that have been challenged (see also, for example, Armstrong, 2005).

In summary, pulling these threads together, and combining insights from organization dynamics with social constructionist thinking, I want to argue the value of conceiving of organizations in processual terms, as a community of meaning, sustained and perpetuated by patterns of communication and inter-action, such patterns being shaped by members' power relations and emotions. The crux of my argument is that 'an' organization can be conceived as a process of networking perpetuated through relationships and through the deployment of discursive resources (language, frameworks of thinking, concepts, assump-tions) as well as communicative practices – the patterns and content of every-day interactions. On the ground this means that the configuration of any organization is perpetuated through patterns of daily communications, the micro-processes and micro-politics of everyday interactions such as meetings, greetings and seating; such as the reception of newcomers, reaction to out-siders, responses to customers or openness to members of other organizations. It lies in the regular communicative acts that sit, for example, around formal meetings, such as where agendas are set, whether the style of engagement is open or a performative pretence, how decisions are reached and whose hands steer the direction. Grand gestures such as where and how the chief executive can be seen or who can speak to a visiting minister are examples of interactions shaped by organization members' power relations, but emotional behaviour will also shape interactions: for example, in the extent to which the chief execu-tive is happy to be upstaged by junior staff or managers in general are open to criticism.

This is the brew, the backdrop in which action learning interventions occur. It is those very communicative acts and the way they are linked with power in a network of relations that make possible particular ways of leading, managing, learning or non-learning. And it is the social, the interactive and the commu-nicative acts which action learning touches. In understanding 'organization' in this way we have greater insight into the organizational development potential of action learning. The ensuing section explores how this might be, in terms of how action learning can be understood to support a social process: as facili-tating action within the social network that constitutes an organization or wider system, and as being a process through which organization members enact new ways of organizing.

The support of a social process

Davies and Kraus (2003) argue that what and whether an individual learns from an experience is affected by factors such as how open they are, their emotion and expectations, prior experience, opportunity to reflect and work on the experience, learning orientation, learned behaviours, formal knowledge, others' observations, access to informed non-participants, and sense-making processes. Lee also highlights the role of emotion and the risk of 'no-change' in citing Vasilyuk (1991): 'all learning that has a transformative effect upon us is derived from a clash between our understanding of the world and our experience, to the extent that learning and change are painful processes of redefinition' (Lee, 2003: 16).

Vince's model of emotions in learning suggests that any novel situation or change provokes at least a degree of anxiety, to which a person may react in a cycle that discourages learning, or that promotes learning. 'Willing ignorance' results from fight/flight, denial, avoidance, defensiveness and resistance. Alternatively a person may face the uncertainty of the novel situation, take risks, struggle with what this brings and reach new insights as a consequence (Vince, 1996). My argument is that part of the potential of action learning is the opportunity, through the social context of the group, to help people through the cycle towards insight and away from willing ignorance (although this is not to ignore that group behaviour towards some individuals can have the reverse effect: see Rigg and Trehan, 1999).

Taking action in the social network

Vince (2004a, b) has also articulated some interesting ideas on how organizing processes, influenced by members' emotions and power relations, either promote possibilities for learning and change or sustain resistances to them. Yolles and Iles (2003) argue that simple input–transformation–output models of individual or organizational development are no use in a context of complexity, power, emotion and the constraints imposed on any planned change of the extent to which the plans accord with people's felt needs. They observe that development in such a context is better served by diagnosis, inquiry and learning, with stakeholders working and learning together, which mirrors the approach of inter-organizational action learning sets. For example, Vince's (2004a, b) perspective on how organizing processes develop around organization members' emotions and power relations suggests that action learning has particular potential for effectiveness within a social network, as a collective process in a specific context for inquiring into actual organizational projects and practices.

The action learning set can be understood in many ways as a microcosm of the organization (Atkins *et al.*, 1996; Reynolds and Trehan, 2001; Rigg and Trehan, 2004). Behaviours played out within the set, such as transference, projection and splitting, provide insights into people's responses to anxiety, ambiguity and risk within the wider organization. Processes within the set provide opportunities for learning about the organization, but also work on these behaviours within the set can generate changes within the organization.

New meanings, new community

I have argued above the value of conceiving of 'organization', in processual terms, as a community of meaning, sustained and perpetuated by everyday communicative acts and patterns of interaction, such patterns being shaped by members' power relations and emotions. The potential of action learning to disrupt an equilibrium and stimulate change beyond the individual is a result of its own discursive, interactive and action-orientated qualities. When organization members engage in action learning for the purpose of leadership development, it is not simply cognitive learning about leadership that they acquire and try to apply; they learn in the course of experimenting with new ways of doing things, redefining problems, maybe subtly altering their patterns of interacting with colleagues, changing the way they run meetings, even the way they organize seating. In other words they deploy different communicative acts, alter the patterning of daily interactions, which accumulates momentum to change the organization dynamic.

This is not to imply that there is a simple or inevitable linear link between new talk, new meaning, different thinking, and new action. As Hardy, Lawrence and Phillips caution, 'exactly *how* do shared understandings, created by conversational narratives and interaction, lead to action?' (1998: 69). Any action that emerges from particular conversational activity and content will be mediated by an individual's identity, skills and emotions, and importantly, as Hardy *et al.* (1998) argue, also by their potential to co-frame the conversation, in other words their power relations. However, the potential of action learning, as participants engage in collaborative or co-operative enquiry, comes from the social nature of shared meaning-making. In other words, action learning affects the very patterns of organizing and herein lies the potential to affect organization-wide or systemic capacity to perform.

Concluding thoughts: implications for public service leadership development

Although there are increasing sums being invested in public leadership development, there remains a significant gap in practical understanding of how individual learning and development can best translate into changed organization or systemic practice. Recent evidence suggests that the strongest impacts on organizations come from interventions with cross-organizational groups, rather than with individuals alone (Chesterman and Horne, 2002; Vince, 2004a, b). The 'organization' may be a single agency, a formal partnership or a multi-agency network. I have argued above how this can be theorized in terms of organizational understanding. The implication of these views is more shared leadership development – opportunities to learn, talk and think that are shared across public sector organizations if not also alongside the private sector as well. The key implication for leadership development is that taking a relational perspective on organizing implies that leaders fundamentally need to become better inter-relators. This chapter has analysed why action learning as a social learning process, has such potential to enable this development.

Relating this context of public leadership back to the heuristic model in Figure 4.1, the complexity for individuals in the public sector needs 'both-and' intentions: both performative learning to improve practice, address problems and enhance capacity; and also emancipatory learning in the sense of provoking transformations in perspective, stimulating new self-insights, increasing awareness of power, of otherness and of powerlessness in the social context of the public policy system. Action learning, as a broad church of approaches with shared principles, has the potential to meet this challenge.

An implication for evaluating the organizational impact of individual learning is that it is simplistic and inadequate to count qualifications or tick off competencies. It is essential to look at the social context, what it is that organization members have learned, how they are trying to work with it, and whether there is anything in the patterns of organizational interactions that blocks them from enacting what they have learned.

Section II

Practice

Developing leaders

The three chapters of this section on 'Practice – developing leaders' are on the theme of action learning employed to develop individual leaders. They relate experiences from different sectors and with senior leaders at different stages of their careers. Chapter 5 conveys Michael Lyons' reflections, in an interview with Clare Rigg, on facilitating learning sets for new local authority chief executives. In Chapter 6 Sue Richards recounts a ten-year-old action learning set of chief probation officers, some established, some new, with evolving membership over the period. In Chapter 7 Frank Blackler and Andy Kennedy describe an action learning programme designed to 'renew and refresh' long serving chief executives in the English National Health Service. What do these chapters have to say about how action learning helps participants develop their leadership capability?

One theme running through all three chapters is the facilitator role and the desirable balance between expert and process facilitation within it. Michael Lyons compares action learning facilitation and coaching or mentoring individuals, when the facilitator is an experienced practitioner, as he was. He talks of a hybrid model that draws from each at different moments, and discusses the value of such an approach to help balance individual and group needs. Sue Richards describes being used as a general public policy expert by the set she facilitated, whose knowledge the group used to help them make sense of their changing professional territory. Also a hybrid, the programme related by Frank Blackler and Andy Kennedy bypassed the dilemma for the individual facilitator by encompassing one-to-one consultations as well as action learning tasks within the design. In explaining the design rationale they provide a valuable articulation of the theoretical underpinning of their programme, based on activity theory. They explain the use of ideas in the learning process drawn from psychoanalytic, attachment and social theory: in particular, notions of 'containment', 'parallel process', 'narrative as a secure base' and 'solidarity with the object'.

Richards illustrates linkages between individual, organizational and systemic development as the leaders she worked with pursued bridges between policy and practice and between the centre of government and localities. The set is interesting in its longevity, with an enduring value for participants, albeit with changing membership over time. She illustrates the importance of the learning set as a peer group, attributing its final demise to the entry of hierarchy into the set, as a result of national restructuring of the probation service and job redistribution.

A final theme, discussed by both Lyons and Richards, is the value of peer supervision for facilitators: someone to question, support and challenge them in similar ways to the role they play with set participants.

5 Local authority chief executive action learning sets

Michael Lyons and Clare Rigg

Introduction

This chapter recounts events and lessons from three action learning sets run by Michael Lyons with new chief executives of UK local authorities during 2002–4. The material is derived from an interview with Michael Lyons (ML) conducted by Clare Rigg (CR) in early 2005 and the chapter is presented in interview format around core themes that explore why and how action learning was used, and in particular Michael Lyons' reflections on coming new to facilitation, but highly experienced as a chief executive.

Action learning – why and how?

CR   Could you explain how these action learning sets began?
ML   Going back to the autumn of 2001 I had just left the position of chief executive of Birmingham City Council and joined INLOGOV [the Institute of Local Government Studies, School of Public Policy, University of Birmingham, UK] as director and was beginning to think through what useful contribution could I make to the working life of the department. One of the earliest landmarks in that was a conversation with Professor Sue Richards there. I raised a personal conviction that one of the things that I felt I could contribute was to share some of the learning of having done the job of chief executive of three big authorities. I felt there had to be something I could share with other people particularly who were new to the role and we talked through how that might be presented.

Action learning was on my agenda right from the beginning and that dates back to an experience way back in 1981 when I was working with West Midlands County Council and we funded a small action learning experiment in something called the Action Resource Centre in Saltley, in Birmingham. That had been preceded by one in Stoke-on-Trent which brought together a group of small enterprises, which had demonstrated quite an extraordinary breakthrough just by getting the MDs of these six companies to form effective action learning sets. And that's where I was first introduced to Reg Revans' thinking and I was captivated.

Starting out – towards a hybrid model of action learning/coaching and mentoring

CR   Did you have specific hopes of things that might be delivered by the interplay of the action learning experience in combination with the transfer of experience participants might gain from working with you?

ML   Oh, yes, I was very clear that they would learn as much from each other so, whilst I acknowledge that this had a degree of hybridity from the beginning, I was also interested in exploring action learning as a tool kit and so we spent a fair bit of time thinking about how could we set this up, learning from previous action learning work about how a group learned from each other, trusted each other. Right from the beginning the thing was intended to concentrate on looking at people early in their job, giving them a chance to bring to their peer group experiences they were having, test them out and to use the group as a problem solving reference group. That was definitely part of the early ambition.

So right from the beginning with the chief executives I saw it as a bit of a hybrid, combining both an interest in action learning but also an interest in experience transfer, in mentoring. In the beginning, what Sue Richards and I agreed was that we would work together, my drawing on her much greater experience of running learning workshops and of management learning and my bringing a recent practitioner's perspective. What we did was to write to incoming chief executives – anybody who was new to the post in the last year – and my memory is that we raised 24 people and extraordinarily 18 of them wrote back to say they were interested. So it was an incredible take-up.

We then divided those folks into three groups doing our best to match similar sized authorities. And also doing our best to match people – there were a couple of people there for whom this was a new appointment but they'd actually been in another chief executive post before. So we threw those more experienced folks together. And that's it really; that's the background.

Having divided them into groups, we then followed the same format for all the three groups which centred on an overnight stay preceded by an afternoon session and followed by a good part of a day session. Sue Richards came to the very first session and did a presentation on the nature of action learning and the relationship of the cycle of action, reflection, learning and re-action. And this was followed by an initial agenda-building session working with the participants on issues they wanted to bring forward to share with colleagues and to then use that structure in the time available to work through those topics. And that very much became the pattern of future sessions. Fairly early in it was agreed that each group would meet three times a year and the whole exercise would run for two years, because we felt that this was the shortest time that you could guarantee getting something out of it but long enough to feel that it was not too much of a commitment in terms of the individual or their authority.

At some time fairly near the beginning of the exercise, I think probably the second set of workshops, Sue and I realized simultaneously that actually these groups didn't need co-facilitation. That had been very important to me; it gave me the confidence to get going, but once we got going it was clear they didn't need two people, and it was rather expensive of our time. So from then on I acted as sole facilitator. Exactly the same format – at the beginning we would always write in advance to say, let us know if there are any issues you are keen to discuss. The first session would be agenda-building, then the remainder of the time divided amongst the items that participants brought to the table. We did experiment once or twice at the suggestion of participants in bringing in someone to make a specific contribution, but it never became a formal part of the process, which I think is illustrative of the fact that these groups were willing to reflect on and change the format if required. The dilemma is that this required prior planning, whereas when these groups worked at their best was when they dealt with what people were feeling and experiencing in real time not what they might have planned for four months before. So I think that's probably why external input never quite became a fixed piece of what we were doing.

The facilitator role – pitfalls and potential of having expertise

CR   Can we talk about your role as the facilitator? From a purist definition of action learning the facilitator is best conceived as a non-subject expert whose primary role is to facilitate the process. With you, you couldn't but have the subject expertise, what has been described as master craftsman or master practitioner, in relation to the participants as apprentices. Could you say a bit more about how you approached the potential tensions of this situation?

ML   Well, I can absolutely understand why the literature and indeed the body of practice points toward being an expert facilitator rather than an expert practitioner because that clearly concentrates on the skills of holding the group together and making sure that people are learning effectively and that all of your energies are directed into creating the learning set and the underlying importance of recognizing that at some time the facilitator might withdraw, so that there isn't a dependency there. So I was aware of that and I was aware that this was going to be a tension and as I set the thing up my original plan was that we might be able to get round this by co-facilitating this but then I realized that this wasn't the solution. So it did become a hybrid.

I am also aware of course of the interaction between the group and me and that there were some things that I warmed to. I was not sitting there passively. I did certainly try to develop a persona in the group of not being directive but basically encouraging discussion and then using a process of summarizing to include my commentary on the discussion that had taken place and that seemed to be appreciated. I won't claim I was always invisible and never offered a view, but it appeared to be that people found it most attractive if I provided a summation after a discussion and a sort of pulling out of learning points for reflection, with a degree of personalization in that. There was definitely a dialogue running through this in which people were valuing an opinion from me as well. I could simultaneously acknowledge it was probably a weakness that I should have so indulged, that it is outside the learning set model, which means energy going out to the facilitator which could have been shared more accurately. Equally it was valued. I think we always did manage to provide the kind of sounding board, the testing, the challenge rather than shaping somebody's solution for them and so it seems to me that that was the thing that I struggled hardest to protect, that people shouldn't feel they have been given an answer but have been helped to question so that any answer which evolved was theirs. And so possibly there were a number of occasions where participants in those different groups went back as a result of discussions, which I contributed to, not with a solution that others or I had given them, but their own one. I think in many ways the kernel of the learning set model was protected and to some extent I just became another member of the learning set, albeit a privileged one, I wouldn't detract from that.

CR   Did you ever find yourself having to hold back from saying, 'I wouldn't do it like that if I were you'?

ML   I started from a very strong view of the limitations of transferable experiences between different local authorities. I used to do a presentation on 'the chief executive as anthropologist' just to emphasize how any local authority is a pretty complex system and whilst it might have some superficial similarity to the one next door in terms of geography and function and size, that's only superficial because the impact of history, different personalities and different structures leads to quite profound differences in culture and behaviours and therefore you should be careful in assuming that what works in one place works in another. So I started with that very strong feeling. I don't think there were many times, I mean there were definitely experiences over the two years where I thought I'm not sure I'd have done it that way but those were pretty equally divided with the feeling that I'm glad that person did because it worked for them, and a feeling of well, what does it matter what I think anyway because there is only one person playing this game, there is only one person on this stage, it's not me and it's not anyone else in the group.

Preoccupations of the chief executives

CR   How did participants use the learning sets?

ML   Before we put the chief executives into groups I asked everyone what were their expectations, what were they hoping to do, what had they been doing previously, and what had they already discovered about the job. So that very much helped me in the shaping of the sets, but it also meant that by the time we had the first set meeting I'd already got a sense of some of the preoccupations across the group.

I think the most important thing to say is that fairly early on the three groups took on quite distinctive characteristics. The group which most totally approximated a traditional action learning set was the group of wholly new chief executives of district councils. That may be because there was greater homogeneity: these people were running authorities of roughly the same size; they had the same set of functions and were all doing it for the first time. Both of the other groups were a combination of counties, unitaries and London boroughs, people doing it for the first and second time, so they were more hybrid in terms of characteristics. The one composed of district chief executives was the one where, not immediately, but certainly before the end of the first year, there was clearly evidence that they were in contact with each other and quite regularly, by email. I don't think they physically met but in the second year that group met up at the Local Government Association conference and the fact that they were part of some other group, this action learning group, was clearly a reason for them getting together at the conference. With the other groups, there was some contact in between meetings, but more intermittent, really, and one group in particular were severely damaged by the experiences of one of their members right from the very first meeting, about which I will say more later. Just very quickly to recap on the other groups, both of them actually worked quite well. Interestingly, the one which in the end appears to have had the longest and most valuable life, you might not have been able to predict that at the beginning because it was actually a bit slow to get beyond information exchange. It started its initial meeting with a fairly technical agenda; people were interested to exchange things they were doing rather than how they were doing them, whereas the two more experienced groups were more quickly into how do you do things and how do I do things and tell me a little bit about how you are attracting external investment – that sort of thing. So the one that started with what some might say a safer agenda, an agenda which was more about an information exchange rather than a more substantial personal commitment to learning and changing, in the end appears to have had the longest life and where interestingly relationships actually were stronger. Maybe because they built up slower. So that would be the distinction I would make between them.

CR   Can you say something about the preoccupations of the groups and the directions they took?

ML   I have a very strong sense that running through all the three groups were about half a dozen common issues. I also have to acknowledge that maybe the issues that I found the most alluring were those I spent most time thinking about between groups. But certainly there was some sort of constancy between all three groups – one being what is the role of the chief executive, the distinctive role? There was a lot of interest in the relationship between the chief executive and the leader of the council and how to get the best out of that relationship. Of course inevitably over the two years we were together, there were some quite sharp experiences of people who were having problems with their leader or in a couple of extreme cases were actually in direct conflict with their leader. So there were a set of issues around that.

Closely related to this but quite separate I think, there was a lot of interest in the extent to which the chief executive should seek to provide leadership to the council. So if the political leadership was seen to be in disarray, lacking in energy, lacking in creativity, the new chief executives coming in were saying 'I have a sense I know what to do here, but is it right for me to; where is the right territory here for me to make my contribution?' In many ways this was the most exciting area, I would now contend, based on my experience and having watched these folks. If the world worked as the model says this is the job of the politicians and it clearly isn't appropriate for chief executives to become the political leadership, but there may be times when the chief executive complements, supplements, stimulates, coaches, and there is no choice in that, it's not something to back off, so long as you are doing it you try to have a sense of not trying to replace but trying to nurture.

CR   It seems an example of a valuable lesson that is very usefully shared through action learning.
ML   Indeed. The very powerful point on what are the exact boundaries of the political process. You can tell that people really don't know what to do in this setting, it's most frightening and there's no doubt in my mind that with the two more experienced groups my being able to say don't worry too much about this, this isn't unknown territory that will open up and swallow you, was very reassuring and helped them to become more bold later on. And if I surveyed them and asked what did you most get out of these two years I am sure they would say that more important than anything else during that period while they were finding their way, it was actually time and time again coming back and finding that what they thought was an exceptional experience was actually shared elsewhere in the group, that it wasn't odd or extreme. That notion of learning through testing and finding an echo was really quite marked and that building of confidence because it had a resonance with other colleagues.

Balancing individual and group needs – when things go awry

ML   The group that worked least well was the one which when we were originally designing them was the group which you might call the most experienced. It included two chief executives of city councils, and one of a county council, but there weren't enough people running those kind of large organizations to comprise a complete set so it meant that this group needed to be completed by other people. I chose them on the basis of their strength of character. There were these three people running these large authorities who were quite experienced and it seemed important to me to have people who could feel confident as their peers, or who would appear potentially as their peers. This was complicated because it meant bringing in people who had substantially less experience. The truth is that the people I brought in without as much experience were not really the problem. The problem revolved around one person, this was Diane [fictitious name], the chief executive of a district council. It was a case of *force majeure* that she was in this group because she would have been a more fitting candidate in one of the other groups, but a neighbouring council chief executive would have been with her which we agreed wasn't appropriate. The only group left to move her into was the more experienced group and indeed there was a bit of pressure from her that this was the right place to be. I was open about how decisions on group membership were being made.

The very first meeting was marked by a most extraordinary revelation about Diane being bullied by her leader. In fact two of the other participants had similar stories but in Diane's case this became a bit of a leitmotif for the next two meetings, I think, looking back on it and in the end she stopped participating. It's a matter of subsequent public knowledge that she later parted acrimoniously from the authority. I don't think it was a problem for the group the first time round but the fact that it bled into subsequent meetings actively disabled the group from really getting going and left a sort of feeling that the original strong business-like approach of getting down to working together wasn't achieved, although I don't think there was anybody there who didn't understand that this was about feelings as much as it was about actions. Nonetheless this group never quite got off on the right footing, putting boundaries around anxiety, and so I think the group was damaged by that.

CR   Did this individual's need detract time away from other people?
ML   It certainly did at the first meeting – an inordinate amount of time. And it did take attention away from other people. People were remarkably positive about the first meeting but at the second meeting things hadn't moved on and Diane was very hungry for attention and care. It was probably at the second meeting where the damage was really done. Indeed the interesting thing was that the other colleagues who had shared the same problems of bullying had actually used the group's advice to sort the thing out in the intervening four months, so there we had a sharp contrast where somebody actually listened to what colleagues said, had been strengthened by peer group advice not to let the thing pass, had gone back and acted remarkably courageously, whereas here we had someone who was locked in a completely different place.

Potential and limitations of action learning for senior leader development

CR   Given the kind of facilitator you were, by which I mean, highly experienced practitioner as well, what are your views on the similarities and differences between the role of action learning facilitator and the role of being a coach or mentor?
ML   There are some frustrations with the action learning model of which the most intensive one was absenteeism. If an action learning set is really going to take off it really needs to draw on almost all of its membership on a consistent

basis. Now I know again all the guidance from earlier practitioners points to that but I would definitely reinforce it. At different times with two of the groups we had difficulty in getting people to every meeting and this became frustrating because the dynamics varied from one to another session. Just every now and again an individual couldn't get to a group and I would try and fill that gap because the format meant that if you missed one then eight months to the next session was quite a long period and I would give them the opportunity to come and have a private session, which although not action learning did provide a degree of continuity and helped to give some back-up to the group arrangements.

When I was thinking this out, one of the things I was going to extrapolate into was other work that I have done since then, as actually I spend more time now coaching and mentoring, and this has been educated by the intensive learning I gained from these action learning sets. With coaching or mentoring it's so much more concentrated, I mean the ability when working one-to-one to affect someone deeply into an issue that is preoccupying them. There were times when that was possible within the action learning sets, but the problem of a facilitator is that you are constantly balancing the needs of the individual who would really like to explore more deeply and you know deserves to explore issues more deeply with the fact that you've got a set of other people who are pretty positively committed to doing this but also have a contract, a quid pro quo: when are we going to get onto my subject that I'm interested in and the trade is quite a conscious part of the debate.

CR   You seem to be saying that, in terms of developing managerial leaders, there is more potential in one-to-one development methods?

ML   I probably personally would say that I am at one with Reg Revans in saying that managers almost by definition ought to be learners and I think that's absolutely right. Any learning activity by people who are managing and directing other people is worthwhile and it almost directly follows from that that actually there may be different learning and different experiments in learning at different times, so I wouldn't say that action learning is inevitably a weaker experience than mentoring but try out both because there might be different things for you. To go back to my group which had problems, you know what I should have done with Diane was to say after the first session, 'Diane, this is such a troubled time you've been through, this nascent embryonic action learning group probably would be overloaded by trying to deal with it – let me be your mentor, your supporter whilst you see if you can sort these issues out then go back into the group once that's sorted, or there's perspective.'

At the initial stage I didn't realize quite how serious the issues were and I didn't realize until somewhat later quite what a detrimental impact that had on other people's perception of the group, but looking back on it now, with the right tools, which is what we are talking about now, I should have been clear that those array of tools were at my disposal; mentoring, coaching as well as facilitation.

Implications for organizational and systemic development

CR Looking beyond individual leadership development, do you have any thoughts on the implications of action learning for organizational and systemic development?

ML Let me talk about Cardiff. You might tell me that this doesn't have a link, but for me it was striking. About a year into the learning sets, Cardiff City Council invited me to chair their corporate governance commission and this was a strange exercise, it was the decision of the council at the suggestion of the then leader that there should be an external look at the way that the council ran itself and in part that was a response to the fact that there was a lot of controversy about something called the 'Echogate' saga. In short it was when a letter was prepared by a senior officer at Cardiff to another Labour politician encouraging them to write to the press to defend the leader who was getting beaten up in the press. Extraordinarily this letter, instead of reaching the member concerned, ended up on the desk of the editor of the newspaper who immediately used it as front page material to question the way the council was being run, and it does raise the issue about why senior officers were involved in the political process and, a small event, but it does suggest that this is not healthy in a democratic organization. And in short the way that the commission was set up was all three leaders, the leaders of the three groups on the council were members of the commission, and external parties. I was invited to chair this and had some say in the category of people we invited.

When I started I didn't think it had any parallels with the action learning set, because essentially we were given the remit by the Council, we were working as a group of people, we had the three leaders who had quite different views of what had been going on in the Council and there were other people, some of them truly external and expert on some part of the community of Cardiff with again their own views of what had been going on. We started our life with the traditional model for a commission, welcoming evidence and reflecting on it, but gradually the process of reflection as opposed to gathering of information grew in significance, not least because the three leaders were there and actually engaged in what became quite an intimate dialogue about their own views of what was going on and how much of this was rooted in history and how much their own behaviour. More and more it felt like an action learning set meeting to discuss how the Council works and how it might work in the future. And I'm sure part of that was the way I was drawing on the other experience and seizing on the opportunity that it seemed to me that the Council was much more likely to change the way it behaved if actually some of the key players understood more clearly and had the chance to explore themselves rather than just concentrating on writing a report. So it really became an extraordinary extended dialogue by a number of people as much as it was a formal commission.

CR That's a really useful insight into the potential for using an action learning approach across whole organizational or even systemic working.

ML   I think so. If you have a group that's completely from one organization or a cluster of organizations working as a family then I think there are a whole set of additional benefits that can be derived as compared with a group of people who come because they play the same role in completely different and separate organizations so you begin to address the inter-relationships between one organization and another. I think Cardiff exhibited just that set of spheres. You had the three leaders, you then had those other people of Cardiff who were learning about what the council did and seeing that actually some of these issues which appeared in the press involved quite complex trade-offs about strong leadership and balance; the question of exactly how Cardiff had got itself into this constitutional and rather odd position, where the whole Council was very weak relative to the leader. This was a much stronger model of one-person leadership than most of the mayoral options on offer. But back to the point which you're exploring on organization development, I've got no doubt at all that the Cardiff exercise would not have been possible if it had not been chaired by someone from outside, which was me. I acted as chair/facilitator but also with other people from outside, for instance from the Local Government Association and the three outside voices were all confident in their own experience and therefore actually very good challenge agents. So the particular cocktail of those people working together and learning together and looking at inter-relationships but in combination with external challenge and investigation you could take that straight into an action learning set.

For me this reinforces the facilitator having some confidence in taking an exploratory role. So I think where this is taking me is to say maybe hybridity is not such a bad thing if it makes for a stronger and more confident challenge in facilitation.

Concluding thoughts on the place for action learning

CR   What key conclusions do you draw and is there anything you would in retrospect have done differently?

ML   Well, it's interesting when you talk to the participants, feedback from all of them was that it was worth doing. But it has to be said that at times attendance was a problem and you have to measure that, did they prioritize it enough that they would always come? In fairness, the first two years of a new chief executive is very hard work and so this is a demanding time to find any space and a number of them were absolutely consistent in attending every occasion. I was left at the end wondering, one group definitely faltered and never made up ground, one group charged on and I wouldn't be surprised if participants actively had communication with each other still. The middle group was more complex because during the life of the group some of them went on for promotion and I suspect that if I asked all of them, I think all of the individuals were buoyed up by the experience of working with their peers, they definitely drew confidence from it which enabled them to move faster, that's my perception. How would I have dealt with it differently? Well, I think there may be some lessons about whether facilitating an action learning set can be combined with a mentoring contribution in a different way. What I've been calling hybridity.

I certainly believe that you need people in a set who are evenly matched. They can only respond to your invitation to join and so they therefore depend upon you to match them accordingly. I think you do need people evenly matched otherwise you never quite get the strength of a group of people who value each other equally.

Finally, I would probably, if I was doing it again, be clearer about supervision for facilitators. Looking back on it that was a weakness really, I should have been going back to someone to discuss the learning and particularly the new experiences I was coming across. I paid attention to this at the start, through the co-facilitation, but then I neglected it later. Because you need to be learning yourself as the facilitator.

6 Learning and leading

Action learning for chief probation officers

Sue Richards

Introduction

This is an account of a learning set which persisted through several different combinations of participants, with one person being a member all the way through. Its members were chief probation officers. It lasted from 1994 until 2004, and was facilitated by the author of this chapter. The chapter is a piece of reflection on the part of the facilitator, weaving together a narrative account of the activities of the set at various stages of its life with the story of the changing circumstances in which participants worked, in the eye of the storm of changes in public management. The author reflects on the process employed within the set, and its benefits and disadvantages.

The draft text was sent to those set members still working to ask for their comments and reflections, and some of their comments have been included. Their names have been changed to protect their confidentiality, although because of their prominence in their profession a determined sleuth could probably work out who they are.

The origins of the set

The probation service has always had a tradition of action learning as part of its own professional training, rooted in social work ideas and the idea of reflective professional practice. Additionally, when this story began, the service itself was very much peer-led, and peer-based development ideas such as the learning set found a natural home there. Professional leadership was provided through an organization called ACOP (the Association of Chief Officers of Probation) whose many working groups on many themes were populated by assistant chief, deputy chief and chief probation officers. In 1994 there were 53 probation areas, all of which had a chief probation officer.

The 53 chief probation officers were each accountable to area committees which consisted predominantly of appointed local magistrates. However, this accountability was in practice couched within the acceptance of the high degree of professional autonomy which was characteristic of public service in the post-war era (Richards, 2001). Area committees tended not to challenge the professional hegemony of probation chiefs, and were not in a position to watch over the interests of the taxpayer. Budgets were set in the Home Office, which provided 80 per cent of the funding, local authorities being required to provide the other 20 per cent. Neither the Home Office nor local authorities were able to exercise much leverage over the service.

By the early 1990s this situation was beginning to look untenable. A decade of Thatcherism had transformed most areas of public service. Even the NHS was experiencing the fundamental changes involved in the internal market. Much of the criminal justice system, however, remained untouched by these events. During the early 1990s all of this changed. Michael Howard's occupancy of the Home Office, and his statement that 'prison works' – implying that the community-based service of probation did not – was a prelude to major initiatives from the Home Office to break the professional autonomy of the probation profession and to establish a more managerial approach, thus bringing it into line with the changes being enacted in other public services.

Creating the learning set

So the writing was on the wall for the probation profession. In 1992, the author was the director of the Public Management Foundation, and had completed an action research project exploring the significance of the concept of the consumer in public service, drawing attention to a shifting balance of power between professionals and managers, facilitated through the emergence of a consumer-oriented service – at least in terms of the rhetoric of legitimation if not yet in practice. The argument was that professional leaders needed to transform themselves into managerial leaders in order to guide their services through these changes in patterns of legitimation. The chair of ACOP asked the author to speak on this subject at the annual conference in Newcastle that year – an event remembered by most for the speech given by the then shadow spokesman on Home Affairs, who promised to be 'tough on crime, tough on the causes of crime' (Labour election slogan, 1992).

Shortly after this, the author was contacted by the person who was to be a member of the set throughout its various emanations. He had been at the ACOP conference and was keen to enhance his own capacity and that of others to respond to the changing environment. On reflection, the choice of facilitator was a crucial determinant of the subsequent operation of the set. A group of professionals seeking to come to terms with and then shape the emerging agenda for their service chose someone with a relevant skill-set to achieve that, leading to the favouring of some sorts of activity and the disfavouring of others. While the facilitator was able to manage the process of action learning, her forte was comparative public management studies and at certain peak times of organizational change this strand predominated. This resulted in both the benefits and the disbenefits of having a facilitator with 'expertise' independent of the expertise of set participants.

The learning set – first generation

The person who provides the thread of continuity throughout this narrative is James, who when the story begins is the deputy chief probation officer in a large probation service, relatively newly appointed, young to reach that level within the service and keen to develop and support his own capacity to work at top levels within the service. James's chief probation officer was someone who was a leading figure on the national stage, frequently away from the locality, and a key task for him was to get a grip on leading and managing the organization and its operational delivery.

Questions of efficiency and effectiveness and good management were crucial to him at the time, as national frameworks for inspection and central government concern for local delivery were being sharpened up. As a new figure on the top management landscape, he was less part of an old world of self-governing professionals, focusing their collective efforts on shaping policy and practice through ACOP, and more focused on service delivery. Growing and developing into the de facto role of chief operating officer – running the inside of the organization while his boss ran the outside – was his first development task and the reason why he had taken the initiative in creating the set.

Two other members of the set could be labelled as well-established members of the cadre of chief probation officers. Emily and Rodney were both chief probation officers for relatively small and rural probation areas, both seen as successful at handling both the external and internal agenda for their organization, adept at networking across the criminal justice world but also paying attention to the effectiveness of the organization. Emily's wry observations on the ways of the world of probation were insightful and knowledgeable. Rodney was intellectually strong, always able to distinguish between the wood and the trees, and a fascinated explorer of the world he inhabited, a naturally reflective practitioner.

Edward was a long-established probation chief, described by James at the start of the set as 'the person we all look up to'. He was chief in a major northern, predominantly urban, probation area. His approach to the work was as a leading professional, carrying forward into his managerial leadership role the professional skills and values – empathy, psychological insight, desire to coach and mentor – to allow the embedded goodness in all to come to the surface and flourish. This approach could be regarded as at the leading edge of thinking about managerial leadership in 2006. In 1994 it looked to some like old-style professionalism.

The last member of the group was Karen. She too had recently been appointed as the deputy chief probation officer of a major urban service, and like James she was young, keen to develop and also working under one of the major national figures in probation. She combined a strong sense of the changing big picture nationally with the need and desire to express herself as a leader in her service. She was clearly the heir apparent, had probably been recruited into the deputy role with that in mind, and was promoted to chief probation officer in the same area soon after the start of the set. Karen conformed to the description of leadership propounded by Julia Middleton, founder of the organization Common Purpose: 'Eyes on the horizon, feet on the ground.'

Method of working

The set functioned at first in a relatively conventional mode. It had come into existence through a process of peer selection and negotiation – although it was funded by the Probation Unit in the Home Office, the policy division carrying an oversight brief for the service as a whole. Probation had a devolved governance structure, but its funding came primarily via the Home Office and this gave the department a locus on development issues. As a collection of peers who belonged to the same professional domain but did not actually work for the same organization, they were well placed to offer each other peer support and challenge off-line.

The set met about three times a year for a 24-hour away-day session. The first few meetings consisted of a gradual process of self-revelation, springing from the joint exploration of organization and management issues that individuals were tackling in their own organizations. These issues covered a wide range of matters, and as the intimacy in the relationships developed, levels of exploration became deep and probing. The two deputy chiefs benefited particularly from having older hands available to reflect on the issues, and this also helped as each of them stepped up a level and grew into the role of chief probation officer. This was a time of mutual benefit from peer support and challenge.

But the focus of the set changed after an initial period of about a year and a half. This is probably rooted in the inception of the set and the choice of facilitator. The context in which early contacts had been made between the facilitator and the set initiator was characterized by interpretations of the changing phenomena of the world of public policy and public service. Initially this had been founded on developing an understanding of the changing nature of public service professionalism, the emergence of public management as a set of ideas behind some of the policy changes, and of the need for professionals to adapt or die – metaphorically.

Set members had chosen as their facilitator someone who was both commentator and academic expert on the changing nature of public management, and also someone with an organizational development/action learning strand to her background. This mixture of 'expert' and 'process facilitator' seemed to be what they wanted and needed. Process facilitator alone would have been good in a relatively unchanging environment, where the expert knowledge held by group members was sufficient in itself. In a case like that process facilitation is what is needed. But probation chiefs felt catapulted into an alien world, and the facilitator had expert knowledge which helped them understand and interpret that world.

So what began to emerge in practice as the set methodology was a mixture of peer support and challenge on issues concerning the management of probation area services, and a wider, more exploratory approach which involved the facilitator bringing in concepts and models in use elsewhere in the public policy system, and the group exploring their applicability to the changing world of probation.

Dominant models in use elsewhere involved the overturning of an approach which rested on the relative autonomy of public service professionals, trusted by politicians and the public to make the right decisions on behalf of society. The pattern and practice of 30 years were giving way to a new order, much more centrally directed by political leaders in government and their agents in Whitehall. This involved senior professionals to position themselves very clearly as managers of professional service rather than as leading professionals, able to make radical shifts within their organizations to meet the new agenda.

The members of the set explored this agenda and their own approach to it, creating for themselves a pathway between the old approach and something they could live with in the new – old values in modern form. Not everyone could or wished to make that journey. Two years after its inception, a shadow fell over the set with the departure of its most established member, Edward. The mood music in the Home Office called for the probation inspectorate to present greater challenge to local area probation services, requiring systems and behaviours that fitted the new paradigm. Edward did not make that transition, and took early retirement following a particularly critical inspection report.

His departure came close to the end of the last Conservative government, and members of the group gave their energies to reflecting on the future role of probation, given the likely election of a government led by the person who had introduced the idea of being 'tough on crime, tough on the causes of crime' at their 1992 conference.

A new agenda and a re-formed learning set

In the dying days of the last Conservative government learning set members gave their attention to the key themes that lay ahead. It became increasingly clear that a greater focus on outcomes would be required in public service. There was a growing discourse about the need to work in a more 'joined-up' way across the boundaries of the silos of public service (Clarke and Stewart, 1997; Richards, 2001). To reflect the changing emphasis, set members decided that they would move away from their existing model of a group of professional peers, and instead construct a cross-professional learning network of perhaps a dozen people, drawn from across the criminal justice system and beyond.

This plan of action came to nothing, however. This was not because of the unattractiveness of the idea, but was caused by the intervention of life events outside the scope of this chapter. The facilitator was unable to make progress in establishing the proposed new criminal justice network. No-one else was commissioned to take this forward during her absence as this had been an agenda which she played a significant role in setting. This situation demonstrates the vulnerability of learning sets as a form of development based on strong personal relationships which are not easily substitutable, given the knowledge and understanding that has been created over time. Individual facilitators are not easily replaceable by others. Because of the unavailability of the facilitator, the existing learning set went into abeyance, and one of its members joined a learning set being run for other probation chiefs. Karen moved across to another set, aware that the support she received from her set had been essential to her own achievement and that it was important for her to find a new source of such support.

The policy agenda for probation made a significant shift in the couple of years following the election of the Labour government of 1997. A commitment to improving the outcomes of the criminal justice system led to the emergence of new ideas about probation structure. New ministers and their civil servants appeared to believe that if only they could exercise more control over probation areas – then controlled through a rather arcane local governance system – then improvements in outcomes could be achieved. The emerging evidence about reoffending rates following both prison and probation were staggeringly high, and this made ministers impatient to devise more effective interventions. A review under the senior civil servant John Halliday examined the case for bringing together the prisons and probation service under a single corrections agency. Although this review did not opt for this solution, it did call for the centralization of the governance of probation, a most fundamental change in its operation. A decision was made to create a National Probation Service (NPS).

In the light of this developing agenda, James again initiated a reforming of the set. One of the features of the change was the reduction in the number of probation areas from 53 to 42, with boundaries coterminous with other boundaries within the criminal justice system. Some 20 of the former chief probation officers decided to take the offer of an early retirement package. Included in this number were both Emily and Rodney who had earlier been members of this set. Those who did not retire were required to attend an assessment centre to ensure that anyone appointed as a new chief officer of probation would be sure to have the right competences for the job.

James approached some other 'established' chiefs who had come through the assessment process, gathering together a group who decided to explore being in a learning set as a way of supporting themselves. In fact Rodney, a member in the earlier history of the set, decided to continue as a member until he reached the point of retirement, reasoning that he needed support to keep his service on track even though he was due to leave it, and his service was due to merge with another.

The other three new members of the set were Jennifer, who was to be the chief officer for a large service in the south of England, Liza, formerly of the probation inspectorate and now to run a medium-sized service which was suffering performance problems, and Janet, chief from another large northern service. Jennifer stayed for a relatively short time, finding that the set did not really meet her development needs. Liza and Janet stayed for the long term.

Liza was strong both intellectually and as a manager of people. Over three years she made some significant improvements in her new service, building its capability by appointing and developing significant numbers of staff at the next level down. At the three-year point she moved into the centre of the National Probation Service to take responsibility for the national leadership of a particularly high-profile area of policy and service.

Janet was an extremely capable manager of people. It is argued that the most significant quality that leaders can display that will persuade their staff to follow them is a genuine concern for staff members' well-being and development (Alimo-Metcalfe, 1998). This does not fit the popular stereotype of leadership, but it does seem to be supported by the empirical evidence about why people follow leaders. Janet is the kind of leader that followers love.

This membership persisted for almost a year in the run-up to the full enactment of the National Probation Service. The agenda during that time was dominated by the issues connected with the new structure. Set members were all supporters of the idea of the National Probation Service, rather than the former model under which they had grown up. They looked forward particularly to the probation service having a recognizable figure to lead it, visible inside and outside probation, and able to make the case for the value of probation work with ministers and their civil servants. They were inspired by the leadership shown by the new National Director of Probation and full of optimism for the future.

What they found harder to deal with, and the issue on which more time was spent than on anything else, was the existence of newly appointed local boards of governance in each of the 42 new probation areas. Chief probation officers in the past had usually taken a fairly dominant role in relation to their old governance structures. They were a 'necessary evil' but too ineffective to be a problem or to get in the way of a professional service run by the professionals.

Under the National Probation Service, new boards of governance were secretary of state appointees, paid for their attendance, and carrying out the role of employer for all staff below chief officer. A new cadre of people was recruited into the probation service to fill these roles, many of them with experience of community leadership of some kind. They were a more formidable structure for governance and the more determined among them sought to anchor probation in the needs of the community and engage chiefs in a local agenda as well as the agenda set nationally through the National Director.

In the first year of operation of this second generation of the set, therefore, the attention of set members was very much focused on sharing ideas and good practice in working with boards, and with seeking to understand how the new national structure for probation would operate. Just before the National Probation Service went live, another significant change happened in set membership. Rodney and Jennifer departed, and three new members joined the set.

The first of these was Caroline, who had been the last person to be appointed as chief probation officer before recruitment had ceased to begin the major changes involved in setting up the NPS. Caroline was put in charge of a service whose performance was very poor. She was young to be appointed as a chief and had had a fast-moving career, constantly seeking new challenges. She was hungry for learning and used the set as a support mechanism, tapping into the experiential knowledge of colleagues who had been there longer, never afraid to be open to new insights and advice.

Simon was a talented and lively former chief probation officer who had come through the assessment process and been assigned to a large and underperforming service, running a non-devolved service in newly devolved Wales. Simon had been a very active member of ACOP and thereby a contributor to the development of professional policy. Under the new arrangements, he found himself twinned with a formidable chair, a former local authority chief executive himself.

The third member of the group to join was Roger: not a professional probation person but a former prison governor and civil servant who had been appointed to lead a very large probation area, merging several previously separate services into one, each of them having its own culture and traditions, systems and processes. Roger's job immediately before this move had been in the preparation of the legislation of the 2000 Act, so he was deeply familiar with the Home Office discussions which underpinned the creation of the national service, and with the provisions of the Act.

The core of this group stayed in place until the set came to an end in 2004. The significant exception to this was Simon, who resigned in 2002, and Jeremy, who entered the group a few months before its close.

Method of working

All group members were facing heavy demands for improvement in their organizational performance, all were faced with a new pattern of local governance, and all were now placed in the position of being personally accountable to the National Director. This was a time of such massive change in their lives that it was hard to know where to turn first. Since they broadly supported the creation of the national service and respected the National Director, herself a former chief officer, this did not at first occupy much of the time, although there was some exploration of the personal shift involved in moving from being the chief probation officer for X and becoming the chief officer for X in the National Probation Service. There were fears of a loss of self-mastery, but a general sense that 'you would be alright as long as you could improve performance in the service'. Some good practice exchange took place over this time.

This view took something of a knock when Simon resigned, or was required to resign. He had not been in post long enough to have failed to improve performance when negotiations took place for his departure. A symbolic sacrifice is sometimes required by top managers who wish to position themselves as

cracking down on performance. Simon may have been perceived as insufficiently loyal by the National Director, continuing to operate as though he were
in a network or peer culture rather than a hierarchy (diMaggio and Powell,
1991). New anxiety in other set members was created by this recognition that
(small 'p') political factors outside your control could determine your fate. This
event may have marked a turning point in support for the National Director
herself in the broader culture of probation. Many staff perceived her to have
transgressed principles of fairness which were still embedded in the culture.

Further anxiety was created by the way the organizational model was interpreted at national level. The key phrase underlying the design of the system,
expressed in the White Paper and embedded in legislation, was 'strong central,
strong local'. This apparently paradoxical statement invited an interpretation
that set a requirement for high-level performance on national targets but scope
for being rooted in local issues and networks, part of local capacity for tackling
crime and the causes of crime.

The structure created to underline this principle meant that there were no
intermediate levels between the 42 chiefs and the National Director, although
there were a number of chief officer-level posts – Strategic Heads – also reporting to the National Director. With around 50 direct reports, a new model of
line management was clearly required.

The National Director was perceived at best to ignore, and at worst to
undermine, the other half of the model, seeming to see the local boards, the
anchor into locality in the strong central model, as an inconvenient and unnec-
essary presence. It may be that this approach simply represented a continuation
on a national scale of the past experience of governance arrangements seen
through the eyes of service professionals. Instead of resourcing local boards to
develop their capacity to be community leaders, they were hemmed into a
corner. Their initial willingness to give their energy to improvement dissi-
pated by being excluded from the process of change. This eventually led the
boards' representative body into opposition mode. For set members it raised
their level of concern and the dissonance of the central and local worlds which
they inhabited.

The innovative organizational model for probation and its application in
practice formed the core agenda for the set. Over a period of two years, each
time they met they considered the nature of this model and what further
evidence they had acquired since last meeting on how it was being interpreted
in practice. They used their daily interactions with the system as data for
inquiry, and attempted to make sense of what was happening, reflecting
together on the key players and their motives and actions, the principles of the
structure and the significance of events.

Some of this evidence came from participants' own interaction with others
in the system, and some of it came from specific inquiries undertaken by them
as a group. The methodology here was to invite key players to dinner during
the 24-hour meeting of the set to discuss relevant aspects of the model. The
National Director herself came to dinner twice, demonstrating the driven,

charismatic individual she was and her commitment to improved service. Other dinner guests included a chief constable, treasury officials, and a succession of strategic heads of the national service. Regrettably, such occasions seemed to add to the stress of the probation service colleagues who came as guests.

At the end of the first year of the national service, the set conducted a stock-take of the operation of the model in practice, and found it wanting in many respects. They took responsibility for enabling others to hear their views, and doing so in such a way that was seen as a positive contribution to improvement. They prepared a presentation to be given at the quarterly meeting of the 50 chief officers of the service and in advance approached the National Director.

Their view was expressed in loyal terms, but was actually a critique of the first year's operation of the national service. Key elements of the critique were that although there had been excellent transformational leadership – inspiring and challenging – this had been let down by the poor quality of transactional processes, leaving the service across the board confused and uncertain. Systems and processes were inadequately thought through. Set members took seriously their joint responsibility as chief officers and briefed the National Director so that she could present the ideas from the stock-take, with them in supportive mode facilitating discussion groups.

Shortly after this, but possibly because senior staff in the Home Office had picked up the same message rather than as a direct result of set members raising the issue, a new structure was introduced into the top team, creating a new tier of three between the National Director and the rest of the 50.

The importance of the system model – strong central, strong local – is not to be underestimated. It rests on a belief that effective probation needs both national programmes and also situational knowledge and networks to engage the community in the process of the rehabilitation of offenders and to build a sense of public confidence in the criminal justice system. The idiosyncratic mode of interpretation of this model meant that this interesting idea for handling central–local relationships was never really tried.

Rather, the management of the service had begun to create a target-driven culture, with national targets such as those related to numbers on behaviour modification programmes – the easily measured targets on throughput. Probation was no different from other centrally driven services in this respect. Quotas for programmes were fulfilled, whether or not individuals were right for the particular programme, thus reducing programme effectiveness. Mean-while, probation reduced its presence in the locality and the partnerships which were needed to achieve better outcomes in the longer term.

Endgame

It is probable that the National Probation Service was always seen by some in the Home Office as a transitional structure. The Halliday report had toyed with the idea of a single correctional service, involving both prison and community punishment and rehabilitation, but had shied away from this as too politically difficult at the time. It appealed to central government officials who perceived the problem with probation to be their lack of control over it. Like other deeply embedded departmental ideas, it was rolled out again when it looked as though the opportunity existed to make it happen. A new more directive Home Secretary after the 2001 election was one factor in the resurgence of the idea, as was the treasury's alarm at the growing cost of prisons and their ineffectiveness in preventing reoffending. The significance of Martin Narey, Director-General of the Prison Service and later second permanent secretary in the Home Office responsible for both prisons and probation, should not be underestimated as a factor leading to change.

The result of this reconfiguration of forces was the review conducted by Patrick Carter, which led to recommendations to set up a National Offender Management Service (NOMS). The problem he was tackling was why, despite vast public expenditure and a relatively punitive sentencing culture, there was such a poor rate of preventing reoffending. Looking at the system 'end to end', he concluded that the levers for improvement were too weak, and that the commissioning of correctional services should be separated from the provision of those services, with contestability being introduced into provision wherever possible. This is a well-established doctrine, based on the ideas of principal–agent theory, akin to the internal market tried in the NHS in the early 1990s.

Carter's vision was of a single commissioning service, buying from a variety of providers of both prisons and community sentences. However, this simple module has been stretched by the realities of Whitehall power politics. While the top management structure of the National Offender Management Service has been put in place, no time was found in the legislative programme to abolish the local statutory boards, so area probation services remain in existence, employing all of the probation staff below chief. It is said that over time the system will evolve to become NOMS, but it is already clear that the prison service will fight hard to retain the commissioning of services within prisons, so what looks likely to remain is a further disjunction in the probation service, with little improvement in the end-to-end management of offenders which justified the change in the first place. The term 'institutional vandalism' comes to mind.

What we are left with is a bit of a mess. The set members could have been of real use to each other in these circumstances, helping each other to get greater clarity on what was happening, but actually they ceased to be a peer group at this point. Three learning set members were appointed as regional offender managers. In one case this looked as though it would involve management of another set member. At the same time, Roger went back into the civil service. It was decided in these circumstances that the set would disband.

Learning sets in a turbulent environment

This learning set had an early life which fitted into the model described by Revans as classic action learning. The set worked as people at more or less peer level brought to the table key issues with which they were grappling, tapping into each other's knowledge and experience to provide feedback and advice on the problem. For a time this was a satisfactory and mutually beneficial way of operating.

However, as the external environment in which probation operated started to take on a more turbulent form, the methodology of the group slipped away from the classic model, and instead moved into inquiry mode in relation to the external environment. This happened early on as a response to the idea of a profession in transition, during the time of the Major government, then in relation to the emergent strategy for probation of the Labour government of 1997. In anticipation of a change of government and then in its early years, the set started to think about the wider issues of effectiveness in criminal justice.

Pretty soon, however, they became consumed by the significance of the changes being made at national level – first the creation of the National Probation Service in 2001 and then the setting up of the National Offender Management System. Most felt secure in their management competencies as chief probation officers, able to perform as required. They helped each other out on specifics, sharing techniques and tools, often in conversations outside the set meetings. The fact that from 1999 they were known to their peers as the 'mature chiefs' group says something about the general tenor of the group. The adjective is used to describe the people who were already chief officers before the onset of the National Probation Service and who got through the assessment process to stay in post.

There were two exceptions to this description in the group. Caroline had been appointed just before NPS and was young and inexperienced. She is, however, an avid and active learner and ensured that she used the resources of the group to help her deal with a problematic service situation. Her openness and desire to learn enabled her to move a long way, resolve many of her service problems, and position herself as a rising star within the national service, just as James and Karen had done right at the beginning of the set. Although we focused primarily on the national agenda, there was always the opportunity to get air-time for individual issues, and Caroline took this opportunity.

Less well served by the focus on the external environment was Roger, the former civil servant. He was seen by the facilitator and set members as a highly esteemed visitor from the world of policy. He had been a key person in framing the legislation which set up the national service, he is a highly intelligent man with strong political skills, as befits someone who has succeeded as a civil servant. What the author of this chapter now realizes in retrospect is that he was given insufficient air-time to bring to the table the management issues that faced him in his service, issues which were challenging in the extreme and for which he had had the wrong apprenticeship.

Instead of working on his areas of lower competence where he needed help, we focused on his areas of high competence where he could be of most use to other set members in helping them understand and navigate the new national system. As the facilitator, the author acknowledges with regret that she allowed her own interest in the functioning of the public policy system to override the needs of a set member. This is a retrospective realization and not one understood at the time. Roger has now left the probation service and gone back into the civil service to work again in the policy domain.

For the author, this situation also justifies the need for peer supervision in action learning facilitation. Having someone to ask questions about the process you are facilitating is very important, and the absence of such a process in this case contributed to the poor service to this one individual. Such peer support and supervision might be particularly important where the set is operating outside the classic model, in a mixed mode involving the facilitator as both process facilitator and management educator, present because of her expertise as well as the process facilitator. Managing the balance between those two roles needs careful attention and the prompting and questioning of others who have been in the same situation.

The story of this learning set carries many messages. Learning sets which contain chief officers from different organizations provide a unique opportunity to admit vulnerability and thus open up to development. The exchange of wisdom between people doing similar jobs in different settings is also of immense value. Despite the reservation just expressed about the dangers of losing sight of the interests of each member in pursuit of the interest of all, there is also great value in such sets trying to build bridges between policy and practice and between the centre of government and localities. Such relationships work best with a robust two-way traffic, and these set members actively pursued that task, for their own benefit and for the wider benefit of the service.

What stopped the set in its tracks was the collapse of the peer principle. Once members related to each other from different positions in a hierarchy, it called into question the very commonality which had previously led to the success of the set. Nothing lasts forever, but while it did, this set was a source of wisdom, fun, insight, kindness and mutuality.

7 The design and evaluation of a leadership programme for experienced chief executives from the health sector[*]

Frank Blackler and Andy Kennedy

Introduction

What ideas should underpin a short, intensive development programme for experienced senior managers working in the public sector? This chapter describes an action learning programme designed to 'renew and refresh' long-serving chief executives in the English National Health Service who were facing considerable performance pressures. An activity theoretical approach was used to help participants stand back from the imperatives of the moment and reflect on the dilemmas of their situations in new ways. Evaluation data suggests that the mix of events included in the programme created a powerful learning experience for most participants. Other theoretical approaches in addition to activity theory are used to explain this outcome. It is suggested that, at times of ongoing change and frustration, programmes such as the one described in the chapter can help participants develop a resilient approach to conflicts and tensions and may stimulate commitment and resolve.

There has been much interest in leadership development in recent years (e.g. Carter *et al.*, 2000; Conger and Benjamin, 1999; James, 2001), but little consensus about appropriate approaches for leader development in the public sector. Recent discussions include Van Wart's (2003) critique of the strongly normative emphasis in relevant US literature, and the report by the UK government's Performance and Innovation Unit (PIU, 2001) which emphasized the difficulties of leader development in situations where criteria of success are contradictory, the responsibilities of elected politicians and full-time managers overlap, and blame-oriented organizational cultures are common. Literature on healthcare leadership typically suggests that leaders must be able to cope with turbulence (see Gilkey, 1999) but Hartman and Crow's (2002) survey of views in North American healthcare settings suggests that there is little consensus about what this might mean for development programmes. In the UK Currie (1999) has provided a powerful critique of the relevance of competence-based approaches in this setting and, as Edmonstone and Western (2002) point out, many questions remain about the type of leaders healthcare organizations need and how best they might be developed.

This chapter describes the development of an activity theoretical approach to the design of a programme commissioned to 'renew and refresh' long-serving chief executives in the NHS. The programme was designed to help participants stand back from the imperatives of the moment and reflect on the dilemmas of their situations in new ways. Evaluation data indicates that the mix of events included in the programme created a powerful learning experience for most participants. Other theoretical approaches, in addition to activity theory, are used to explain this outcome. It is concluded that a programme based on activity theory, using an action learning approach that includes significant opportunities for reflection, can help participants develop a resilient approach to the conflicts and tensions in their organizations and re-engage with their objectives.

Managers at the centre of a storm; the NHS and its chief executives

The chief executives described in this chapter are the, usually non-medical, managers responsible for managing hospitals, community healthcare organizations and regional health authorities in the English National Health Service. They are amongst the most highly paid managers in the UK's public sector and occupy pivotal boundary-spanning positions which require them to push forward policies that may be unpopular. CEs are responsible to government both for the finances and for the clinical performance of their organizations; they must enact national priorities for healthcare and lead local change programmes; develop good working relations with the many professional groups working in their organizations; work with the chair of their board; build relationships with relevant local agencies to develop services for the public; and generally foster public confidence in the NHS in line with governmental imperatives.

The NHS provides healthcare services to all citizens, most of which remain free at the time of use. It is centrally funded through general taxation and is organized so that government can exercise tight controls. It is the largest employer in Europe with a workforce of around one million. The inevitable complexity of an organization of this size is compounded, in the first place, by tensions associated with the intrinsic nature of healthcare work and, second, with the difficulties associated with the particular organization of the NHS in the UK. Regarding the former, workers in healthcare experience an ongoing proximity to human suffering that can provoke strong, potentially dysfunctional, institutional defences against anxiety (Menzies, 1959; Hinshelwood and Skogstad, 2000). Regarding the latter, as documented by Ham (1999), Timmins (1999) and Klein (2001), since the creation of the NHS governments have experienced ongoing difficulties in reconciling the priorities of healthcare professionals, patients and taxpayers, whilst ensuring an equitable delivery of services across the country.

As Klein (2001) pointed out, the economic and political costs to British governments of problems in the NHS have risen dramatically in recent years. This was much in evidence between early 2000 to early 2003 when the programme discussed here was run, as problems in the NHS moved to the centre stage of British politics. Stung by press reports of problems in the NHS, the New Labour government became determined to invest heavily in it, push through a radical and long-term programme of reforms, specify national standards of care, monitor progress and demonstrate early progress to a sceptical public. Detailed targets of performance, some of which were to prove controversial, were introduced with little consultation.

The significance of these events for chief executives in the NHS was considerable. A small number were to lose their positions because of reorganization; all were required to conform to a complex, and relentlessly demanding, regime of performance inspection. This ranged from daily reviews on issues of high political priority (such as waiting times for emergency treatments) to the publication of national 'league tables' of hospital performance. Performance review systems have been central to the management of public services in the UK for more than a decade (see Power, 1994), but the uncompromising regime developed to monitor the NHS at this time was new. Press and media reports began to appear suggesting that government action had created a 'bullying culture' (e.g. BBC/Institute of Healthcare Management Survey, 2002) and the chairman of the British Medical Association was to state that pressures on NHS managers had become 'obscene' and that 'the fundamental NHS principle of care based on need and need alone has been superseded by the principle of care based on numbers' (*The Guardian*, 1 July 2003). Greener's (2003) academic analysis of the situation similarly concluded that centrally developed performance indicators had provoked a distortion of effort within the service as a whole and were placing tremendous pressure on chief executives.

Finally in this section it should be noted that the concept of management is, in itself, controversial within the NHS. One reason for this is the direct challenge to the power of clinicians that CEs represent (see discussions by Strong and Robinson, 1990; Hunter, 1996; and Ferlie *et al.*, 1996). Another is that politicians have found it convenient to distance themselves from the failures of the system they control by scapegoating managers. For example, at the launch of the New Labour government's reform plan for the NHS, the Secretary of State for Health stated: 'Managers do not have a God-given right to manage, unless you get the structures right you won't get the delivery' (Eaton, 2001: 10). The *Health Service Journal* (a weekly magazine read widely in the NHS) has regularly printed articles on the insecurities faced by chief executives (Cole, 2000, 2001 and 2002). One of these summarized the general situation facing chief executives by saying: 'Life for the average NHS chief executive is nasty, brutish and short. Like football managers, they find that a generous salary often comes at the price of chronic insecurity and the constant risk of being shown the door' (Cole, 2001: 24).

The programme specification and the design rationale

In 1999 officials in the central NHS Executive commissioned the development programme discussed here. It was to be designed for CEs who had been in post for at least seven years (something of an achievement in itself). The commissioners held high expectations for the programme. Although they initially anticipated that CEs would only attend a programme of this kind for a very few days, nonetheless they specified a wide range of learning outcomes including the development of new leadership skills, improved capacities for organizational learning and the rebalancing of work/life relationships. The programme specification warned that NHS chief executives are a demanding group: 'any programme for senior chief executives must recognize that they are discriminating, even sceptical, clients who have considerable experience, knowledge, understanding and skills'. The programme must be 'challenging, credible and capable of capturing their interest'.

At an early stage we decided that it would be inappropriate to design the programme as an academic course (given the needs and motivation of the client group), as a competency-based programme (given their skills and track records), or primarily as an experiential group programme (given the tight restrictions on the length of the programme). Our expectation was that the members of the client group were likely to respond well to an action learning approach, and that such an approach could be used to support group as well as individual learning, and critical reflections as well as practical discussions.

It was quickly to become clear, however, that whilst it was not difficult to think of interesting things that the chief executives might be given to do, it was much harder to be explicit about why we were choosing to include some possibilities while rejecting others. In the absence of a framework to help us make these decisions we found ourselves continually having to revisit the priorities we were developing for the programme in order to think how best these could be achieved.

To help with this issue two approaches to learning theory seemed most likely to be useful: work-based theories of action learning and activity theory. Work-based theories are rooted in the writings of Dewey, Habermas, Revans and Schön, and are well known in the management literature. Marsick and O'Neil's (1999) review of work in this tradition identified three major 'schools' within it: all share a concern with how people can 'learn how to learn' although they differ in their relative concern with learning for pragmatic problem-solving versus critical review. Given the frenetic problem-solving environment of the NHS (where, as Pettigrew *et al.* (1992: 228) observed, 'endemic short-termism and over reaction' is the norm), we wished to design a development programme that would be a process of reflection and review. Early critical approaches to action learning (e.g. Mezirow, 1991) focused primarily on personal values; more recently writers in this tradition have emphasized the social basis of knowledge and the value of public reflection (Hatton and Smith, 1995; Reynolds, 1998). Raelin (2000: 13) summarized the assumptions of such writers: through talk and reflection people can learn to recognize their taken-for-granted values, appreciate the connections between their own practices and the organizational contexts in which they are embedded, and participate in a learning process 'that may transform their world by their very participation in it'. Helpful though we found Raelin's review of how such ideas have been applied to management development we felt that in the complex and uncertain situation of the NHS this general framework was insufficiently precise. We wanted to be clearer about what should be understood by reflective practice, what might prompt such reflection, and how the move from mental process to innovative practices might be understood and supported.

Activity theorists have focused on the relationships between personal and institutional change more directly. The approach has its origins in Russian psychology in the work of Vygotsky, Leont'ev and Luria, and in the writings of Marx and Hegel (see Engeström *et al.*, 1999). Activity theory has been influential in educational circles (e.g. Cole *et al.*, 1978; Wertsch, 1979), although it has been less well known in organization studies (see Blackler *et al.* (2000) for a comparison with better-known approaches to learning in this area). Writers in this tradition draw attention to the importance of the learning of language and dialogue, but they emphasize too the significance of other factors for practices, such as tools and equipment, formal and informal procedures, and the division of labour (Engeström, 1987). Also central to the approach is the notion of 'object of activity', i.e. the physical entity that people are addressing, or the project they are working on. Objects can be relatively easy to identify in craft or manual work (e.g. Keller and Keller's (1993) discussion of a blacksmith's preoccupation with the spoon he was hammering), but they can be more difficult to specify in more complex work situations.

A distinctive feature of activity theory is the way it draws attention to the developments that take place in systems of activity over time. Over long periods systems of activity change their character as objects and infrastructures develop (see Blackler *et al.*'s (1999) account of changes in manufacturing industry). The significance of such developments can be obvious in retrospect, but as such developments occur they feel hesitant and uncertain. Activity theory suggests that developments in activity are driven by people's attempts to resolve the shortcomings, tensions and dilemmas within the activity system. As people recognize tensions within their practices they may begin to reconfigure their activity systems by developing new objects of activity. 'Expansive learning' is the term activity theorists have adopted to describe this learning cycle (Engeström, 1987, 1996). Such learning is likely to occur when people reflect on their overall system of activity (how it developed historically, how it functions currently), acknowledge key tensions within it, consider what pragmatically might be attempted at the local level to resolve them and, with others, develop new approaches in practice.

This general orientation alerted us to a dimension of development generally overlooked in the management learning literature and helped us to give the programme direction. First, it encouraged us to locate the particular events overtaking the NHS through 2000–3 in a longer-term context. As we have described, new policies were transforming the service over this period as government urgently responded to the escalating economic and political costs of the NHS. At the same time factors such as advances in medical technologies, the application of new information technologies, shifts in the demography of the population, new patterns of illness, and changing citizen attitudes towards the NHS suggest that uncertainties, debates, power struggles and policy changes are likely to be a feature of the NHS for many years to come (Harrison and Dixon, 2000).

Second, the approach emphasizes that inherent dilemmas are the driving force for changes in activity systems. When these dilemmas are acute and the consequences of failure are powerful it can be expected that participants can feel overwhelmed and that their learning will be inhibited. We anticipated (and, as discussed below, our suspicions were to be confirmed) that this was likely to be true of some NHS chief executives.

Figure 7.1 summarizes principles we took from activity theory and outlines their implications for leader development programmes: we aimed to help participants stand back from the imperatives of the moment and reflect on the dilemmas of their situations in new ways. Finally, the emphasis in both work based theories of action learning and activity theory on the importance of reflection as part of the learning process encouraged us to build boundaried periods of reflection into the programme.

The programme

The programme was designed as a modular, part-time programme for cohorts of around 16 participants. Its basic structure was established for the first cohort who began the programme early in 2000. In the light of experiences in delivering it a number of modifications were made to the original design. The version outlined on Figure 7.2 was delivered to the fourth, fifth and sixth cohorts who passed through the programme between late 2001 and early 2003, i.e. at the time when the reorganization of the NHS was proceeding apace. The course was structured around three themes: 'Reflections on self', 'Reflections on organizing', and 'Reflections on leadership'. All three themes were featured at each stage of the programme, with the emphasis moving from 'Reflections on self' at the start of the programme, through 'Reflections on organizing' in the middle section to 'Reflections on leadership' in the final stage.

Because of the limited time available for the programme in each module it was necessary to create a climate of enquiry and experimentation with a minimum of delay. Accordingly, a variety of inputs were included at the start of each module and at key points subsequently to catch participants' attention, and to challenge or inform. These events are shown in italics on Figure 7.2. In designing these events we relied heavily on inputs from outside contributors from the arts, humanities and social sciences, as well as contributions from visiting managers, many of whom were from outside the NHS.

Activity theory orientation	Implications for leader development programmes
Knowledge is not 'acquired' or 'absorbed'. Rather *knowing* is an active, creative process associated with pragmatic activity. It involves the use and development of linguistic, material, and social resources and takes place within particular communities and historical contexts. Learning is not only manifest in the exercise of new skills and actions but it also occurs at the level of activities. In complex organizations and at times of change people can lose sight of the overall project or 'object of the activity' in which they are engaged and may feel disempowered or overwhelmed by developments over which they have no control. Activity systems are never free of tensions, and collective development depends upon the ways in which people deal with them. The process is not driven by a well-developed 'blueprint for action', but early ideas are developed through actions. Such learning is likely to question established routines and vested interests, and to challenge imaginations. It may provoke a radically expanded appreciation of possibilities than in the previous form of the activity.	Participants should work, with others, on relevant practical activities. Such work should be undertaken in a way that will stimulate the development of a 'learning community'. The life of the learning community might usefully be extended beyond the life of the programme. Opportunities should be provided for participants to recognize and, with others, to reflect upon the object of their work activities and the means through which they are addressing them. Such recognition can be stimulated by exposure to the different ways in which people approach similar activities, and also by exposure to unfamiliar contexts and activities. Opportunities can be created to help people to recognize and address disturbances in their activity systems and develop new objects and activity systems. They should be encouraged to consider how and why their activities have changed over time, and to reflect on current tensions within them. They should consider also the implications for them personally of the emerging situation. With others they should debate and experiment with ideas about how activities might be enacted in new ways. Events of this kind can be expected to stimulate a search for new concepts and examples of new ways of working.

Figure 7.1 An activity theoretical approach to learning and change.

The key learning events on the programme, however, involved participants working actively, either with a personal tutor, or with colleagues in small groups, or with colleagues in the full group, on a variety of pressing problems, and in reflecting on the processes involved.

Further details about the structure and content of the programme are summarized in Appendix 1. A note on the dilemmas that, towards the end of the programme, participants chose to discuss explicitly is provided in Appendix 2.

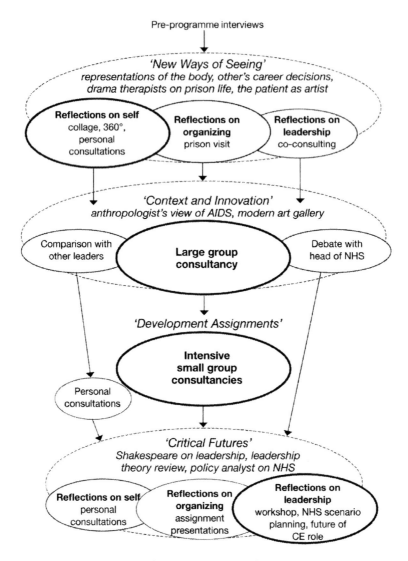

Figure 7.2 The structure of the NHS senior chief executive programme. Elements relying on participants' active involvement are circled by a solid line. Elements designed to support a culture of enquiry are shown in italics.

Evaluation studies

The NHS undertook two small evaluation studies and towards the end of 2002 we commissioned an independent researcher ourselves to study opinions. Typical of the early informal feedback that we received was the following note sent by a participant to the NHS Executive. He was halfway through the programme when he wrote:

I take my own personal development seriously and have worked for a succession of chairmen who support me, but I hadn't actually been on a structured development programme since my MBA in the mid 1980s. I had heard good feedback from colleagues who had been through the first wave and this encouraged me to put my name down for the senior chief executive programme.

I've always been a strong supporter of targeted programmes for chief executives. The job is uniquely difficult. There is an enormous wealth of government expectation and a huge amount of personal and organizational pressure. It can undermine your ability to see the wood for the trees. All chief executives should have some operational focus, but the current level of personal accountability and emphasis on targets means that we are being sucked into operational management more than is healthy for our organizations. There is often not enough time to reflect and plan more strategically.

The programme has helped me to step back and rebalance. I have valued the chance to look at issues in different ways. We have heard contributions from all sorts of speakers, including art historians, social scientists, and people from the public sector. We have done a piece of consultancy for the metropolitan police which allowed us to compare and contrast experience with them.

The moment that stays with me is when we visited a young offender's institute, around the time that there was publicity about locking up children at a younger age than before. It is shattering, especially if you have teenage children yourself, to meet 14 year olds and see them begin their first custodial sentence. You can only wonder at the series of circumstances that led them there.

The key learning for me has not been the difficulty, but the importance of taking time out. The first week of the programme coincided with the publication of the Alder Hey report [which dealt with a scandal in a children's hospital] so those of us running acute trusts were on the phone every few hours. On the previous wave, the petrol crisis had the same effect on participants.

The mutual reinforcement and peer support reminded me that although local issues can seem particularly difficult, many others are grappling with similar issues. As to longer term benefits, I expect these to emerge as I go away and absorb the learning. I think of it as work in progress.

It is vital that this kind of programme is maintained and extended to other senior staff in leadership roles. I've been luckier than some but development for many people is haphazard. We can't leave something so important to local circumstances and chance.

More formal systematic evaluation of the programme began at the end of 2001 when 11 (out of the total of 32) participants from the second and third cohorts met to discuss the programme with its commissioners. Notes from the meeting stated that the programme was 'valued by the whole group present as being timely and delivering its objectives'. The opportunities it created for reflection, the value to participants of spending time with a diverse group of colleagues, and the relevance of the programme to those who were having to make a change of direction were all praised. The consultancy assignments were valued. Participants felt that the programme had developed their managerial skills although 'it was not always apparent to participants that this was the case at the time'. There was some feeling that there had been insufficient time for reflection in the first module (a problem that was later addressed) and disagreement about the comparative value of elements of the programme (shown in italics on Figure 7.2) that had been included to create a climate of challenge and enquiry.

A year later staff from the NHS Executive interviewed by phone another eight participants (from the total of 28 people) who participated in the fourth and fifth cohorts. Feedback was similar and half the people interviewed specifically stated that the programme had increased their determination to continue in their roles. Notes from the interviews are summarized in Figure 7.3.

Towards the end of the third year of the programme the writers organized a further evaluation, hiring an experienced post-doctoral researcher to visit 15 participants selected at random from the first five (out of six) cohorts. Her discussions with programme participants were wide-ranging, discussing the impact of the programme outcomes in the light of their specific career stage and job problems, exploring how the programme had influenced participants' thinking and actions, and exploring any lasting effects. The interviews were recorded and transcribed. A summary of the transcriptions is provided in Table 7.1.

There are many similarities between the data for our own evaluation and those carried out by the NHS, but it is possible to extract more detail from our evaluation. Two of the 15 people interviewed were under extreme pressure over the months of the programme; both reported that they had enjoyed aspects of it but had not benefited very much. Five others had had to take important career decisions around the time of the programme; all of these said the programme had helped them rethink their preferences and options. The others said the programme had helped them reflect on work issues as well as personal ones. Seven discussed how the programme helped them develop new approaches and had stimulated their resolve; one reported how she had been depressed as a result of discussions during the programme which had undermined her faith in the leadership of senior staff at the Department of Health.

Discussion

Whilst the programme evidently proved useful for many of the participants, questions remain about the ways in which it supported their learning and what the broader implications of this case might be.

When we embarked on the design of the programme we were not sure where it would lead. Activity theory proved very helpful in alerting us to the learning potential of encouraging people to locate events in a broader context and to concentrate on the tensions and dilemmas characteristic of their situations. What

General comments

General comments included:

'Large chunks were especially good, a high return on the cost.'

'I've never experienced anything quite like it, it was very productive.'

'I have pursued many opportunities and am very interested in personal development but this was really quite an extraordinary experience. It was an extraordinary personal experience.'

'Delighted with it. Achieved status by being on it. Have recommended it to others.'

Opportunity to reflect

All eight respondents mentioned a major benefit of the programme was the opportunities it provided for reflection. Example comments:

'It allowed you to step back and see the wood for the trees.'

'It was a good time for reflection, time to consider work/life balance – managerially, intellectually and spiritually it was very restful, provided recuperation, stopped us in our tracks.'

'The course provided an opportunity for time out to relax and time to reflect on one's own style, approach and agenda. The prison visit was an eye opener, the Tate Modern just created an opportunity to look at things from a different perspective.'

Opportunity to network, work with, and learn from colleagues

Seven of the eight mentioned these. Example comments:

'Found it useful because of the content but more importantly the people on the course.'

'Being with a similar group of chief executives where we were all in the same position and could be honest and it was OK to say that at the time work was tiring or I felt confused or angry. I didn't have to apologise to myself for being cynical or despondent but I could be real with the group and myself.'

'It is intensely personal and creates a network of communications sufficient to help you in the future.'

Determination to continue

Four of the eight stated that the programme strengthened their resolve to continue in their jobs and take on difficult issues. Example comments:

'The course gave me confidence to implement change despite resistance and certainly left its mark on me.'

'The programme is subversive because you challenge politicians.'

'If I had not gone on the course I probably would not still be with the NHS.'

Specific likes and dislikes

The full group consultancy and the small group assignments were much praised, as were a number of specific sessions. Opinion was divided on the value of the lecture from the art historian, the collage exercise and the visit to the modern art gallery.

Figure 7.3 Responses to the NHS telephone survey (8 participants).

we did not anticipate was the strength of feeling that this process would sometimes generate. Bazerman's (2001) observation that the emotional aspects of collaboration and learning have been largely overlooked by researchers working in the Vygotsky tradition resonates with our experiences. To understand these aspects of the learning process in this case we found ideas from psychoanalytic, attachment and social theory helpful; in particular, notions of 'containment', 'parallel process', 'narrative as a secure base' and 'solidarity with the object'.

Table 7.1 Authors' evaluation (15 participants)

Approach to programme	Reference number, from which cohort, time since course	Circumstances of each interviewee	Interview summarized
A. Interviewees who did not benefit greatly from the programme			
Underconsiderable pressure during programme, and found it difficult to stand back from the day-to-day	1. Cohort 3. Interviewed 13 months after programme	CE of hospital at the centre of high profile enquiry. Programme of interest but of secondary priority	Had trouble standing back from the day-to-day during the six months of the programme to reflect on himself. Enjoyed reflecting on the wider environment affecting the public sector. Used assignment to unwind
	2. Cohort 5. Interview 2 months after programme	Not yet settled in new job as head of hospital facing difficulties. At an earlier stage in his career than other participants and wondered if it was right programme for him	Found it difficult to stand back from the day-to-day. But the programme reminded him there is life outside the NHS. Has tried to improve his life–work balance subsequently. Subsequently has reflected intermittently
B. Interviewees who focused primarily on their personal situations			
(a) In process of making career choice at the time of the programme; used the programme as a resource in this	3. Cohort 1. 25 months	Anticipating need to move on from Hospital Trust (probably within the NHS)	Programme greatly influenced her thinking about what she wanted to do, think through her work–life balance, and career after 50. Praises tutor, and co-participants who helped her develop a new perspective
	4. Cohort 2. 19 months	Knew he wanted to move on from Hospital Trust (unsure if would stay in the NHS or not)	Programme helped him reflect, away from day-to-day pressures. Learned about others' career decisions, learned from colleagues. Later changed his job. Life–work balance better now. Is more confident. Continues reflecting
	5. Cohort 3. 14 months	Aware of impending restructuring and loss of jobs like his, and the need to reconsider his future	Programme mix provided a time to think through available career options in a different way. (Later was not too bothered by failure to get senior position and happy to take a 12-month project, with better life balance than before. Considers it may soon be time to leave the NHS.) Continues to remember discussions about the changing nature of leadership in the NHS

(b) Important career decision made shortly before start of programme; used the programme to reflect on it		
6. Cohort 5. 3 months	Restructuring meant loss of job. At time of programme had recently failed to achieve more senior post	Programme helped her bounce back from failure to get senior job. Mentioned supportive colleagues and stimulating and broadening events. Helped her to remain buoyant as she led her organization to closure. Has improved her life–work balance. Now in policy development role. Continues to reflect
7. Cohort 5. 2 months	At the time of the programme had recently left Hospital Trust to work as CE elsewhere in the NHS	Used the programme to reflect on whether he had made the right decision in leaving a hospital trust for his present, less hectic, job. Decided he had. Says he is not a reflector and has not done it since, but valued the experience

C. Interviewees who focused on their organization and the NHS as well as on their personal situations

Programme used for 'renewal and refreshment' more broadly		
8. Cohort 1. 26 months since programme	Asked to audit the first design of the programme as known to be sceptical. Later had to face job change as NHS was restructured	During programme began to think what he was going to do in the next few years, about broad changes in the NHS, and where his talents would fit in. Benefited from being with others on the programme. The consultancy helped him see his own organization differently
9. Cohort 2. 14 months	Expected to learn about life balance. Later faced a reorganization of his Trust	Praised the value of colleagues, mentoring, the assignments, collage. Programme confirmed his direction. Is now more confident and reflective in his role. Gave him new perspectives. Has a better life–work balance.
10. Cohort 2. 19 months	Participated in the programme around the time that the 10-year plan for the NHS was announced. Opportunity to review his organization in this context	Rethought the place of his organization and the service it provides in the NHS, and his strategy for integrating it more closely. Rethought his leadership style. Reworked his life–work balance. Felt a more rounded individual as a result of the programme. Enjoyed the varied elements of the programme and contacts with colleagues. Continues to reflect
11. Cohort 3. 12 months	Expected time for reflection. Later his hospital faced poor national rating (which he worked to improve)	The programme provided an opportunity to reflect on career and life–work balance, one particular session and the assignment had a big impact. Rethought ideas about change. He now focuses on the 'why' not just the 'how'. Continued to reflect

continued

Table 7.1 Continued

Approach to programme	Reference number, from which cohort, time since course	Circumstances of each interviewee	Interview summarized
	12. Cohort 3. 13 months	At the time of the programme about to take over merged Hospital Trust in difficulty	Programme came at the right time as soon to move to a new position. Assignment useful regarding transfer of practices. Learned from (varied) supportive colleagues. Life–work balance still poor. At time of interview was under considerable pressure, but the programme had helped him to think 'I can only do my best'
	13. Cohort 4. 7 months	Approached the programme as a break from work pressure, to meet new colleagues, and to reflect on future options	Provided a rare opportunity to reflect. Became cynical about the motives of people at the centre of the NHS. Learned to take a strategic view, and became determined to develop his organization's perspective on priorities. Rethought his approach to leadership. Began to think through his personal future options
	14. Cohort 4. 7 months	At the time of the programme moved into difficult new job. Expected the programme to help him develop skills and understandings relevant to the new position	Provided space for reflection at a crucial time. Learned the need for a more delegatory approach to leadership in the new job. Learned to think 'outside the NHS box' and to take time to understand complex problems. Developed a broader network of colleagues. Spoke of the impotence CEs felt in the face of a radical change policy but of how he came back from the programme with more energy and passion. Programme stimulated thoughts (and confidence) about what his next career move might be
	15 Cohort 5. 3 months	Had recently been headhunted but had decided to stay on in a Hospital Trust post where she has been very successful	Enjoyed assignments and saw much in them applicable to the NHS. Devastated by the impression that the NHS leadership do not understand the situation facing CEs. After the programme felt her job had become joyless; worked with coach on this. Determined to see job through but wonders about staying in the (new) public sector

(a) Containment   The programme released time for people who led exception-ally busy lives to take time out to focus on themselves, and the evaluation data suggests this was much welcomed. Our conclusion was that the general ambi-ence of the residential modules and the design of specific events within them created a boundaried environment within which personal reflection could take place safely. Factors such as a well-designed programme with effective timekeeping and timetabled for appropriate reflection appeared to inspire con-fidence for serious work on personal issues. The one-to-one consultations with staff were a significant opportunity for some of the participants. Also relevant in this respect was the co-consulting exercise we developed in the first residen-tial module (which encouraged participants to discuss intractable problems they faced), and a scenario-planning exercise we used in the last (which helped them reflect upon their reactions to plausible, but unwelcome, developments that might overtake the service). Typically, participants emerged from such exercises with new ideas about how to address problems and with new hope for success. Bion's (1961) notion of the 'container', where a consultant system absorbs the anxiety projected into it and allows the client to re-assimilate it in a more bearable form, captures a key aspect of the learning environment that, we felt, the programme provided.

(b) Parallel process   The term parallel process was coined by Searles (1955: 135) to describe how the 'processes at work currently in the relationship between patient and therapist are often reflected in the relationship between therapist and supervisor'. The programme described here may be seen as providing a therapeutic experience, in which CEs had an opportunity to examine the conflict and contradictions of their jobs in the safe and containing environment provided by the course, and also to model this experience in the whole group consultancy and in the small group assignments, where they learned that other organizations experience conflicts and dilemmas that are equally as fraught as their own. A major learning experience from these aspects of the programme was that such conflicts and dilemmas are unlikely to have a simple resolution, but that ways need to be found to live with them and so to survive them. This learning they took back to the course and finally back to their own working environments, where containing and surviving the anxieties of their work could be seen as priorities. In this way learning took place in a series of parallel processes: on the course, in the consultancy and the assign-ments, finally being transferred back to the working environment.

(c) Narrative as a secure base   A recurring theme in the evaluation data sum-marized above are the tributes participants paid to their colleagues on the programme. Our record of how the various cohorts developed through the programme is provided in Appendix 3. At the start of the programme conver-sations between participants (some of whom seemed quite depressed) often focused on the frustrations of the moment; by its conclusion discussions seemed more balanced, with positive and negative aspects of their work being

discussed together, sometimes in a humorous way. What was happening bears comparison, we think, with Papadopoulos' (1999) notion of 'storied communities'. Papadopoulos was interested in explaining how victims of oppression could not only survive, but might actually benefit from such experiences, perhaps becoming an inspiration to others. He suggests that a key ingredient of the learning that can take place is the narratives that spontaneously arise between those sharing the oppression. Such stories can, he suggests, function as a 'secure base' (a term he borrows from Bowlby's 1973 and 1988 theory of attachment): when people develop a coherent narrative they gain a sense of security and psychological resilience. Understood in this way resilience is less a question of personality, more a feature of relations between individuals and their communities. The interpretation resonates with our impression of what occurred between the chief executives: narratives that the participants shared provided an opportunity for them to re-engage with their problems in a manner that seemed almost playful.

(d) Solidarity with the object   The evaluation data summarized on Figure 7.3 and Table 7.1 indicate that, as a result of their participation in the programme, some participants felt more committed to their work. In our efforts to understand why this might be the case we found the papers by Knorr Cetina (1997) and Knorr Cetina and Bruegger (2000) helpful. Knorr Cetina argues that people can develop relations with certain kinds of objects (she calls them 'knowledge objects') which can be as intimate as the relations they develop with each other. In explaining this she adopts arguments from Heidegger which suggest that knowledge objects are never fully understood but constantly invite new interpretations; then, using arguments from Lacan, she suggests that this unfolding independence of the knowledge object can inspire profound feelings in those who work with the object. Knorr Cetina's account of a research scientist's passion for the objects she was studying and the obsessive involvement of a group of financial traders with the markets in which they were working echoed the involvement the NHS CEs showed for their work. In activity theoretical terms, the object of CEs' attention can be described as the environment in which healthcare services are provided. As we discussed earlier, this is a multifaceted and contested terrain, with procedures and priorities currently being imposed on CEs, some of which were distracting, others misguided. Our impression was that the programme helped the participants stand back from such frustrations and regain a clearer picture of the changing object and their involvement with it.

Interestingly, there were a number of differences between early and later cohorts. Although they were enthusiastic about much of the programme, members of earlier cohorts appeared to experience more difficulty in using the learning opportunities that it provided than did later participants. For example, worries about external perceptions of the programme ('Is it a pre-retirement course?') were raised more often by earlier participants, who tended to idealize some contributors and dismiss others more often than members of later cohorts, to find fault with the hotel arrangements, resist reflecting on group process, and leave early or arrive late than was true of members of later cohorts. There were, we felt, perhaps three reasons for this. First, as we learned more about what the programme could achieve and how it might most effectively be delivered, we were able to strengthen its design and delivery. Second, the growing reputation of the programme changed people's approach to it and it appeared easier for later cohorts to become more involved at an earlier stage. Third, the growing confidence of the staff both in the programme and in participants' abilities to make good use of it may also have contributed to the change in mood.

Conclusion

To summarize, chief executives in the NHS work in an ambiguous and conflictual environment and must face a series of personal and organizational risks. We have described how activity theory helped us give shape to a leadership programme intended to refresh long-serving CEs; we anticipated that critical reflection could emerge from a focus on pragmatic concerns, and that exercises which help participants reflect on the complexity of their activity system would be useful. Using this orientation we endeavoured to develop a mix of events that would support new perspectives amongst chief executives on personal issues and career matters, organizational problems, institutional tensions and leadership roles.

The experience of running the programme made us aware of the heavy demands that shifts in complex activity systems can make on those involved. Reflection on the emotional aspects of the learning associated with the programme discussed here was instructive. As participants focused on the tensions that are an inevitable part of their work it appeared to us that they moved away from an attitude, seemingly common at the start of the programme, that their jobs would be fine if only the everyday dilemmas and problems they faced could be overcome, towards a recognition (sometimes explicitly stated at the end of the programme) that their job was dealing with these problems and dilemmas which might never be truly resolved. This 'figure ground' reversal was invigorating to those involved, for some re-igniting a passion for the work.

While there were exceptional pressures on NHS chief executives at the time of this programme we do not believe their situation is unique. Changes in the organization of contemporary economies and work systems suggest that radical shifts in the nature of activity systems may be relatively common at the present time, and leaders in public, private and voluntary sector organizations face pressures and constraints that may be demoralizing. The major point to emerge from the experiences reported in this chapter is that an appropriately designed action learning programme can rekindle commitment and resolve.

Acknowledgements

Many thanks to Sharon Turnbull for undertaking the interview survey summarized here and to Sarah Blackler for her comments on an earlier version of this chapter. Thanks too to David Knowles, Julia Davies and Pat Brand for their advice and help in delivering the programme.

Appendix 1

A summary of the programme is as follows. *Module 1* was entitled 'New Ways of Seeing'. It extended over four days. Prior to the start of the module participants were each interviewed about their career history and aspirations by a member of the programme faculty, and arrangements were made for an independent agency to collect material for a '360-degree feedback' exercise. After a general welcome to the programme, *Day 1* of the first residential module began with a discussion of procedural rules, which introduced the importance of reflection to the design of the programme and drew people's attention to various ways in which the process would be supported throughout the programme. Then an art historian presented a slide show to illustrate how representations of the body have changed over recent decades. Next, participants each created a collage of their lives, then discussed them in small groups. In the early evening a guest manager from outside the health service was interviewed in front of the group about key life and career decisions he had made and how he had faced the difficulties they posed. Finally on that day, participants were each given the confidential 360-degree feedback report and some guidance on preparing for a personal consultation the next morning. *Day 2* began with personal consultations between a staff member and individual participants, continuing the discussions that had already begun on work and life issues. A session was conducted by two drama therapists who, in anticipation of the afternoon's event, discussed their work in juvenile prisons and their impressions of life in such institutions. After lunch, accompanied by a specialist in the sociology of prisons, the group spent a few hours in a juvenile prison, talking to officers, professionals and the prison governor. On returning to the training centre participants debated the dilemmas of prison management and related what they had seen to the dilemmas of healthcare management. *Day 3* began with a lecture on how changes in work organizations might be understood from a social science perspective, before moving to a small group co-consulting exercise that focused on intractable problems that participants faced. The evening included a patient's perspective on the NHS, with a presentation of paintings introduced by an artist (Michele Angelo Petrone) which symbolically represented his experience of being a cancer patient. *Day 4* began with a second interview with a visiting manager about key life/career decisions (on this occasion a manager from the health service). This was followed with a session introducing the range of possible assignments on offer to participants. A plenary review concluded the module.

Module 2, entitled 'Context and Innovation', took place about six weeks later and lasted five days. Following a welcome session, *Day 1* began with a preliminary discussion about the dilemmas of organizational consulting. This was followed by a social anthropologist describing her study of AIDS in southern Africa, requesting the views of the group about what might be done in this very difficult situation. Next, participants were briefed on a consultancy exercise arranged for the full group. A senior client presented background information on a complex organizational problem to the group, then subgroups formed to explore particular aspects of the overall problem with members of his top team. (On different occasions the consultancy was undertaken in the London Metropolitan Police, the London Diocese of the Church of England, BBC Radio and Westminster City Local Authority.) *Day 2* and half of *Day 3* were taken up with fieldwork on the problems. In the afternoon of Day 3 participants met with the head of the NHS to discuss leadership issues. In the early evening they were taken on a guided tour of the Tate Modern art gallery (led by the art historian who contributed to Module 1). *Day 4* began with a session that invited participants to discuss how they were approaching the consultancy; after this participants worked on the presentation they would make to the client group. In the afternoon the group presented the conclusions of their consultancy to the client group. Later a guest manager from outside the NHS talked of his experiences in managing in the public sector. The day concluded with a formal dinner to which guests were invited. *Day 5* began with a session led by a visiting top manager from the Scottish NHS who discussed his approach to reconciling competing interest groups in the public sector and how he coped with the personal pressures of his job. The module concluded with a plenary review that continued discussions on the way the group had worked together on the consultancy.

In the three or four months before the final residential module a varied range of *development assignments* were offered to each cohort. All were designed as consultancy assignments. Over an intensive few days working in twos, threes or fours participants explored complex organizational problems, some of which resembled problems they experienced themselves, others of which were new to them, then presented their analysis and recommendations to a senior client. Assignments were arranged in private or voluntary organizations in England and Europe. Others to address issues associated with the organization of healthcare services were arranged in Africa, Australia, Central Europe, Eastern Europe, North America, Scandinavia and South America.

Before the final module participants were each offered a further personal consultation. *Module 3*, 'Critical Futures', extended over three days. Staggered throughout the module were periods that were set aside for participants to present reports of their work on the development assignments to the full group. Time was also set aside for each participant to have a final personal consultation session. Participants watched a video of Richard Branagh's version of 'Henry V' the evening before the module started. On *Day 1* they discussed how Shakespeare explored leadership in the play with a leading Shakespearian scholar. A review of current approaches to leadership followed, then a workshop in which participants discussed leadership issues of current importance in the NHS. On *Day 2* a health policy theorist introduced his analysis of tensions and change in the NHS before participants worked on an exercise to develop alternative plausible scenarios for the future of the service. Small groups worked to develop short presentations on the likely demands such scenarios implied for the chief executive role. A final dinner concluded this day. On the morning of *Day 3* small groups each presented their analyses of the future of the CE role to a panel of distinguished public and healthcare sector managers, who commented on what had been said as a prelude to a general discussion. The programme concluded with a plenary review.

Appendix 2

In the last module of the programme, as part of their discussion of the future of the CE role, participants were encouraged to identify current dilemmas and tensions that they needed to confront. Here are lists produced by three different small groups from different cohorts:

Group (i)

- CEs need a clear long-term vision but are under intense short-term pressures.
- There is a gap between the rhetoric of government and the situation on the front line that CEs have to manage.
- They must:
  - focus on change but acknowledge the importance of continuity;
  - balance their passion for the job with other aspects of their lives;
  - hold others accountable and also let go of detailed controls;
  - balance risk adversity with an awareness of important options;
  - work in partnership but recognize that some of the developments they help introduce will produce losers.

Group (ii)

- CEs serve multiple constituencies.
- They must:
  - balance priorities imposed from outside against those raised from within;
  - face weekly and monthly priorities as well as acting to solve long-term issues;
  - match the demands of micro-leadership with those of macro-leadership;
  - accept a growing role as civil leaders (a role that they have little or no experience of);

- address the clash between expectations of government and those of clinicians;
- face the fact that current strategies are determined centrally, but that local innovation is essential;
- recognize that their organizations are not perfect.

Group (iii)

- CEs need to act according to their principles in the face of high personal risks.
- They must:

  - build partnerships for the long term while meeting short-term performance agendas;
  - help build long-term visions whilst achieving short-term gains;
  - remain resilient, optimistic and enthusiastic in the face of extreme complexity;
  - develop their credibility by delivering on the agendas of others, but not overlook their own;
  - deal with failures whilst avoiding a blame culture;
  - make space for reflection and self-awareness in the face of intense work pressures;
  - build a team that both challenges and complements the CE.

Appendix 3

As we note in the body of the chapter, each cohort passing through the programme developed its own distinctive character but there were marked similarities in the ways different cohorts engaged in the programme. Early conversations between participants at the start of the programme featured the stresses of the moment and the frustrations and pressures that many were experiencing. Many of the chief executives appeared somewhat depressed by the way events were developing in the service. Although they are senior players in the NHS many of them indicated how divorced they felt from the reorganization that was gathering pace around them. There was always very strong support for the government's objectives for change amongst the group (in particular, participants strongly welcomed the extra investment the government was providing and the way the plan sought to place patients at the centre of the system). But as, through the life of the programme, the approach the government was developing became clear, many participants indicated that they were unhappy about the way the changes were being introduced. In particular, they were unhappy with the way politicians reacted to pressure from the tabloid newspapers and, later, with the way targets and timetables were being imposed on them. At a time when politicians were calling for better leadership in the NHS, the frustration of the chief executives at the way their leadership position was being undermined was clear. (A postal survey by Walshe and Smith (2001) suggested that such misgivings about the way that the NHS was being reorganized were not confined to participants in the programme reported here but were widespread amongst chief executives around this time.)

The full group consultancy in the second module typically stimulated much collective effort. Participants were obviously concerned to make a success of the consultancy, worked hard to collaborate together and got along well. Later, they were obviously pleased and gratified by the reception their work received. A session with the head of the NHS during this module acted as a focus for subsequent discussions about leadership in the service. In the period after the second module the small group development assignments, some of which were undertaken abroad, attracted considerable interest and commitment. Personal consultations with staff held around that period were frequently dominated by discussions about how much they had enjoyed them, what they had achieved, and broader lessons learned.

Most participants evidently approached the concluding residential module with enthusiasm. Small group presentations at the conclusion of this event on dilemmas and the future of the chief executive role varied; whilst some were relatively slight, others were insightful, humorous and ironic. Participants appeared greatly to welcome the opportunity this module provided for them to stand back from the pressures of the moment and reconsider the emerging dilemmas of their positions. Overall their roles seemed more balanced than had been the case at the start of the programme, with both positive and negative aspects of their work now being discussed at the same time. Different individuals undoubtedly varied in the ways they moved to resolve their problems, but it was noticeable that by the conclusion of the programme many talked of the continuing enthusiasm they felt for their work and the opportunities it offered for them to make a mark. Whilst acknowledging their inevitable responsibilities to meet government targets they spoke with conviction about the importance of their work in creating an environment in which effective healthcare services could be provided despite the increasingly difficult circumstances most were facing. Some spoke of the need to widen the discussion about the conflicts and dilemmas that were emerging within the service, to help their staff to address such problems productively.

Note

* This chapter was originally published in 2004 as 'The design and evaluation of a leadership programme' by Frank Blackler and Andy Kennedy in the journal *Management Learning* 35(2): 181–203, and is reprinted here by permission of Sage Publications.

Section III

Practice

Developing organizations

The next three chapters, 8–10, are accounts of action learning interventions where the primary objective was to achieve organization development. All three provide illustrations of how action learning is used within organizations, and in diverse ways. Carol Yapp, in Chapter 8, discusses work with an established authority divisional management team. Geoff Mead, in Chapter 9, describes cross-organizational action learning within the police service, designed to improve organizational performance through improving the quality of their leadership. And in Chapter 10 Pam Fox, Clare Rigg and Martin Willis describe an initiative that brought together senior officers from local authorities judged to be poorly performing by the UK government's Comprehensive Performance Assessment (CPA) framework, with the objective of contributing to their organizations' turnaround.

Carol Yapp is critically reflective on how she facilitated the team, which initially embraced action learning as a means of exploring collaboration with external partners, but ultimately chose to avoid the discomfort and tension within their own collaborative relations that the process threw up. She reflects on the role of internal facilitator, and whether she was constrained by her own pre-assumptions of the individuals. Her account raises issues of the extent and timing of facilitators' confrontation and challenge, and on being aware as a facilitator of one's own level of discomfort. This context illustrates some of the tensions of doing process work with established groups where the pull to avoid disturbing existing relationships by exploring how they work can be strong. It also illustrates an issue for internal organization development, where the apparently egalitarian relations within an action learning set cut across the organization hierarchy. In such a context, participants judge the cost of being open and direct. Geoff Mead in his account of working within the police service also highlights the importance of being alert to the politics and practicalities of doing collaborative inquiry in an overtly hierarchical organization. His group included members in boss–staff relationships. Both Yapp and Mead illustrate the process of paying careful attention to the groundwork of setting up action learning and of managing the micro-politics of gaining support from powerful players.

One of the issues raised by Mead's chapter, as well as by Fox *et al.*, is that of the relationship of the group with the wider organization, and of group members within the group and outside. Mead draws on the Habermasian concept of communicative space, in which the group provides space to explore splits between 'system' (in the sense of organizational world) and 'lifeworld'. The idea is echoed by Fox *et al.*, even though the intention of action learning in these turnaround sets very much emphasized organization improvement and formally included relatively little personal space. A key theme in all three chapters is how, in order to maintain a link between the group, its members and the wider organization, facilitators and action learning participants themselves have to be politically astute as to how they gain support, and avoid blockage, for the ideas they develop as a result of the action learning process.

8   Levels of action learning, and holding groups to the experience

Carol Yapp

I have enough experience of action learning to know that when it works well, it can have the kind of fundamental impact on management practice that most other vehicles for learning cannot achieve. However, I long ago came to the conclusion that facilitating learning sets, like management, is mostly an art – and it is tricky. There are no absolute guarantees that it will work, there are many reasons for it being a more challenging process than most learning interventions, and it does not suit every situation.

We often learn most powerfully from reflecting on our less successful interventions, and this chapter represents my attempt to learn from one of mine – a particular development intervention with a group of senior managers in an English local authority. In looking back, there seem to be some key points in the process that if managed differently may have led to a more successful outcome. I have changed my own practice as a result of my reflections – part of my long-term, iterative, learning through action. What follows is some background, a description of events, my reflections, my speculations on what I could or should have done instead, and my conclusions for practice.

Context

At the time, I was an 'employee and organizational development manager' in the local authority concerned. It was a large metropolitan borough with 13,000 employees, and substantial challenges in the community of 250,000 people. External inspection and assessment of performance were starting to bite very hard, and the publication of the subsequent judgements made the process all the more potent. Performance and all the processes that were believed to create or develop it took on a new significance.

Training and development was one of those processes, and a development initiative was designed and commissioned for the most senior managers – Directors and Heads of Service. It started with a 360 degree feedback programme that was intended to be followed by themed action learning sets, the themes being based on the overall team profile. The programme began well but was not followed through (which could be the subject of another chapter); however, one of the Heads of Service decided to take the 360 degree programme into her division. Her management team of 13 people all went through the assessment, and they had both individual feedback reports and a team profile. The overall team profile was very healthy but they wanted to use it to develop, and be even more effective as a whole team.

This was a corporate division whose role was linked significantly, if not entirely, to the improvement agenda. It was a relatively young division that had a mix of newly appointed people – externally and internally promoted staff, and some 'captured' staff who had been in improvement roles in the service departments. The latter now reported directly to this corporate division. Part of their role was to promote and support the implementation of the corporate improvement agenda in departments. Anyone who has worked in a large organization will realize the significance of this as an issue. It is rare that any service embraces corporate policy, however rational it might seem to those in the centre – but that is another story. Here the corporate/departmental issue is context. Nevertheless, at the very least this can create tensions within 'outposted' roles – particularly for those whose loyalties had previously been pledged to a department. At the very best they have split loyalties, at worst they are disguising a loyalty to one or the other or, rarely, overtly dismissing one agenda in favour of the other.

Despite the organizational tensions inherent in the division's role, it was rapidly gaining a distinct identity both within the division and across the organization. The divisional head was ambitious for her service and intended it to perform, be seen to perform, and to deliver on its brief. She was determined that the organization was going to improve against the all-important, and all-encompassing, external assessment criteria.

I had worked, or was still working, quite closely with a number of individuals within the team – through past or current roles and often within inter-disciplinary projects. I therefore knew there were issues that did not get expressed within the team meetings. Some of these issues were to do with styles of working, and others were to do with tensions in the relationships with departments. But I was pretty certain, given the right conditions, they would be able to articulate them and they could be worked through.

The first pre-meeting: how they might take team development forward; the suggestion of action learning and how it could work

The head of division invited me to one of her management team meetings to join in the debate about how they might take team development forward – based on the 360 degree feedback profile.

They had not decided what they wanted specifically to develop. I talked generally about options, conventional direct training courses and its various guises, and also mentioned action learning – initially describing it as a process of working with their knowledge and experience, as well as external input if they so wished – and how it could work in practice. I suggested it would be best to decide what they wanted to work on before choosing a training/learning option. They committed to discussing this at their next meeting, and also asked me to attend to describe in more detail how action learning in particular might work. I remember feeling that there was a high degree of interest in it, but also a rather high degree of caution.

The second pre-meeting: the focus for the development; a visual model of how an action learning process could work for them; suggestion of further options and levels

I attended their next meeting and had prepared a visual model of how an action learning process could work for them (see Figure 8.1), to supplement the verbal explanation I had given at the previous meeting. The meeting started with the debate about what they should focus any development activity on. The team profile had been strong against the 360 degree model criteria, with no significant weaknesses. However, a team member had been given the task of reviewing the profile, and determining what the team's weaker points were.

They presented a piece of very analytical work. The profile had shown that 'managing the job' and 'follow up' were relatively weak. However, if customer and employee surveys and feedback were taken into account, improving 'collaborative working' would have the most potential in improving the performance of the team. It was argued that an additional argument for focusing on this issue was that their role could only be pursued through working collaboratively – departments did not respond to dicta from the corporate centre. There was a short discussion where views were expressed in favour and against focusing on this area of development. A couple of team members thought the team were actually very good at working collaboratively, within

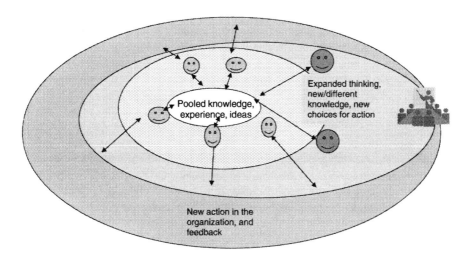

Figure 8.1 Basic action learning process.

the team, the division, and with other departments. Others felt there was a lot to be done in all of those areas, and most definitely within the team.

The decision was taken to go with 'collaboration'. No further objections were raised, and though I looked around the table for any sense of discomfort with this decision no-one displayed any signs of being unhappy. The meeting turned to me to describe the action learning option to them again, this time with the simple visual aid that I hoped would help clarify the process for those who seemed cautious and/or unclear. I work on the premise that action learning now has many guises and, though not pure in origin, are so close to the spirit of the original model to deserve the title – though arguably the first model I describe does not include the programmed learning of Revans' original. I developed this typology to help the team make a choice. I described two possible approaches.

Option 1: Pooling and working with their existing knowledge and experience, there would be a series of meetings scheduled over six months working with their joint knowledge and experience, aimed at improving their collaborative working with departments in real time – as they go along – trying things out, finding new approaches that worked better. This would include sharing individual practice, reviewing collective strategies, uncovering tacit knowledge and making it explicit.

Option 2: Using existing knowledge and experience, as in Option 1, plus the addition of some external views and experience and theoretical input – inviting other people in similar roles to talk about their practice, and/or people who teach on the subject.

The overall aim would be to arrive at new or different ideas for action, collectively and individually, and ultimately to produce more effective practice. People who had initial reservations seemed more comfortable. I think it felt more tangible and the focus on improvement had been made very explicit. And then I had another idea. Given the choice of focus for the development – collaboration – they could take the action learning process to another level by reflecting on, and learning from, their own collaborative processes as a team, in their action learning set.

Choosing to address the issue of collaboration made the choice of action learning particularly appropriate – there was a lot of synergy to be had. I gave a mild health warning by indicating that it was not always comfortable for a group to look inwardly at itself, but I felt they were sufficiently well established and already open enough with themselves to be OK. The idea of synergy was very appealing to a group of people whose jobs were about efficiency and effectiveness, but the original sense of discomfort about a process they were not familiar with returned. I was asked to arrange a meeting of the management group within a couple of weeks to explain further.

Pre-meetings 3–7: briefing on options for levels of action learning; and a health warning

It turned out to be impossible to get all the team together in the timeframe I had been given. I arranged three separate meetings – which turned into five because some people were unable to attend on the day. I was slightly concerned at this point at the last-minute cancellations. However, this was hardly unusual behaviour in the organization, particularly when the issue was learning and development. Managers were locked into a continual process of prioritizing and reprioritizing time and commitments. It was difficult to tell whether this was due to the uncontrollable pressures of their jobs, or a symptom of something less excusable – giving the appearance of commitment, but having no intention of following through. It took a good deal of persistence on my part, but I managed to brief everyone but one individual – who, rather than meet, said he would go along with whatever the team decided as a way forward.

In these briefing meetings, my remit was to describe the options open to the team in terms of approaches to action learning. I decided to present them in terms of levels and depth (see Table 8.1). I had already described to them the model incorporated as Level 1 of pooling their existing knowledge and experience, with the possible addition of external views and experience or theoretical input. Levels 2 and 3 were options that were progressively working with the experiences of the action learning set in working collaboratively. Level 2 would incorporate Level 1 with the additional requirement for them to look inwardly at their own experience of working collaboratively in the action learning set. The final level, Level 3, would add the dimension of taking into account the feelings and emotions generated by trying to work collaboratively as a team, and exploring their impact on task achievement.

I was careful to draw parallels with, as well as differentiate, these approaches from others that were currently being used within the organization, or that they may have experienced before. For example, the chief executive had referred publicly to his own experience of action learning. On the surface at least, the process had followed Revan's original description and use of action learning, and did not therefore have the collective dimension available, and perhaps desirable, to them as a team. The typology I described is represented in Table 8.1.

Table 8.1 Action learning options – levels and depth

Action learning options – levels and depth
Level 1 (a) Pooling and working with the knowledge and experience existing within the action learning set; (b) pooling own existing knowledge and experience plus external views, experience and theoretical input.
Level 2 Reflecting on the collaborative effort within the action learning set itself, unpacking the steps it goes through to achieve the task collaboratively.
Level 3 Taking account of, and working with, the emotions and feelings generated by trying to work collaboratively, and their impact on the task.

The health warning

My personal belief is that real and effective learning for action in organizations can only be achieved if learning groups operate at/include Level 3. However, my experience of this as a facilitator, and as a participant in action learning sets, obliged me to make explicit the personal discomfort that the process can generate. It had to be a conscious choice. If they chose not to go there, I would facilitate the process at whatever level they were comfortable.

I took care to describe the difference between Levels 2 and 3. I gave examples of how at Level 2 they could reflect on their own collaborative process, and define the stages/steps they took themselves as a group – careful to keep these steps at a 'task' level. To bring a rather brief and innocuous-looking statement to life ('taking account of, and working with, the emotions and feelings generated by trying to work collaboratively, and their impact on the task'), I chose to illustrate the key difference between Levels 2 and 3 by describing a personal experience of working in an action learning set on a group task. This was still like describing the taste of an orange to someone who had never even heard of one, but I hoped it would give a sense of what the taste might be like.

I described how at a particular point it had been very challenging for me; it had involved anger and a strength of emotion that I had not anticipated, that almost led to my withdrawal from the group and the task. I hoped this would bring alive the notion of the power and relevance of emotions to task achievement and effectiveness in organizations. I ran the risk of appearing at least a little neurotic, particularly as a woman. However, I also knew that this was a fairly frequent feature of working life and that individuals would admit to withdrawing their cooperation from others privately, but would never admit it publicly. Public admission of allowing feelings to get in the way of fulfilling 'rational' role requirements would appear 'unprofessional' – and so would any admission of even having such feelings. I showed them Vince's (1996) model of emotions in learning to rationalize and unpick the process I went through – my personal experience being that it is absolutely spot-on.

I described how an issue developed with another member of the set that I could not seem to work through with them. I left a meeting, swore a lot (to myself), avoided going, defined the problem as the other individual concerned, and almost resolved not to go again. But a sense of responsibility and guilt made me struggle through the issues and, ultimately, gain some real insight and new strategies for working with people. It had been a hugely empowering piece of development for me. It was obviously a more detailed description than has been given here.

To the uninitiated this sounds overdramatic, and I related this story with some humour. But I was also careful to say I could laugh about it 'now' – it definitely was not funny at the time. It was almost by accident that I 'struggled' and worked through it; I could have stayed in 'willing ignorance' (as Vince terms it), rather than work through my discomfort. I could have left or avoided the group instead.

So this was not an easy option – it could sometimes be very personal. It was their choice – I was telling them it could be uncomfortable – and if they were not up for that, it was OK. While I was recounting my story the body language of the people listening appeared consistently to be a mixture of fascination and surprise. I was not sure how to interpret it, but was erring on the side of them thinking I was rather eccentric. However, to my surprise, the general agreement at the end of the briefings was that they would like to go ahead with action learning, and operate at Level 3. My health warning seemed to have encouraged rather than deterred them.

Pre-meeting 8: checking the decision on action learning options

I attended their next management team meeting to check on the collective decision on how they would like to move forward. No-one had changed their mind, they were willing and felt able to address any discomfort within the group if it arose, and they were open to personal, constructive challenge if that arose too. There was one proviso for one individual: they did not have to tell everyone everything about themselves; their personal business was their business. I suggested someone from the team might like to work with me to set up the group: dates, times and initial structure. Three people volunteered, but only one was able to keep our appointment to meet.

Pre-meeting 9: structuring the programme

The team member and myself devised a timetable of six monthly meetings and a structure for the 'preliminary meeting'. It was a large group, 13, and to ease them into the process we designed the first meeting to be highly structured and in a format that they were familiar with – a mixture of syndicate and large group working. The agenda was designed to check and reinforce the purpose and desired outcome, agreeing the timetable and end date, space to talk about ground rules for how the group would like to operate and, finally, start to define 'collaboration'. At this stage I was relieved that we were close to starting the programme. Though not inclined to rush headlong into development interventions – I had a feeling that there was an element of this team that was unusually cautious. However, as the date for the session drew close, it was postponed and reset for several weeks ahead.

Session 1 (or meeting 10): the start

When this first session finally went ahead, everything went smoothly and there was lots of healthy discussion in groups. The design worked well, and it was so highly structured it almost ran itself – I mostly observed, but occasionally clarified low-level queries about the tasks. I had described how I saw my role as facilitator at the start, i.e. not to lead the group, but to help them learn from their own collaborative process.

It came to the plenary, and finally the discussion on 'what collaboration means for us'. As the discussion developed it reopened the debate about whether they should be working on collaboration at all. I observed to the group that they had already had the debate, and asked what they thought revisiting the decision meant. There was no direct response to my question. The previous debate was replayed exactly as it had been previously and they came to the same decision again, to go ahead with collaboration.

We discussed how they wanted to use the next session, and they decided to share individual past experiences and learning from successful and unsuccessful attempts at collaborative working (Level 1).

Session 2 (or meeting 11): sharing individual experiences (Level 1 – avoiding Level 2)

The next session happened according to schedule. People were sharing, some being more revealing of past experiences that they considered to be personal errors of judgement. I observed. Towards the end of the allotted time I asked them to start to distil some of the learning. The first comment hinted at a change of collaborative practice for the division. This prompted and reopened the debate about whether what they were doing was already very good. I commented to the group that the debate had reopened after having made the decision twice already. There was a brief pause, then they replayed their arguments, and the decision was again made to go ahead.

Time had run out, there was no chance to challenge the group further, and the session was rounded off by people saying how they felt about it. Everyone said how useful they had found the discussion, how much they enjoyed it, and how good it was to get together as a team and talk about other things than tasks, and targets in their business plan. Finally we turned to the format for the next meeting. Two individuals felt it would be useful to look at some theory on team working, and said they would prepare a paper based on some work they had each explored in the course of their masters degrees.

Session 3 (or meeting 12): papers on team working, and avoidance

After a brief warm-up, the meeting began with two people introducing the rest of the team to the ideas in their chosen paper about team working. Very shortly into the discussion one individual suggested that they were already good at team work and collaboration. There was a flurry of debate and they settled on collaboration again. The question was then quickly raised of how to move forward. I made the decision here not to suggest a way forward. My rationale was that the task was to work together on improving their collaborative practices. Therefore, the choice of how they moved forward – and how they made that choice – was part of their own live process of working collaboratively together. We were into Level 2 and I should not interfere with that process; it would not be theirs if I did.

They all looked to me, and I briefly described the rationale for it being their choice on how to move forward, and reiterated that my role as a facilitator was not to lead but help them learn from the process of working collaboratively together. There was a pause, someone suggested a way forward, then someone else said they were confused. I explained again. There was another attempt by a different individual to move it forward and then the debate about whether they should be working on 'collaboration' started again, but this time in a much more animated way. I started to say something – intending to make the observation that they had made this decision at least four times already – to question what they thought that was about. I was cut off in mid-sentence by one of the group, who went on to talk quite forcibly about why they did not need to develop: 'We're a great team.'

Others expressed confusion over the process and one individual expressed frustration about them being confused – 'What's there to be confused about?' Another said she was concerned about the level of tension in the group and was worried for the group – it was 'unpleasant'. We were starting to get into Level 3. Someone tried to move it forward again and then we were back to 'We don't need to work on collaboration.' They looked to me and I finished what I had started to say, deciding to keep it at Level 2: they had made this decision at least four times already and what did they think that was about? In case it is not obvious, I was reflecting back to them that there could be an issue here about how they made decisions that either was not obvious under 'normal' circumstances, or, if there was something about this particular situation that had rendered the decision ineffective, what was it? What was the problem with their efforts to work collaboratively, to move forward?

The whole group were clearly uncomfortable. We were at the end of the allotted time. Someone said they would have to go very shortly and it was quickly decided to end the meeting there, as they were clearly 'getting nowhere'. Nothing could have been further from the truth. I made a mental note to pick up the decision-making issues right at the start of the next meeting (Level 2), and also to address the tension and feelings generated (Level 3). However, someone made a further suggestion that at their next management team meeting perhaps they should consider taking a break from the planned sessions, because they were all really busy at the moment. They could pick it up later in the year. I had lost it. Despite my efforts to be explicit during the pre-meetings about emotions, tendencies to avoid them, and their importance, the group had beaten a very hasty retreat at the first signs.

After the collapse

A few days later I was seeing the head of division about another matter but we started naturally to discuss the last session. She had been fascinated by the experience. It was fairly clear to me during the session that she understood the idea of group process: if not right at the start, soon afterwards. Her choice not to intervene or attempt to explain was interesting in itself, and made for the 'right' reasons. As the formal leader of the team, she chose not be the default when the group became stuck. She said it felt like the door kept opening but just as it looked as though it would open completely, it closed again. I expressed concern about discussing the group without them being party to the discussion, and she wanted to be careful about that too. But she was concerned for the individual who had done most of the (overt) challenging – how he might have felt afterwards – and asked me to speak to him to make sure he felt OK. I agreed, but before I could do anything about it, he appeared in my office and asked if we could have a chat.

He said he was told very forcibly by one of the group members that his behaviour towards me had been immensely rude, and that he should apologize. This was the individual who had interrupted me in mid-sentence. I assured him that I was not offended. I did not think it was ethical to talk about the group but would have been happy to help him unpick his contribution, and to talk in general terms about the action learning process, but he chose to focus on our 'interaction' and checking that I was OK. I reassured him.

Unsurprisingly the decision at their management team was that they should take a break. I doubt whether the team would have picked it up again, but I happened to leave the organization before there was an opportunity.

Reflections: 'I could haves' and 'I shouldn't haves'

There are so many perspectives from which one could analyse and reflect on this story, but for the purposes of this chapter, for practitioners of action learning, it is: could I have done anything better as a facilitator that would have led to a more successful outcome for this group?

I misjudged them as a group of people

Perhaps had they been completely unknown to me, I would have made fewer assumptions. As indicated earlier I had worked, or was still working, quite closely with most of them. I knew there were issues that did not get expressed within the team meetings. I knew what some of those issues were, and I thought there would be a willingness and the ability to work them through. But the team relationship was much more delicate than I had anticipated. Most particularly, individuals who I thought would be fine with disagreement most definitely were not. Some reacted openly to any signs of an issue being uncomfortable – people getting mildly animated in discussion or signs of 'emotion' – by labelling it as inappropriate behaviour. Others withdrew.

I could have paid more attention to important team norms

There was something else I knew really well about the group but had not paid sufficient attention to. They often used the term 'glass half-full' almost as a mantra, they placed a great deal of emphasis on being upbeat, and the normal response to the first sign of tension was that someone would crack a joke. I 'knew' this in advance, and there were sufficient signs during the whole process for a complete stranger to pick that up. Of course none of this is unique to this group but it was very pronounced. I did not give this sufficient weight. However, I thought I had prepared the ground quite well. I did not expect them to move into 'flight' so quickly and easily – but in retrospect perhaps I should have done.

Perhaps I should not have let them out of the room at session 3

At least I should not have let them go without a sense of how what had just happened fitted with the levels of action learning I had described. I could have reiterated the levels at which we agreed the set would operate, particularly Levels 2 and 3. I could also have offered my perspective on what had happened, if only for them to challenge, and to engage them in a discussion about it. Perhaps I could have helped them to feel that it was normal/not unusual, helped them to meet their quite human need to feel more comfortable before they left, say it was OK, or given them a task-type route out.

Perhaps I could have been clearer

I could have been clearer about the difference between 'task' processes and 'group' process in advance by giving more examples. But I am always reluctant to give examples of task or group processes in these circumstances. I see it as akin to asking a leading question, or saying this is how you do it: groups can attach themselves to examples, start focusing on them, or use them as instructions. On balance it may have been a lesser risk. And I could have given a re-explanation of why I would not interfere as the facilitator in terms of direction.

I could have picked up the issue of remaking the decision much earlier

I could perhaps have done this in session 1 or 2, when they were working within the safety of a fairly familiar structure, and kept it at an analytical level – and could have facilitated a new decision. But I was playing the long game, trying to introduce them gently, letting an issue go if they were reluctant to address it. Or was I avoiding challenging the group harder because that would have been uncomfortable for me? Was working with people I knew, using this style of facilitation, just too challenging for me? It was hard to watch the group process, people I liked, beginning to expose their feelings and feeling embarrassed, even just a little.

Or, I could have played an even longer game

I could have helped them get started in session 3, reminded them of what they had agreed and done already, their previous reflections and learning points, and assisted them to build conclusions for the way forward in that session. By doing that the group's collaborative process issues would have emerged later, but they may also have been less clear, clouded by my role in constructing the process. It would also not have overcome the problem of unresolved conflict over the basic notion of what they were there to work on – collaboration.

I could have had a debriefing with the head of division

I put it off, partly because I did not want to discuss the group in the absence of the group – I do not think it is ethical and, without a dialogue with all of the people involved, it would be silly to pretend that any accurate analysis of what happened could be made from my observations alone. But there was a level at which we could have discussed it that would have been helpful, with care. It would also have been appropriate and desirable to have more concern for my own credibility, as well as the ethics of the situation.

I could have pushed them to meet again

I could have pushed at least for a debriefing – if only to ensure they got an opportunity to take some learning from it, and perhaps more importantly to unravel their confusion. I decided to wait for a while and see if they got back to it – hoping. They did not.

Conclusions for practice

It was a pretty careful and substantial setting-up process, from the 'classic' training needs analysis, choosing the development tool, building the 'contract', gaining agreement, warming people up to an unfamiliar approach, through to implementation. For it not to have come to a successful conclusion was disappointing. However, even though I described the process carefully, and included a very explicit health warning, the actual experience of this type of process is always surprising to people – which also illustrates the importance of experiential learning. Having information in our heads is not enough; it can only become real knowledge and understanding when we test this information in practice.

Facilitating learning in groups of this nature is not an easy option, and neither is it an exact science. Choosing interventions in the meetings, and the timing of them, is a matter of judgement. If a group chooses flight as a response to discomfort, and there are no sanctions, then sometimes there is very little that can be done. However, there are a number of lessons that I can usefully draw from this experience, but three in particular will inform my future practice: addressing discomfort and tension; session containment; and holding groups to their 'contract'.

Addressing discomfort and tension

Directly addressing discomfort in a group is always hard for the group members, at whatever point in a meeting or in an overall programme. Decisions on whether to let them pass should be taken with care. There are lots of reasons for not challenging at any given point (above), and fewer but riskier reasons to do so. I also now appreciate my own personal reluctance to hold people in their discomfort long enough to learn from it, particularly people I like very much. But in future I shall err on the side of challenging sooner rather than later. The most powerful learning lies in these moments of discomfort. They are rarely addressed in the course of normal organizational life. Action learning sets of this nature are almost unique opportunities to push through this barrier, and address underlying group and, therefore, organizational issues. Of course this would increase the risk of flight, which makes my second and third learning points all the more important.

Session containment

It is often the way of group process that important events happen right at the end of the allotted time for a meeting. I intend never to let the group leave a session on an unexplored point of discomfort. Though on one level the space between meetings can be seen as useful time to reflect and unpack what has happened in a group, many people find this extremely difficult. It can become an opportunity for mental as well as physical flight – an individual rationalization of events through the lens of their current practice and worldview, rather than a chance to test them. Even if group members protest, or individuals leave, I shall make certain that at least some debriefing takes place. They will have something specific, a focus for their reflection, that would not be easy to dismiss or rationalize as 'we're clearly getting nowhere'.

Contract reiteration

Some people come to an instinctive understanding of the idea of group process – that is, all that happens beneath the surface in a group that helps or hinders task achievement. Others find it difficult to grasp or just simply dismiss its importance. I feel reiterating what a group has contracted to do will help on two levels. For those who find the concept difficult to grasp, it will help them to understand – to relate the practice and the experience to the abstract articulation of the idea. For those who do not accept the notion either of group process or its importance, or are anxious to extract themselves for other reasons, revisiting the 'contract' may hold them to the experience. It is an issue to be explored in its own right, if people withdraw from painstakingly carefully set-up agreements. Being required to explain their views and the resulting discussion would be learning for the group, even if only in making the boundaries for the interactions explicit. For some, being required to explain their views and their wish to withdraw may be a greater discomfort than staying with the programme. I say this with some care as it could be perceived as coercion, but the intention would be to help people stay with the process long enough to make their motives, choices and impact more conscious.

There are never any guarantees of success, but in my view when this style of learning does work it has more impact than any other I know, and having insight into ourselves, our own practice, and our interactions with others, is good for its own sake. However, it is difficult to think of, or even imagine, a job in public service management that does not require an individual to work collaboratively with many others, often in very complex circumstances. If we are honest with ourselves, we know how very hard this can be, and how unfortunate, even in the best of organizations, the consequences can be for services and communities. Technical proficiency can only take us so far. And, of course, it is not only services and vulnerable people in our communities that are affected. Managers impact directly on their staff, and vice versa, and have a huge role in creating the culture and practice in, and between, organizations as a whole.

I have great respect for public sector managers, and the role of the public sector – but we can all be better. This type of work is about my own commitment and small contribution to creating reflexive, honest and human practice in our organizations, and from them to the community – whilst holding myself to the same standard.

9 Developing ourselves as police leaders

How can we inquire collaboratively in a hierarchical organization?*

Geoff Mead

Introduction

This chapter gives a practical account of an 18-month long *action inquiry* project, in which the author facilitated (and co-inquired with) a mixed group of police managers with the intention of improving our own leadership practices. Six phases of the inquiry are identified: doing the groundwork, getting the group together, creating a safe environment, sustaining the inquiry, accounting for the learning, and bridging the gaps. It is argued that such forms of collaborative inquiry are particularly well suited to addressing the uniquely complex phenomenon of leadership, and some tangible benefits for members of the project and for the organization as a whole are identified. Particular attention is paid to the politics and practicalities of doing collaborative inquiry in an overtly hierarchical organization, concluding that *action inquiry* must be crafted to its particular circumstances and context to realize its considerable potential to help us improve both individual practice and organizational performance.

Improving the quality of leadership is a crucial issue for the police service. Learning *about* theories of leadership is not enough. What really matters is for each of us to understand and improve our own unique practice as leaders': this was the challenge taken up by a mixed group of police managers (including the author) in the Hertfordshire Constabulary in an 18-month-long action inquiry – 'Developing Ourselves as Leaders'. For most participants, the results have been positive, exciting and tangible (though hard to quantify). However, we also found that doing collaborative inquiry in the police context had particular problems – not least that of creating a safe learning environment in an overtly hierarchical organization in which neither the democratic and emergent processes of collaborative inquiry nor the kind of transformative learning claimed by some members of the Action Inquiry Group (AIG) sit comfortably.

This chapter will examine some of these difficulties and our attempts to overcome them – hopefully in a way that will prove useful to readers contemplating or actually doing collaborative inquiry in an organizational setting. I shall say something about the rationale behind choosing an action inquiry approach before considering some of the politics and practicalities of the 'Developing Ourselves as Leaders' project in more detail. Finally, some tentative conclusions will be offered on the basis of this experience.

Why action inquiry?

As an educator and senior police manager, I have long been interested in the challenges inherent in police leadership and leadership development (see, for example: Mead, 1988, 1990, 1995). By 1998, I had come to the view that all methods of leadership development are based on assumptions (usually implicit) about the nature of leadership. Warren Bennis, one of the most respected and enduring commentators on the subject, described leadership as the most studied and least understood phenomenon in social science (Bennis, 1989). In fact, though common usage sometimes requires it, the word 'leadership' has little meaning in the abstract. We might even say that it only acquires meaning in action – 'leading' as opposed to 'leadership'.

My assumptions about leadership reflect this basic epistemological position. I take it that leadership is an active process, not an abstract quality. Leadership is not the prerogative of the few but is distributed throughout the organization: exercised day-to-day by many at all levels. Nor is it a zero-sum game in which the more I lead, the more you follow. Rather, it is a complex and often paradoxical practice, uniquely exercised by each of us in particular circumstances, which we can develop and improve over time.

It therefore follows that effective methods of leadership development must be able to support a multiplicity of individual inquiries whilst holding a common focus (in this case, that of developing ourselves as leaders). They will benefit from diversity of membership – particularly in relation to ethnic origin, gender, level and area of responsibility, police and support staff. Because practice changes over time, it requires an iterative process not a one-off event. And because practice is multi-dimensional it is essential to work holistically across all four domains – experiential, imaginal, propositional and practical (Heron, 1992, 1996).

Thus, when I wanted to offer a leadership development programme to the Hertfordshire Constabulary as part of my Ph.D. research, some form of collaborative action inquiry capable of encompassing all these dimensions and domains seemed to be called for. Drawing on writer-practitioners such as Donald Schön (1983), Mike Pedler (1981), William Torbert (1991, 2001), John Heron (1992, 1996), Peter Reason (1988, 1994; Reason and Rowan 1981; Reason and Bradbury 2001) and Jack Whitehead (1993), I adopted the nomenclature of action inquiry to describe what I envisaged: practitioners coming together as a community of inquiry, encouraging and challenging each other as they engaged in real-time, real-life development over several cycles of action and reflection, with the process of the group designed co-operatively to meet emerging themes and interests. I hoped too that the term action inquiry would be sufficiently understandable and intriguing to attract potential co-inquirers.

Politics and practicalities

As Coghlan and Brannick (2001: 64) observe: 'While doing any research in an organization is very political, doing research in and on your own organization is particularly so . . . Indeed it might [even] be considered subversive.' Although my experience of doing research was limited, I had got my fingers burned often enough as a senior police manager to be very aware of organizational sensitivities and the need to avoid activating its 'immune response' to the action inquiry project. In the event, political dynamics moved into the foreground on several occasions. Rather than cluster them together, I prefer to consider them in the particular contexts in which they arose.

In hindsight, I can identify six main phases of the action inquiry – outlined in Table 9.1. In this section, I will follow them in rough chronological order, highlighting the politics and practicalities of doing the 'Developing Ourselves as Leaders' project.

Doing the groundwork

The process of seeking sponsorship and support for the project began in late 1997, about a year before the AIG was initiated, when Peter Sharpe (then Chief Constable of the Hertfordshire Constabulary) agreed to support my application for a Bramshill Fellowship. I wanted to obtain a fellowship for two reasons: because it represented a commitment to fund my studies and, even more importantly, because it would give my research some official recognition

Table 9.1 Phases of the 'Developing Ourselves as Leaders' action inquiry

Phase	Theme	Main activities	Timeframe
1	Doing the groundwork	Personal sanction from Chief Constable Consultation with influential peers Getting support from HR and Training	Sept. 1997 to Sept. 1998
2	Getting the group together	Letter of invitation to 300+ managers Briefings for 50+ potential participants Set-up meeting for committed members	Oct. 1998 to Feb. 1999
3	Creating a safe environment	Establishing my role as co-facilitator Contracting 'ground rules' for the group Sharing personal stories, hopes, fears	Feb. 1999 to April 1999
4	Sustaining the inquiry	Developing individual inquiry questions Meetings every six to eight weeks Holding each other to account	April 1999 to June 2000
5	Accounting for the learning	Individual papers from members Extended review of learning Multiple, creative techniques	Oct. 1999 to Feb. 2000
6	Bridging the gaps	Feeding back results to organization Presentations at police conferences Independent evaluation of project	May 2000 and ongoing

and legitimacy. We were both keen to ensure that I would provide some 'return' for this investment in my development, and my plan included a proposal to conduct some form of collaborative action research (at that time, in the area of men and masculinities) in the Hertfordshire Constabulary.

The Chief Constable's endorsement of my Bramshill Fellowship sanctioned the project in principle and proved invaluable when I began to sound out other potential supporters during the summer of 1998. By this time I was outside the organization, seconded to National Police Training, and I was anxious to 'test the waters' back in Hertfordshire. Over the course of several weeks I had long conversations with several erstwhile colleagues who I felt would be open-minded and sympathetic, whose judgement I trusted and whom I knew to be influential 'opinion-formers' in the organization. They were happy to lend their personal support to a collaborative inquiry process (indeed, two of them subsequently joined the group) but encouraged me to reconsider my intended focus on men and masculinities – which they saw as too narrow, confrontational and exclusive.

Their views tended to confirm my own doubts about the readiness of other members of the organization to tackle this issue head on. It occurred to me that a more creative approach would be to invite men and women into a space that, by its very nature (i.e. community, collaboration and diminished sense of hierarchy) would challenge deep-seated notions of hegemonic masculinity. Gender issues, including masculinity, might emerge naturally in such a group if they were really as significant in the organization as I imagined them to be.

So I reformulated my proposal to cover a more general inquiry into leadership practice among men and women across the organization – 'Developing Ourselves as Leaders' – and subsequently put it to the training manager and head of human resources on that basis. They were both quite excited by the idea and willing to support it, provided it was offered as a complementary development activity clearly outside the scope of the existing structures for management development. This degree of 'distancing' from mainstream training activity was understandable and probably quite helpful in differentiating it in the minds of potential co-inquirers.

Even as a senior 'insider', getting high-level support for the action inquiry project required persistent and delicate negotiations. Powerful players needed to be convinced of the potential benefits of this approach and reassured that, though challenging, it did not represent a fundamental threat to the organization. In managing the micro-politics of these interactions, I found it helpful to present myself as a 'tempered radical' (Meyerson and Scully, 1995): as someone authentically committed to the mission and goals of the organization who is also seeking to bring about radical change in some aspects of the way it does business. This ambivalence – this state of living contradiction – is a powerful spur to action but, as I have written elsewhere, can also be an uncomfortable and uneasy position to occupy.

It no doubt helped that I was also able to call on my track record as director of other successful management and leadership development programmes to establish my credibility and competence in the field. Despite these credentials, doing the groundwork was a slow and painstaking business – but absolutely essential to securing the levels of access and support it would take to get the project off the ground.

Getting the group together

By October 1998 we were ready to launch the group. Working closely with Roger Barrett, the Force Development Manager, a letter of invitation was drafted, refined and sent out to over 300 middle and senior managers through-out the Hertfordshire Constabulary. We wanted to offer the chance of partici-pating to as wide a range of people as possible without being overwhelmed by potential participants. So, after much debate, we set eligibility criteria based on rank or grade. Although setting an arbitrary cut-off, these grounds had some logic and were defensible in terms of existing organizational practice.

Between 50 and 60 people responded to the letter by coming to one of the briefing sessions, some of them familiar faces, some new to me – men and women, police officers and civilian support staff of many ranks and grades. To the non-police reader this may not seem particularly noteworthy but such heterogeneity is still comparatively rare in police management and leadership development programmes. The briefings were designed to help people make a positive decision to opt in to the action inquiry or to decide, without any stigma, that it was not for them. The underlying principle was that of volun-tary, informed self-selection. I spoke a little about the rationale for offering this opportunity to focus on leadership and said something about the participative and democratic ethos of action inquiry. I talked about the possibility of transformative learning and asked people to decide if they wanted to take part using their head (Do you have enough information? Does it make sense for you to do it?), heart (Are you intrigued, curious, drawn? Does it feel right for you to do it?), and will (Are you able and willing to meet the commitment? Do you really want to do it?).

I then told the story of 'Jumping Mouse' – a wonderful Native American tale of journeying, sacrifice and transformation (Storm, 1972). It is a long story – twenty minutes or so – and telling it felt like a risky thing to do. The possibility of ridicule was high. Nevertheless, I had been talking in a fairly conventional way about a radically different way of learning and I wanted to be more congruent. It was a defining moment. As I looked at the audience I saw some eyes glaze over whilst others began to sparkle with interest – choices were being made. We closed the session with questions and a general discussion and everyone was given a short paper reiterating the main points of the briefing and a reply slip with which to notify their decision within three weeks.

Sixteen people confirmed their intention to take part and we arranged a preliminary meeting in mid-February 1999 to resolve any outstanding issues and to set up the inquiry group. Not everyone could make the meeting (a consistent and seemingly inevitable feature of organizational life), but there were enough of us to share some hopes and expectations and to arrange a series of meetings over the coming year, beginning with a two-day residential event in April to kick-start the inquiry process.

By staging the process of self-selection (invitation, briefing, written reply, preliminary meeting), and with a bit of good luck, we had managed to recruit a manageable number of committed people. It also turned out that the final group was well mixed in terms of police officers (eight) and civilian support staff (eight), and in terms of men (ten) and women (six). There was also a wide spread of police ranks and civilian support staff grades from many different specialities and locations. We could not have asked for a more promising start.

Creating a safe environment

This issue was always present to some degree, and was figural in the early stages of group formation, and again, towards the end, when we considered how to feed back our learning to the organization and beyond. It featured strongly at our inaugural residential event in April 1999. Twelve of us came together at the Police Staff College, Bramshill, from Friday lunchtime to Saturday teatime (a fair blend, we thought, of work and personal time). As we moved through the weekend, three main issues about the safety of the learning environment arose:

- Within the group – how did group members want to behave towards each other and be treated?
- My role as facilitator – how would I offer leadership and to what extent would I participate as a co-inquirer?
- Outside the group – what were the appropriate boundaries with the organization and how could they be maintained?

We addressed the first issue in several ways: sharing our hopes, fears and life stories in a series of creative exercises, gradually deepening trust and empathy by taking small risks, allaying some of our concerns by building relationships and getting to know each other. We also spent some time midway through the process generating ground rules for the group, such as:

- confidentiality – we own our own stories
- feedback – challenge with respect
- listening – allow others to speak uninterrupted
- honesty – tell it like it is
- pro-activity – take responsibility for our own learning
- process – flexible, fun and realistic.

The list is neither surprising nor startlingly original. What matters is that these agreements were generated organically by the group on the basis of shared experience. We knew what they meant for us and we never needed to refer to them again.

I found the second issue – my role in the group – a particularly knotty one at first. Clearly I had initiated and convened the group. I was the only person with prior knowledge and experience of collaborative inquiry and, as if this was not enough, I also held the most senior rank/grade. Concerned that these factors might distort the group dynamics and make it impossible to establish peer relationships, I had played down my role at our preliminary meeting in February, stepping out of the limelight for fear of dominating the group. Unfortunately it left the stage bare, so that our meeting was stilted and confusing. It was 'good enough' not to put too many people off (though three of them did drop out afterwards) but we could so easily have fallen at this first hurdle. I debriefed the experience with Roger and consciously decided to play a more active role (though still rather tentatively) at the residential event in April.

Two things occurred that weekend that shaped my subsequent role in the group. On Saturday morning, two members of the group challenged me to stop 'playing small' and encouraged me, in the words of Nelson Mandela, to allow myself to be 'brilliant, talented and fabulous', to 'let your own light shine'. They made it very clear that they did not need me to stand aside for them to be powerful too. It was a lesson I hope never to forget. Thank you Judy and Carol.

On Saturday afternoon, as we coached each other in formulating our individual inquiry questions, I offered: 'How can I lead [in] this process of action inquiry with authenticity, integrity and joy?' By making my leadership within the group an object of inquiry, any taboos or awkwardness around it seemed to fall away and I continued to lead wholeheartedly (if sometimes inexpertly) for the remainder of the project. The fact that I had so publicly committed myself as a co-inquirer did much, I believe, to reduce the distortion of hierarchical power in the group. I was personally powerful but not because of my rank.

The third issue – that of the relationship of the group with the wider organization – also manifested itself in several ways. Although all members of the group had identified themselves as exercising leadership in the organization, and all were committed to working in its best interests, for some there were also strong feelings of alienation – a concern that 'I can't be me' in the workplace and an equally strong desire to 'be me' in the AIG. There was a feeling of unease and a fear of making oneself vulnerable by stepping outside cultural norms.

Some members of the group were actually in hierarchical working relationships (there were three boss–subordinate dyads/triads in the group). Could they deal openly and honestly with each other in the group – and what effect would that have on their outside relationships? For the most part, the 'confidentiality contract' and sensitive mutual exploration of these edges defused potential problems – though one member did withdraw from the group because he felt that his presence was inhibiting a more junior colleague. As the group became more established there were few, if any, signs of reticence or reservations about these outside working relationships.

The issues of authenticity and alienation, however, continued to be a puzzle. Why should we (for I shared some of these feelings) be so concerned about the tensions and contradictions between our personal and professional personas? Why were we so driven to explore them? What underlay our intuitive sense that finding some resolution of these dilemmas was crucial to improving our effectiveness as leaders? Paradoxically, it seems that some of the very qualities and activities that are required to achieve high standards of organizational performance – originality, creativity, co-operation and relationship-building – are not highly valued in a 'command and control' culture.

At the time, Roger Harrison's notions of organizational alignment and attunement helped me make sense of this phenomenon. Alignment refers to the focusing of individual effort and will on organizational objectives, attunement to promoting healthy relationships and quality of life within the organization. He argues (Harrison, 1983) that a healthy, effective organization will find a balance between these two dimensions. Perhaps, in a highly aligned organization, the AIG was providing much-needed opportunities for attunement. The supportive behaviour that was so apparent among group members would suggest that this was so. Indeed, as one reader of an earlier draft of this article suggested, perhaps the most radical (and useful) thing we did was simply to create a space within the organization in which we could 'be ourselves'.

More recently, I have found support for this suggestion in Jurgen Habermas's notion of 'communicative spaces': 'in which people come together to explore problems and issues, always holding open the question of whether they will commit themselves to the authentic and binding work of mutual understanding and consensus' (Kemmis, 2001: 100). It is this, says Habermas, that makes communicative action and the healing of the system–lifeworld split possible. It might also help to explain how the strong personal focus in the action inquiry group contributed to some very tangible organizational benefits.

Sustaining the inquiry

Of course, every collaborative inquiry will follow its own unique path, but a number of practical issues arose in sustaining ours, which may be of interest. The first, to which I have already alluded, was the difficulty of getting everyone to meetings. We held five interim meetings, six to eight weeks apart, with an extended review of our learning at a second residential event in January 2000. We never had a 'full house' and no one (not even me) managed to get to all the sessions, so we could not afford to be too rigid about what constituted membership of the group. A few dropped out never to return, one person 'joined' halfway through and some stayed on the fringe. Nevertheless, there was an identifiable core of ten who remained deeply involved throughout. Work pressures often impinged on meeting times despite pre-arranging the dates of meetings for the whole year – and without such advance planning it is doubtful whether any of the meetings would have been sufficiently well attended to be worthwhile.

At the residential event in April, each member of the AIG formulated his or her own individual inquiry question under the umbrella: 'How can I improve the way I exercise leadership in the Hertfordshire Constabulary?' The focus on our own practice informed each subsequent cycle of action and reflection. As individual inquiries gathered momentum, I found that it took a considerable amount of energy and attention to hold the whole process together. Although we shared the tasks of arranging venues and of 'rounding people up' for meetings, a good deal of the work came my way – from negotiating a budget to cover our costs for the year, to writing innumerable letters keeping members in touch with developments and making sure that those who could not get to particular meetings were kept in the picture.

We found that the simple act of sharing our stories, telling each other how we had been getting on with our inquiries, was enormously powerful – both to deepen the relationships between us and as a way of holding ourselves and each other to account. We quickly got into the habit of tape-recording our sessions and sending copies of relevant sections of the tapes to individuals to aid further reflection. Most sessions began with an extended 'check in' of this sort, and then followed whatever themes emerged. On one occasion, following a 'spin-off' meeting arranged by several women members of the group, this led to a fascinating exploration of gender and leadership. We learned to trust the process of action inquiry and that, in an organizational setting at least, it needs to be sustained by careful cultivation and lots of energy.

Accounting for the learning

Although much of the time we concentrated on supporting each other in our individual inquiries, we were also curious to see what common themes were emerging. This desire seemed to arise quite naturally after about six months, and we agreed that each of us would write about what we were learning about our own leadership practice as a result of our inquiries and circulate it within the group. In the event, nine papers were produced, which we took to our meeting in October 1999. We discussed each paper in turn, checking for clarification, offering feedback to the author and noting our own reaction. A few days later, Roger and I met to listen to the tape recording from which we distilled what seemed to be key statements and themes, which in turn were circulated to the group for comment and consideration. Our 'mid-term paper' proved to be an extremely useful exercise both in terms of getting a feel for where the group had got to and of providing a mirror to individual members.

Our paths then diverged once more until we came together for an extended review of our learning at the second residential event in January 2000. (See Figure 9.1 for an illustration of the patterns of convergence and divergence during the inquiry.) Again, we met from Friday lunchtime until Saturday teatime at Bramshill – eight of us – collaboratively designing the process on the basis of some questions and principles we had decided previously. We used three different activities to provide accounts of our learning. First, we all

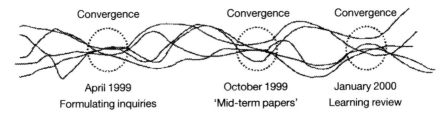

Figure 9.1 Convergence and divergence in the action inquiry process.

brought objects symbolizing what we had learned about ourselves as leaders. Each of us, in turn, displayed the object on a central table and spoke about what it meant. The 'presentations' were recorded on videotape and the objects gathered together for the weekend to represent and hold the energy of the group.

Second, we each made a brief statement in response to the question: 'How has your practice as a leader changed and improved through the AIG process?' and were then interviewed by a colleague in a 'goldfish bowl' setting so that other members of the group could also listen and respond. The interviews were sympathetic but challenging – friends acting as enemies (and as friends). These were tape-recorded and subsequently transcribed.

Third, we spent some time making visual representations – pictures and collages – responding to the question: 'What has the story of the AIG looked like for me?' These were then displayed round the room and we took it in turns to speak about our images, using the video camera once more to record the event. The material from all three activities was later copied, transcribed and fed back as a record of the learning and as a stimulus to further action.

We closed the meeting by reviewing what we wanted to share about our learning with others, whom we wanted to share it with, and how we could make it safe to do so. As in the early stages of the inquiry, strong concerns were expressed about how 'the organization' would react to what we had been doing. By this time, however, we had come to believe that it was possible to bridge the gaps – provided we were politically 'savvy' going about it. For example:

- Challenge but do not confront or criticize.
- Choose the right audiences (15 per cent is enough).
- Continue to respect individual confidences.
- Seek the new Chief Constable's seal of approval.
- Use the learning to add value to existing programmes.
- Maintain contact with each other for mutual support.
- Be content to sow seeds – do not try to do it all at once.

Finally each of us made public commitments to take specific actions to begin the process of communicating our learning to others in our own organization, and beyond to other researchers and practitioners.

Bridging the gaps

From the organization's point of view, the most immediate benefits of the inquiry are to be found in the improved leadership practices of its members, though of course there are so many variables in human behaviour that, whilst one can ascribe these benefits to the AIG, one cannot 'prove' the connection. In police-speak, we may have reasonable grounds to suspect, but we cannot prove the case beyond all reasonable doubt. Fortunately, there is considerable room for manoeuvre between these two standards – perhaps we could be satisfied with 'on the balance of probabilities'?

Although I have expressed it rather flippantly, what we discovered, as soon as we began to try to communicate what we had been doing, were some significant epistemological gaps: major differences in our understandings of what constitutes useful and valid knowledge. Guy Claxton (1997) speaks about a propensity to believe that people have only learned something if they can codify and reproduce it (which may go some way towards explaining the current fashion for leadership competency frameworks and the like). But that would be to oversimplify the matter – what we met, as we sought to communicate our learning, was not hostility but a mixture of interest, pragmatism and scepticism.

I personally briefed our new Chief Constable in May 2000. He expressed considerable enthusiasm about promoting 'leadership' in the Constabulary and urged me to speak with the head of human resources to make practical arrangements for bringing the benefits of the research back into the organization. I did so in June, and we agreed in principle that I would advise and 'shadow' an in-house facilitator if another action inquiry group was formed. To date this has not happened, but I have become more closely involved in some other leadership development initiatives in Hertfordshire.

Seeking a wider audience, with three other members of the AIG, I offered a workshop on 'Developing Ourselves as Leaders' at the high-profile 2000 ACPO Research Conference. We expected about 15 participants, but found that there was a huge interest in the workshop – over 40 delegates came to our session – where we described the process of the AIG, presented some of our individual and collective learning, and made ourselves available for small group discussions. We had some lively debates. Delegates were not unsympathetic but most were somewhat sceptical. Typical of their comments were: 'I can see that you are all very enthusiastic and believe that you have learned a lot, but can you prove it?' 'How have you evaluated the impact of the course [sic] on organizational effectiveness?' 'Yes, I believe you but I'd never be able to sell it back in force without some sort of evaluation.'

This was a blow – what better evidence of the effectiveness of the process could there be than us four living examples presenting our learning to the conference? If these delegates, broadly representative of the UK police service, were not convinced, what chance did we have of persuading others of the value of our approach? But these arguments also pointed the way to how we might begin to bridge some of the gaps. On the advice of one delegate, I approached the Home Office Research Unit with the suggestion that they might fund an independent evaluation of the impact of the AIG. I am happy to say that, after some delay, they agreed that this would be a useful strand of their overall research programme and the evaluation took place.

One stipulation of the invitation to tender was that the research should be conducted in a way that is congruent with our own collaborative methodology and contributes to our further learning. As a result, the researcher presented the provisional findings to the AIG for discussion and feedback as part of the analysis. The independent evaluation is a high-risk strategy, and one could argue that no external examination could ever capture the richness of our experience, but if its findings tend to confirm our claims of improved leadership practice, we may be at least halfway across the bridge.

An even more ambitious attempt to influence public policy was sending a short case study on the AIG to the Cabinet Office Performance and Innovation Unit as a contribution to their research and still-awaited report on Public Service Leadership. Within a couple of weeks I found myself sitting round a Whitehall table with members of the 'Prime Minister's Leadership Project' team. There was some interest in our work and a shortened version of the case study (which I never saw) was included in early drafts of the report (which I also never saw). Although it was dropped from later drafts 'on grounds of space', the Cabinet Office accepted a proposal to deliver the learning set element of their Public Service Leadership Scheme through facilitated action inquiry groups which I oversaw for the ensuing three years (see Chapter 11 of this book). Our work in the 'Developing Ourselves as Leaders' project has provided the foundation from which we can extend the focus on leadership practice and the improvement of service delivery across the public sector.

Conclusions

Did we manage to inquire collaboratively? I think the answer is a qualified 'Yes'. There is ample evidence in the transcripts of our meetings and in the accounts of our learning to substantiate the claim that, at the individual level, we created and took opportunities for transformational learning: learning that was grounded in our day-to-day practice as we variously engaged with the demands of delivering a high-quality service in the complex environment of contemporary policing.

The emerging findings of the independent evaluation confirms these claims, suggesting that members of the AIG have been assessed by colleagues as having become calmer, better able to work under pressure and more strategic in their outlook. Nearly all members of the action inquiry group described the process as worthwhile and rewarding. Here are some of their comments recorded at our penultimate meeting:

> 'Now I have really got some sense of direction as you can see in this picture . . .'

'I need a helping hand sometimes to get to where I want to go . . . that's when I come to the group.'

'We shared our inquiries and from that came the learning and the feedback.'

'The thing about this has been the honesty . . . in these sessions we have said when we disagree and why we disagree with somebody.'

'It is about light and focus and being able to find your way through the dark.'

In case this is beginning to sound like yet another 'victory narrative' of action research (MacLure, 1996), I should point out that it did not work for everyone. Several members of the group dropped out – generally pleading lack of time, though one said she was bringing 'too much emotional baggage' to the group and that her continued presence might interfere with other people's learning. Although I think she was mistaken in this regard and overly self-critical, one has to respect her decision to withdraw.

Furthermore, it would be fair to say that – as yet – our collective learning has had less impact. We are still struggling to communicate the benefits of a collaborative approach to leadership development to a wider police audience, hampered by a training orthodoxy that places a high value on *uniformity* (role definitions and competency frameworks), *compulsion* (if it works, everyone should do it), and *assessment* (preferably pass or fail). Perhaps the independent evaluation of our work will lend weight to our own voices. We have certainly learned that, as sense-making and knowledge creation move into the public domain, they can become highly politicized and the potential difficulties of conducting collaborative inquiry in a hierarchical organization such as the police service should not be underestimated.

For me personally it has been an immensely satisfying experience. I have become a much more confident and effective practitioner of collaborative learning, more willing to 'let my light shine' and more conscious of the choices and choice-points in such a process. We, for example, were quite a closed group: we adopted an informal, loose approach to the action-research cycle and we focused quite strongly on our individual leadership practices. Had we communicated more openly with others during the life of the group (say by publicizing our 'mid-term paper'), had we adopted a more rigorous pattern of action-research, had we addressed systemic leadership issues, we may have had fewer (and narrower) gaps to bridge later on. Yet I am not sure I would make many different choices if faced with similar circumstances. Members of the group came with strong personal agendas, which demanded a high level of safety, and thus confidentiality, in the early stages – and I was reluctant to reinforce the prevailing hierarchical culture by imposing too much structure or discipline on our proceedings.

Action inquiry is not a standard technique that can be applied (like a coat of paint) to meet every need. It is a sophisticated and powerful approach to human inquiry, with enormous potential to help us improve both individual practice and organizational performance. To realize this potential it must be crafted to its particular circumstances and context. There are no guarantees of success but, with a little courage and a lot of determination, a little imagination and a lot of energy, much is possible.

Acknowledgements

I would like to thank Peter Sharpe and Paul Acres, Chief Constables of the Hertfordshire Constabulary, and Pauline Lawrence, Head of Human Resources, for their personal and institutional support for the project – without them it would never have got off the ground. I would also like to acknowledge the support and encouragement of Peter Reason, Judi Marshall, Jack Whitehead and other colleagues at the Centre for Action Research into Professional Practice at Bath University who have somehow managed to sharpen my critical judgement without dampening my enthusiasm.

I extend my most profound gratitude and admiration to the friends and colleagues who joined me in the 'Developing Ourselves as Leaders' action inquiry group and who courageously and tenaciously inquired into their own leadership practices whilst simultaneously teaching me how to facilitate a collaborative process. Thank you Mark, Carol, Phil, Dawn, Roger, Tim, Heather, Bernard, Peter, Judy, Gary, Dave and Barry – without you there would have been no inquiry and no learning. I hope you feel that this chapter does justice to our shared experience.

Note

* This chapter originally appeared as Mead (2002). It is reprinted here with permission from the publisher Kluwer Academic Press/Plenum Publishers.

10 Supporting organizational turnaround in local authorities[*]

Pam Fox, Clare Rigg and Martin Willis

Introduction

In December 2002, 15 local authorities in England were judged by the British Audit Commission under the government's Comprehensive Performance Assessment (CPA) to be poor or otherwise so weak in their corporate perform-ance as to need to engage in radical recovery planning, or organization turn-around. Various forms of intervention were offered, or imposed, to help senior managers and local politicians with the recovery and improvement process in their authorities. One of these interventions was action learning sets run with senior managers during 2003 to 2004. Four sets ran, focusing on specific areas of activity, covering human resource management, finance and performance management, and we, the authors of this chapter, each facilitated one or two sets. This chapter aims to convey how action learning was used to contribute to organization turnaround. It is written from our perspective as facilitators and is our interpretation of events. It is based on material collected from participants and recorded by us during the life of the sets, as gathered through ongoing feedback, facilitator diaries and a final participant survey.

The chapter begins with background on how the action learning sets were initiated, how they worked, their preoccupations and the role of the facilitator, before discussing two main themes which the work illustrates. The first of these is the contribution of action learning to organization turnaround, both to the processes of organization change, and also in providing space for individuals to make sense of their personal feelings about being judged as failing and to regain a sense of influence. The second theme is the multiple stakeholder context of this kind of cross-organizational action learning and the resultant issues raised.

Why action learning? The context of turnaround in local authorities

The challenges facing local authorities in achieving rapid turnaround are complex. Not only is radical rethinking and change required, but dynamic external influences mean the goalposts do not stop moving. There is no steady state end-point; rather the intention is that the turned-around authority will move to a state of ongoing improvement and innovation. Research on local authority turnaround to date (Boyne, 2003; Hughes *et al.*, 2004) has focused particularly on the role of changes in top managerial and political leadership in catalysing turnaround, coupled with external support and challenge for these actors. However, sustaining change requires the diffusion of new practices, values and behaviours throughout all levels of an authority. A capacity to experiment and learn needs to become a widespread organizational norm, which is perhaps an even greater challenge.

An additional aspect of the turnaround context was the subjectivity imbuing the CPA process, as explicated by Boyne and Enticott (2004) and Boyne *et al.* (2004). The resultant context was one where senior organization members' orientation to turnaround interventions were often ambivalent, in part embracing the external drive for improvement, but simultaneously carrying a sense of being coerced and personally judged, by a process with contested objectivity.

Action learning is used as a tool across the public and private sectors to enhance performance and improve quality. However, it was chosen as an intervention method in this instance because of its particular applicability in contexts where people have difficult organizational issues to address, which do not have an obvious correct solution like a jigsaw puzzle. This is an apt description of any turnaround agenda (Mellahi *et al.*, 2002), where the roots of problems are multifaceted and complex, but particularly for a local authority where improvement confronts managers and elected members with multiple, systemic fronts to work on, and where external support from other agencies needs to be complemented by an internal capacity to learn through practice.

These four action learning sets were part of the long-term study of recovery in local government, 'Learning from the Experience of Recovery', carried out by the Institute of Local Government Studies (INLOGOV) at the University of Birmingham and partners on behalf of the UK Office of the Deputy Prime Minister (ODPM) (see Hughes *et al.*, 2004). The sets were instigated for two primary objectives. The first was the ODPM's prime objective of delivering improved organization performance. To this end the intention was to provide peer support for change managers in recovering councils and to provide an opportunity for individual reflection and development in relation to their roles in managing the turnaround or recovery. It was intended that the sets would offer an important resource through which change managers could share experiences, test understandings and refine their strategies.

The second objective for using action learning was to provide a means of gathering data on the realities of the recovery process from the perspective of change managers, and especially on the way in which the process of improvement is played out through a series of individual relationships over time, through the detailed focus on the emerging role of key actors in the organization. As such the action learning sets were seen as a research tool to complement the other data collection methods (interviews, surveys, observation and documentary analysis) being used in the study.

As action learning sets that drew participants from across different local authorities, this is an example of cross-organizational action learning, which raises some specific issues for operationalizing action learning that are distinct from intra-organizational action learning. Key was the existence of multiple stakeholders with differing and potentially conflicting interests, as will be explored below.

Forming the sets

When forming these turnaround sets we were alert to the fact that they could either be composed of authorities that are in similar performance bands or with membership that cut across different performance bands. The idea that a set might be composed entirely of those from authorities judged to be poor and weak could attract some scepticism, if dismissively perceived as 'the inept leading the incompetent'. However, there were three arguments to counter this. First, in general, action learning set participants derive most benefit when they are peers working on related problems/opportunities, rather than participants working on widely different issues or at varying levels of challenge. This also avoids the potential for the 'halo effect', where participants shy away from challenging other individuals in the action learning set who are perceived as successful and beyond critique. Second, this presumption ignores the evidence on 'poor' councils also containing good-quality services. And, third, perspectives from excellent organizations, whether local authority or other sector, could be introduced to a turnaround set, by bringing in individuals for specific and timely 'expert input' without them being a member of the set. On this basis it was decided membership of the action learning sets would be entirely drawn from the 15 English local authorities engaged in recovery planning. All 15 were invited to send officers to one or more themed action learning sets. The costs of running the sets were covered by the ODPM and authorities had only to cover the costs of staff time and travel. The sets were promoted in late 2002 and spring 2003 to each of the councils through a range of channels with which they were already involved as part of their guided recovery planning. All 15 authorities engaged in recovery or turnaround had internal change managers, who project-managed their authority's recovery programme; an ODPM representative, known as the 'lead official' who was an external monitor/adviser; as well as access to various support groups like the Local Government Association Improvement Support Group. For more on the full panoply of intervention instruments, see Hughes *et al.* (2004).

In total seven of the 15 authorities elected to participate and were represented in at least one of the sets, with five councils sending someone to all of them. As a result, all the sets had between five and seven participants. Geographically the sets drew membership from authorities in south-west England through London and the Midlands, up to the north and east of England. This also had implications for the sets' meeting logistics, and certainly meant participants were too spread out to meet physically outside the set times. Whilst the business of action learning sets is frequently, and traditionally, generated by the participants, this project was an example of its application to pre-established themes. These were selected by INLOGOV and the ODPM on the basis of prior evidence of the root causes of failing authorities. Consequently, four action learning sets commenced in April 2003, one for each of the directors or lead managers of finance, performance, recovery and human resources. From the perspective of the funder, the ODPM, there was a desire for quick and visible outcomes. The result was a defined programme, not only with pre-determined themes, but of six meetings over a 12–15 month period, albeit with later scope for extension. To build up momentum meetings were deliberately scheduled more frequently at the start, moving from monthly for the first three months to three-monthly thereafter.

Participants' initial expectations

Why did set participants become involved? The rationale of individual managers for participating was invariably to be seen by central government assessors to be availing of any opportunity to help their authority's recovery process. As such they were generally not 'informed buyers' coming to action learning with any prior experience of what it might produce, but they came very much carrying a sense of corporate responsibility of making the time productive for their authority. When asked at the initial meeting what their objectives and expectations were, the dominant view of participants was that they saw the rationale for involvement as learning so that they could better contribute to their authority's turnaround and improvement. They were explicit in not seeing their participation as something primarily for their own individual benefit. A commonly expressed concern by participants was that the group should not be a simple talking shop, but that it should be useful to their work roles.

Participants' starting focus, therefore, was very much in line with that of the ODPM as client, on using action learning with the intention of enhancing organization performance.

What did the groups do?

Early preoccupations

Despite participants' espoused desire to use the action learning sets for the benefit of their organization, their initial preoccupations showed the sets clearly provided important individual emotional support, particularly early on. First meetings saw considerable outpourings of feelings about the process of being labelled as poor or so weak as to be deemed unlikely to improve. Participants expressed a sense of having been 'kicked in the teeth' and voiced feelings of unfairness about the CPA process, often focusing on the very marginal scoring that had resulted in their 'poor' rating. Some participants of the sets expressed a sense of feeling personally wounded by the feedback. In facilitating early on we chose to enable that personal space within the sets, and indeed this early exchange had a therapeutic effect, which in our view facilitated the focus to move on quickly in most cases. Subsequent exchanges between ALS (action learning set) participants also identified that there were elements of good practice in each authority, which helped them feel their own situation was not all irretrievable doom and gloom. Being able to share experiences of the subjectivities of the CPA judgements, as well as draw on external commentary on them, helped to create a sense of the possibility of doing things. In this way participants clearly found in the action learning sets a communicative space in which it was possible to express feelings of being bruised, hurt, misjudged or coerced, and to regain a sense of influence.

There was one exception in one ALS, an example of a source of resistance to critical reflection that can be quite common in action learning: 'harking back to the golden era'. From this one individual there was a degree of idolizing perceived past experiences, looking back on elements of their organization, particularly the management team that they were part of, as beyond critique. Challenge to this resistance came from other group members and exposure to external ideas and practices, drawn from other organizations and sectors.

Evolving focus

Participants of the action learning sets were largely self-selecting in that they joined on the basis of their interest in the pre-established theme which a particular set was to cover (finance, human resources, etc.). However, once they were established the particular inquiry or issue on which the participants of the sets worked were generated on the basis of participants' perception primarily of what they thought would be of value to the authority in which they worked.

There were a number of different ways in which the action learning sets provided both individual and organizational learning. Some of the meeting time was taken up with participants reviewing with their colleagues what they were doing within their job role and receiving constructive scrutiny on the thinking underlying those actions. At other times external people were invited from other local authorities or private sector companies to talk about the way they did things in their context. This would be followed by set members examining the application of relevant practices to their own authorities. In some sessions the facilitator would lead a session, presenting a review of practice and/or research into a particular theme that participants had pre-determined. Again this was used to provoke participant reflections on the implications for their own practice. The fourth main way of working was by individuals identifying lines of inquiry to be pursued between meetings of the action learning sets, the results of which would be brought back for discussion and to distil the learning at a future meeting of the set. Examples of such inquiry questions include: How are performance targets helping or hindering allocation of resources and effort? How best can performance management be used to deliver target outcomes? What different models of human resource management exist? How do I lead change more effectively? How do I improve my work with elected members? How can improvement be sustained?

Widening horizons

By about the fourth meeting, ALS participants were looking outside their respective councils to experience elsewhere, either in excellent authorities or in the private sector. Key learning from these was that these excellent authorities were doing distinctive things that marked them apart, but, reassuringly, that the distance was not unassailable, in that what they did was often quite simple and replicable. For example, the financial management ALS saw a simple transparent planning process being used in an excellent authority, which initially led some to question the value of the process being requested by their ODPM lead official, which they described as heavy-handed and mechanistic. However, this provoked a discussion as to whether they had to get the detailed process right first before they could reach a stage of simpler systems. This helped them see a bigger picture, to move beyond a mechanistic working through of recovery plans and towards seeing recovery in the wider context of developing a vision for their area.

Implications of multiple stakeholders

These sets, as has been outlined above, were created fundamentally to deliver organization improvements, what can be characterized in Reason and Bradbury's (2001) terms as third-person inquiry, rather than primarily to focus on individual self-reflection, or first-person inquiry. The key implication to highlight here is that this meant there were three other stakeholders besides the participants themselves, whose involvement influenced the action learning sets even though not as action learning set participants. First, there were the local authority senior managers, whose commitment to the project was important, in particular the extent to which they were willing to engage with their authority's set participant(s) when they tried to implement ideas generated by the action learning process. Included in the second category were those other organization members who were involved in internal changes but not party to the action learning process. The third stakeholder was the client, the ODPM, who funded the whole programme and was intent on seeing improvements.

This project was an interesting example of the use of action learning in a consultancy context, where it was commissioned by a client (ODPM) on behalf of councils, who between them had expectations of visible and speedy results. The client's willingness to fund action learning was because of anticipated gains such as faster performance improvements, quicker sharing of knowledge, avoidance of each authority reinventing the same wheel and clearer identification of systemic blocks to turnaround. This sense of 'non-participating-client-owned' action learning is also different from the traditional Revans style of participant-owned and -directed action learning (Revans, 1982). It places a different pressure on the facilitator who is pulled in the direction of both the participants' best interests and the client's brief. In our case we also had a third pull: to meet the research objectives of INLOGOV.

The consequence of this complex stakeholder network was to present participants in the action learning sets with a number of tensions and difficulties. A key one was uncertainty in the early stage over who was in control of the recovery process, and to what extent local authority leaders could assert their direction. Another example was of feeling powerless in situations where there was conflicting advice and judgement by external agencies and no clear resolution. However, as the recovery process progressed, some participants of the ALSs became more assertive about how they engaged with external guidance.

A further difficulty involved other organization members who were essential to the turnaround process although not involved in the action learning and not leading the recovery. ALS participants expressed concern that key human aspects of the turnaround were being forgotten in the externally driven model of recovery, particularly staff feelings, perception and morale. For example, some managers who had thought they were part of the solution felt that, with the incoming of new managers, they were being construed as part of the problem. Where authorities were still receiving blanket criticism without acknowledgement of effort or pockets of achievement, it was feared that this could have implications for sustaining improvement if staff motivation could not be raised. ALS participants were particularly concerned by shifts such as changing interim managers or new inexperienced political leadership.

Differing views were expressed on the role of local politicians in the recovery process. Some saw recovery as being primarily a managerial process, driven by central government, over which local politicians had little control and in which they played a marginal role. Others indicated that their elected members had a key role, particularly where a dramatic change in political control had followed the CPA results, and appeared to catalyse the turnaround process.

Role of the facilitator/set adviser

A core premise of Revans' principles of action learning is that participants themselves have the expertise to reach solutions, but that they can be assisted by a facilitator to engage in more rigorous thinking and better problem diagnosis so as to develop better-quality solutions. The primary skill for a facilitator is the ability to ask questions of sufficient challenge to provoke new thinking.

Two of the four action learning sets (those on human resource management and on financial management) were facilitated by two full-time academics from INLOGOV with broad experience of action learning, both of whom had worked in local government. The two other learning sets were facilitated by a principal associate with INLOGOV who had a local authority background but also a detailed knowledge of action learning. At the outset the facilitator role was defined to participants as:

- providing a structure for the meetings;
- steering the group's style of operation to produce good-quality questioning and to draw participants back from rushing to offer advice without adequate diagnostic review or reflection;
- modelling the above in our own style of questioning;
- encouraging the group to establish and maintain ground rules, such as confidentiality and turn-taking.

We saw our purpose as neither to sit in judgement of the participants, nor to act as experts telling them how to do their jobs, but we also found that the role changed over the duration of the learning sets. Whilst initially we sought to provide a structure to manage the timings and control contributions, we gradually aimed to make members of the sets aware of the self-monitoring of behaviours required for a balance between taking from the set and giving. Tackling any individuals who dominated or side-tracked the discussion, or who avoided self-reflection, gradually became the responsibility of set participants as well as that of the facilitators.

In the early stages facilitation required holding a space open for participants to communicate their feelings about the CPA judgements and the recovery or turnaround process. This was followed by a more task-orientated role, sometimes providing the 'P' (of Revans' specialized knowledge, 1982), or more frequently drawing on our networks to source it from outside. Here, it was useful to have a good understanding of the wider public policy and service system and valuable to have a contextual understanding of local government.

We found that facilitation required holding in balance responding to participants' expressed wishes – for example, to investigate specific aspects of local authority financial management – and recognizing when there might be a more significant individual issue to address behind the pull to action. For example, we had to be alert to the possibility that the espoused desire to prioritize 'getting things done' on behalf of the authority actually masked common management drivers which limit learning because they militate against reflection, openness and questioning, such as an impulse to instant activity, compulsion to feel in control, or desire to be seen as strong and all-knowing.

Value to the participants

When the action learning sets were evaluated, participants were positive about their engagement across the board. They said that they had gained knowledge and developed new networks both within the ALS and also beyond, with other excellent authorities and the private sector. Many said they had developed increased confidence in themselves, could act more assertively and felt better able to challenge. Most said they had made changes to their working practices as a result of their engagement in the action learning process. The following comments are illustrative of the feedback:

'I have enjoyed and benefited from the process, made several interesting contacts, and found your [the facilitator's] knowledge and resource network helpful in my and my Council's development.'

'Better understanding of other Local Authorities and practices they have adopted.'

'More confidence to challenge or question colleagues.'

'Confirmation of "Best Practice" for some of our organizational Practices and Procedures.'

'A relaxed atmosphere appeared to enable people to open up and talk about the realities of situations rather than hiding behind formal talk.'

'I have used what I have learned in budget consultation methodology for the 2004/5 budget.'

'The process used for budget consultation has generally been more effective and feedback has been good from consultees.'

The action learning set participants were overwhelmingly committed to their respective authority's improvement and accepting of the need for radical changes, even if for a few there was an initial reluctance to accept CPA ratings. Energy for recovery and improvement grew without exception, particularly as they saw real results being produced. Participants in the action learning sets said they found the action learning process useful both organizationally and to them as individuals in contributing to their authority's turnaround.

Signing up for recovery through inter-organizational action learning – concluding observations

The four action learning sets produced some important insights into the factors that influence the success of action learning sets run on an inter-organizational basis, and run in a context of recovery and turnaround where there is external pressure to participate.

In a context of inter-organizational action learning, there is always a risk that participants can become so involved in the work of their action learning set or in their own individual development that they become detached from their organization. Where the objective is organization capacity-building, this could clearly be problematic. In this instance such a risk was clearly heightened by the gaze of the external client, the ODPM, and although the risk never materialized, it was important for facilitators to be alert to the possibility.

If one danger is separation between set participants and their organizations, this project also showed that another risk is that action learning set participants are not properly supported within their organization. Support is likely to include, for example, adequate time to fully engage in the action learning process; backing to experiment and lead on turnaround projects; or access to the ear of the Chief Executive and/or most senior managers. Not only does the individual lose out, but the organization does not benefit if there are no supported connections between the individual's action learning and the wider organization: for example, dissemination routes for communicating the learning through the authority. A related issue is that organizations and individuals gain most when action learning group participants have appropriate status and ability to influence and implement change. They need to be people who have real issues to work on and ideally who have a client in the organization who wants to see results. In a public sector turnaround context this is further complicated by the existence of external stakeholders such as central government in the form of ODPM.

Action learning needs commitment and consistent engagement from participants to be successful. Other participants as well as the employing organizations are likely to lose out when commitment is not total or attendance is inconsistent. With these turnaround sets, there was an early danger that in being compelled to participate there might be questionable commitment from participants. In the event attendance and participation were not significant issues. In the first weeks there were two or three individuals from other authorities who expressed interest in participating, but they never materialized. However, for those who did engage, there was a definite sense in the initial stages, until the ALSs had proved their value, of participants being present because they felt they had to be seen to be taking advantage of any turnaround support, rather than because they had particularly chosen or were committed to the action learning process.

This experience with action learning illustrates the value of holding space for individual concerns and issues, even where the design prioritizes organization outcomes. The support structure of an action learning set, including sharing with others from similar contexts, helps motivate and maintain momentum through what can be difficult times for them and their organization; it enables individuals to express and explore problems that may be sensitive or confidential and be experimental with solutions. Action learning can provide a safe environment for individuals to explore issues away from the gaze of external supervisors. It can also validate the role and skill of individuals in a context when they may be feeling bruised from the experience of being defined as part of a poorly performing organization. The 'critical friend' process encourages individuals to be self-reflective of aspects of their practice that may need to change. One of the conclusions from this project is that third-person inquiry could not really begin without first-person communicative space. We would argue that the two are interconnected. If there is no such space, it is likely that thinking on organization issues will continue to be obscured by unresolved individual concerns.

The initiative demonstrates that action learning has some particular contributions to make in a turnaround context, particularly as part of supporting individual capacity-building. Turnaround is radical and has to be staged. There may well be some clearing out initially, but the process of improvement needs a second stage of capacity-building with the people that remain. It is their resourcefulness on which improvement depends. As this chapter has shown, many are likely to feel 'beaten up': perhaps uncertain whether they are part of the future solution or are seen as part of the problem. Action learning has an important contribution to making people value themselves and regain a sense of influence. Yet the focus of public policy improvement interventions is organizational: recovery and improvement plans; systems; targets; overall capacity. The key implication from this chapter for organizational turnaround is that leaping to third-person interventions, and aiming for organizational change first, will not work without first giving some time to first-person inquiry and the individual reflective space.

Note

* This paper arises from a research and action learning programme entitled 'Learning from the Experience of Recovery' commissioned by the UK government's Office of the Deputy Prime Minister, in association with the Audit Commission, the Local Government Association, and the Improvement and Development Agency. The views of the authors do not necessarily represent those of the commissioning bodies. Further details can be found at: http://www.inlogov.bham.ac.uk/research/expofrecovery.htm (accessed 11 March 2006).

Section IV

Practice

Networks and partnerships: developing the public policy system

A joined-up approach to public policy issues and service delivery is almost universally espoused. It is unquestionable that many 'wicked' issues continue to challenge public services, without respect for organizational boundaries. But mechanisms for resource allocation remain departmentally compartmentalized whilst accountability and performance management arrangements continue to pull against inter-agency working. In practice collaboration with others who have differing organizational cultural norms and systems is not straightforward. Members are confronted with the need to learn about each other's values, priorities and practices in order to pursue the holy grail of better joined-up working. We see it as a lost opportunity that so few voices have taken a systemic perspective to explicitly envisage the development of leadership as a route for enhancing organizational capacity to work across boundaries and to improve joined-up thinking, so as to strengthen the public service system more widely.

In this section, Chapters 11–13 present three accounts of action learning employed as a systemic intervention, used with the primary aim of developing the public service system more broadly. In Chapter 11 Geoff Mead describes the UK Public Service Leaders Scheme (PSLS) established in 2002 for rising leaders across central and local government, health, police and defence organizations. Chapter 12, by Martin Willis, is an account of four partnership action learning sets designed to develop collaborative relationships across health and social care, as part of the UK Department of Health-funded Social Care Leadership Development Initiative (SCLDI). In Chapter 13 David Coghlan and Paul Coughlan offer different insights which are particularly pertinent to the new world of public service provision in which managers increasingly engage in private–public partnerships and supplier relationships.

A key issue raised by Geoff Mead's chapter, which is echoed in several others throughout the book and revisited in the final chapter, is the potential friction between an intention of systematic collaborative inquiry into public service leadership and what individual participants prioritize: what Mead interprets, in Habermasian terms, as a boundary crisis between system and lifeworld (Habermas, 1987).

Mead's chapter illustrates the systemic value of inter-organizational action learning, with the cross-organizational learning PSLS participants developed through their action inquiry group exchanges and visits. Martin Willis extends this theme, illustrating how cross-organizational action learning can help forge collaborative working relationships, in that participants learn to 'lead-in-partnership' rather than learning about 'leadership for partnership'. In this sense the action learning experience is not a dry run; it is the space to begin to 'do' partnership, which involves both sharing power and giving clear messages about boundaries.

A key theme of this section is learning and innovation across a network. Commonly this is conceived of in top-down ways such as dissemination of best practice, bench-marking against the best, learning from the experts. Even in the modified version of this concept which is implicit in UK ideas such as the Beacon Council scheme, where good practice examples were picked out and people invited to come and observe them, the idea of sitting at the feet of people who know better still prevails. The old distinction between invention and innovation applies here. The challenge is not to have the good idea in the first place, it is to change organizational practice on a permanent and self-sustaining basis. Coghlan and Coughlan illustrate an example of a peer-based non-linear and organic approach to innovation and change, which is more likely to have success than more traditional top-down approaches implied in the term 'disseminating best practice'. Their second case study illustrates private sector practice of collaboration across the contractual divide. Managing quality up and down the supply chain is not a new idea in the private sector, and this case illustrates adoption of a peer-directed problem-solving approach, with the addition of reflection and learning so that not only do they solve the problem but they also improve their capacity to solve future problems. For the public sector, the significance of this case is the infrequency with which the public sector acts in this way. Public officials seem to feel constrained, rightly or wrongly, by the legal framework through which competition is managed and by a stereotypical simplistic perception of how the private sector approaches competition.

11 Developing public service leaders through action inquiry

Geoff Mead

Introduction

In 2001, in response to governmental concerns about the quality of public service leadership, the Cabinet Office established the Public Service Leaders Scheme (PSLS) for rising leaders in central and local government, the National Health Service, the police and voluntary organizations. At the time of writing, some 250 public service leaders have taken part in the programme, which includes, as a mandatory element, participation in facilitated action inquiry groups. The author has been involved in the scheme since its inception, designing the action inquiry group element of the programme, selecting and supporting the facilitators of the 21 groups over the lifetime of the scheme, monitoring performance and undertaking an overall quality assurance role.

Regrettably, book chapters and journal articles on leadership development schemes are sometimes presented as 'victory narratives' (MacLure, 1996) charting the inexorably successful implementation of a project from design to evaluation. In this chapter, I want to sidestep the academic convention of impersonal third-person language and pseudo-objectivity to give a more personal account. I want to go below the surface of a large-scale action inquiry-based programme to explore what happened (if not 'what really happened' then 'what might have happened') and how, whilst not taking the form that was originally intended, the outcomes for many of the participants seem to have been significant and positive.

In the light of this practical exploration, I also want to consider some theoretical perspectives that may offer useful insights to designers, facilitators, sponsors and members of such schemes. In particular, I will draw upon the ideas of the conflicting logics of system and lifeworld first propounded by social theorist Jurgen Habermas to explore the nature of the learning environment created in the action inquiry groups (Habermas, 1987). I will also refer to notions of leadership maturity and of the four territories of experience – visioning, strategizing, performing and assessing (Fisher and Rooke, 2000; Torbert, 2004) – when considering, respectively, participants' leadership development needs and the tensions that can occur between different stakeholders in a complex programme like the Public Service Leaders Scheme.

First, though, some background information to set the scene and establish the context for the action inquiry groups.

Context

Although commissioned by the Cabinet Office, the PSLS was designed and is delivered by a consortium of suppliers: CMPS Civil Service College, the University of Birmingham (INLOGOV) and Clutterbuck Associates on a commercial basis. The scheme – as described to potential applicants on the PSLS website (www.publicserviceleadersscheme.gov.uk) – is intended to develop a new generation of public service leaders with the appropriate skills, abilities, knowledge and experience to work effectively in positions of leadership within – and across – the public sector.

The programme, following the original design brief, is comprised of several related elements. Participants attend a two-day foundation event to introduce them to the programme and make an initial identification of learning and development needs through small group exercises and the results of a 360 degree feedback tool (Transformational Leadership Questionnaire™). On the basis of this information, and in dialogue with their organizational sponsor, they prepare a written personal learning contract against which to gauge and evidence their development over their time on the scheme. Participants are expected to attend at least 80 per cent of the nine two- or three-day residential network learning events, with input on leadership and public service delivery issues by high-profile practitioners (and the occasional academic) and large group inquiry processes such as organizational and city raids, world café, and open space technology.[1] All participants have the opportunity to select a mentor from a pool of trained volunteers, mostly senior public service leaders, and all have access to the virtual learning centre, an on-line repository of information, articles and notices of events. As part of the programme, participants are expected to arrange a period of interchange in another organization, probably in a sector different from their own. Finally, all participants are expected to work as members of facilitated action inquiry groups, which meet six times a year. To help them navigate this complex programme and to take advantage of the whole range of its offerings, participants are assigned to nominated personal development advisers drawn from the Cabinet Office secretariat. Readers who would like to know more about the overall scheme than this brief overview provides may wish to refer to the PSLS website for a more comprehensive description of the various elements, as I shall henceforth focus on the action inquiry groups themselves.

What is action inquiry?

The term action inquiry was first used by consultant and academic Bill Torbert (1999, 2004) as a development of action science as practised by Chris Argyris (Argyris *et al.*, 1985). He uses the term to describe: 'a moment to moment way of living whereby we attune ourselves through inquiry to acting in an increasingly timely and wise fashion for the development of the families, teams, and organizations in which we participate' (Torbert, 2004: 2). I adopted the nomenclature of action inquiry in a looser though related sense, and coined the phrase action inquiry group (Mead, 2002) to describe a process I initiated with police leaders in the Hertfordshire Constabulary during the period 1997–2001 (see Chapter 9 of this book):

> [a group of] practitioners coming together as a community of inquiry, encouraging and challenging each other as they engaged in real-time, real-life development over several cycles of action and reflection with the process of the group designed co-operatively to meet emerging themes and interests.
>
> (Mead, 2002: 193)

In designing the action inquiry group element of the PSLS I naturally built upon the experience of convening and facilitating this inquiry into police leadership. I was also strongly influenced by the tradition of *action research* represented by the Centre for Action Research in Professional Practice at the University of Bath (see, for example, Reason, 1988, 1994; Reason and Bradbury, 2001) where I completed my doctorate and where I now teach as a visiting fellow. Whilst not incompatible with *action learning* (Revans, 1998) and *self-managed learning* (Cunningham, 1994) action research has, perhaps, a broader practical scope and deeper theoretical roots than most approaches to adult learning. Having said that, there is no established methodology for action inquiry groups per se, and the novel attempt to craft a vehicle uniquely fitted for the needs of the PSLS participants allowed much scope for creative design.

When introducing the concept to facilitators and participants, the distinctive features of action inquiry groups were described as:

- cycles of action and reflection
- ongoing inquiry questions
- focus on improving practice
- the possibility of collaborative inquiries
- an egalitarian and participative ethos
- valuing many different ways of knowing.

I envisaged that – under the broad umbrella inquiry question 'How can we improve the quality of our practice as public service leaders?' – participants would identify specific inquiry questions about their own practice as leaders that they wanted to address in the action inquiry groups either as first-person, second-person or third-person inquiries (Reason and Bradbury, 2001) where:

- first-person inquiry focuses on changing one's individual practice and behaviour;

- second-person inquiry engages two or more people in exploring mutual concerns;
- third-person inquiry seeks wider systemic change with others outside the inquiry group.

I also explained that the action inquiry groups were intended to provide:

- continuity and a sense of community
- a safe and challenging space
- personal and professional development
- individual and collective learning
- long-term cross-sector relationships
- integration with other elements of PSLS.

The facilitator's role was not to be a content expert but to support the group's learning process. Their function was described as:

- to add value by holding the focus, guiding the process, and giving high-quality feedback;
- to help you reflect and apply new learning to real-life situations;
- to encourage you to focus on improving your leadership practice;
- to help you take increasing responsibility for your own learning and development.

This then was our starting point. Nothing if not ambitious, but not too far removed from the kinds of statements one might make about many different kinds of action learning process. For the first cohort, I imagined that the groups would quickly identify themes of common interest to work on as second-person or third-person inquiries and that they might then follow roughly parallel developmental paths, steered by their facilitators and monitored by me through regular meta-set meetings of the facilitators, which I would convene and chair. There would, I thought, be no shortage of tangible output from the groups to demonstrate their progress and reassure the scheme's sponsors. Facilitation of the groups would be testing but largely unproblematic and I was confident that all the facilitators (eight for the first cohort) would be equal to the task and stick with their groups throughout their projected three-year lifecycle. But, like true love, it seems that the course of true learning never does run smooth and the next four years were to challenge many of our practices and assumptions about developing public service leaders through action inquiry.

Action inquiry groups

After a little more information about the composition and structure of the action inquiry groups, I would like to get closer to the messier reality of engaging 250 people in 21 groups each lasting three years.

PSLS participants are drawn mainly from central government (civil service), local government and the National Health Service, with a small minority of police and voluntary sector representatives. Each of the three cohorts to date has had an approximately even number of men and women overall, though this has varied between sectors, with (as with so many such schemes) disproportionately few members from visible ethnic minorities. Typically, participants occupied middle management roles when they entered the scheme and many were promoted once or twice during their time on the programme. Many had originally been recruited through some kind of fast-track scheme and all had been identified by their sponsoring organizations as having the potential to progress to senior public service leadership roles. They ranged in age from late twenties to late forties with a substantial majority in their thirties.

Each action inquiry group had 11 or 12 members and a professional external facilitator drawn from staff and associates of the supplier consortium. This is considerably more than the typical six to eight members of conventional action learning sets. The choice was fuelled partly by financial considerations but more by the desire to build greater diversity and resilience into each group. A larger group requires creative facilitation (sometimes working, for example, individually, in pairs or in sub-groups) if participants are to get a reasonable amount of 'airtime' at each meeting. In hindsight, this suited some groups and facilitators better than others, though over time, as some members left the PSLS and others were unable to get to all the meetings of the action inquiry group, most groups developed a stable core of up to ten attendees.

Several simple criteria were used to guide the composition of the groups. First, an attempt was made to cluster participants geographically to ease the burden of travel and to encourage personal contact between meetings. Second, members were selected to provide maximum diversity of sector and professional background. Third, without applying quotas, a reasonable gender balance was sought. Finally, participants were invited to swap groups if they felt that the proposed membership was unsuitable for any reason (and a few did indeed take this option). These arrangements appear to have suited most participants reasonably well, though the real value of geographical clustering was questioned by some in practice.

The groups meet six times a year. During the first year, three (and during the second year, one) of these meetings are half-days timed to coincide with the network learning events mentioned above. All other meetings are full days, timed for the mutual convenience of participants and facilitators and they are hosted by group members, usually at their place of work. Again, economic considerations limit the number of meetings, which is no more than adequate to sustain momentum. Participants and facilitators agree that the half-day meetings are barely long enough, though it is difficult to see how they could be extended without adversely affecting the remainder of the network learning event schedule. However, from the point of view of supporting and monitoring the whole process during the early stages, bringing all the groups together during the three network learning events in the first year of the programme enabled us to schedule parallel meta-set meetings of all the action inquiry group facilitators, which proved invaluable.

It was agreed with the sponsors of the scheme that the content of action inquiry group meetings is confidential and that the facilitators play no part in assessing participants' performance. Nevertheless, it is clearly essential to monitor the progress of each group and evaluate the effectiveness of all elements of the PSLS. The activities of the groups were monitored through direct feedback from facilitators at the meta-set meetings, and by use of a simple pro-forma completed by facilitators after each action inquiry group meeting. Several facilitators decided to share the content of these forms with the members of their groups and none of the forms went beyond me as the person with accountability to the client for this element of the scheme. Twice a year, I synthesized this information in an anonymous report to the sponsors of the scheme for whom, without some such form of reporting, the action inquiry groups would have remained 'a black box' (as one member of the Cabinet Office secretariat once put it to me). Participants were enabled to give direct feedback on their experience through evaluation forms (when the meetings coincided with network learning events) and through a whole-programme evaluation process conducted by external consultants on behalf of the sponsors. A further route, about which I shall say more later, was through an appreciative evaluation exercise in which participants were invited to identify in what ways the process had been helpful and how the groups worked when 'at their best'.

The map is not the territory

As a semanticist, Alfred Korzybski once memorably said, 'the map is not the territory' (Korzybski, 1941), and this became increasingly evident in respect of the action inquiry groups as time went on. In this section I will outline and reflect upon some significant ways in which the actuality of the process departed from my initial (and what now seem somewhat naïve) assumptions about how this element of the PSLS would work in practice.

The first signs of the 'messiness' of the process appeared at the very first meeting of cohort 1's action inquiry groups at the beginning of the programme. It quickly became clear that whilst some groups relished the prospect of following their own learning agendas, others felt daunted by the openness of the design, and I repeatedly found myself called upon to explain the purpose of the groups. 'But what do you actually want us to do?' was a common plea from those who wanted more direction. My response, either in person or through their facilitator, was to encourage them to take their time to establish their individual learning needs and common interests to allow themes for co-operative inquiry (Heron, 1996; Reason and Heron, 1999) to emerge. Over time, most groups did indeed find some common interests to focus on as well as their individual issues but, in hindsight, the expectation that this would happen smoothly and naturally proved unrealistic. Some of the themes that emerged in the first cohort were:

- managing the interface between policy and service delivery
- ways of improving motivation in public services
- being transformational in a transactional world
- work–life balance – how to be an effective leader and stay sane.

In the light of the difficulty some groups had in establishing and taking forward such co-operative inquiries, the advice to cohorts 2 and 3 was to concentrate on developing high-quality inquiries into their own leadership practice (a shift of emphasis from second-person inquiry to supporting each other's first-person inquiries).

It also quickly became apparent that facilitating the action inquiry groups through such an open and emergent process was extremely demanding for the facilitators. All of them were competent and experienced at facilitating group learning processes but we found that generic facilitation skills were not enough to manage the complexities of this process (despite two days' preparatory briefing and regular ongoing supervision in their meta-set). The first 12 months of the scheme saw quite a high – and unplanned – turnover of facilitators, causing some disruption in affected groups. Three out of the eight left for various reasons during the early stages and a concerted effort was made to replace them with facilitators with greater specific experience of action inquiry. Over time the team of facilitators stabilized and developed greater confidence as they learned from their experience of facilitating the action inquiry groups. For subsequent cohorts, some facilitators were invited to take on second groups (thus providing continuity across cohorts) and some new facilitators, including several associates of the Centre for Action Research in Professional Practice at the University of Bath, were recruited to bring fresh ideas and further specific expertise into the team. This practice seemed to work well and, although not without difficulties, facilitating the second and third cohorts has not proved to be quite so problematic.

At the time of writing, the first two cohorts have now completed the rolling three-year programme and the third cohort is entering its final year. A further unanticipated issue has been the effect of the longevity of the action inquiry groups. A common experience has been a slump in energy and enthusiasm towards the end of the second year (exacerbated by the departure of some participants who for funding or other reasons opted to leave the PSLS at that point). However, this has also resulted in most groups reducing to a core of committed members determined to make the most of their final year. Having noticed this phenomenon with cohort 1, we have encouraged a resurgence of interest in cohorts 2 and 3, by holding a café society-type event at which all the action inquiry groups share with each other what they have been doing and quiz each other about future plans. Here is a small sample of what cohort 3 groups said to each other at the most recent café society event about what they wanted to do in their final year:

• have more individual time at meetings
• have a consistent commitment to meeting targets
• follow through better after action inquiry group meetings
• check where we are each up to against graduation criteria
• carry on meeting after PSLS.

Working with such groups over an extended period of three years was pretty much unknown territory and we have come to accept they will have a different rhythm and pace from groups that meet for shorter periods. Generally we experienced the energy of the groups ebbing and flowing something like the pattern shown in Figure 11.1. After initial excitement there seems to be a period of reaction when the purpose and value of the group is called into question. This usually picks up fairly quickly so that by the end of the first year and the beginning of the second the groups are finding their own way forward. Uncertainty about the future and the disruptive effect of some members leaving the group towards the end of the second year causes energy to slump, until those that are left renew their commitment. By the end of the third year, most groups are on a 'high' and some have continued to meet informally after the end of the three-year programme.

We had anticipated that some PSLS participants would graduate from the scheme at the end of the second year as they achieved the learning goals agreed in their personal learning contracts. However, we had not foreseen the wide range of personal circumstances that made it difficult (and sometimes impossible) for members to attend and play a full part in the action inquiry groups. As well as the usual quota of births, marriages, divorces, even deaths, most PSLS participants changed jobs at least once and sometimes twice or more during the programme, usually on promotion. Making the time and space to

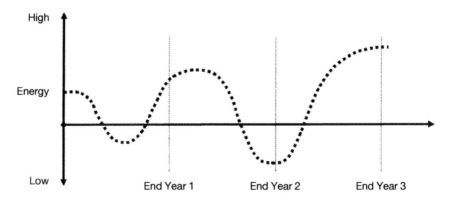

Figure 11.1 Action inquiry groups – energy.

attend six action inquiry group meetings a year proved to be a commitment not all could manage, and it was quite clear that the process would only succeed if participants could see significant benefits from attending. Perhaps this fuelled what we might term 'the pull to the personal' experienced in most groups, where the distinctions between work and the rest of life soon dissolved. This was such a strong phenomenon in the groups that I shall return to it later in the chapter when I offer some more detailed reflections on the process of the action inquiry groups.

Having imagined that each cohort of action inquiry groups would follow broadly similar paths of inquiry, co-ordinated through the work of the facilitators and through my overall supervision of their work in the meta-set, we found that each group identified subtly different needs and each soon developed its own unique style and way of working. Whilst this was not of itself undesirable, it did cause tensions in terms of our accountability to the Cabinet Office secretariat who, as the client, understandably wanted to know what benefits participants were getting from this not inexpensive element of the scheme. This brings up an important point about the perspectives of the different stakeholders in the PSLS generally and the action inquiry groups in particular.

One way of looking at this is through the 'four territories of experience' proposed by Fisher, Torbert and others (Fisher and Rooke, 2000; Torbert, 2004) as critical for effective action in the world: visioning, strategizing, performing and assessing. By their definition, visioning is concerned with long-term intentions, purposes and aims; strategizing with planning and implementing overall delivery; performing with acting in pursuit of role-defined responsibilities; assessing with observed behavioural consequences and the effects of action.

When these categories of action are aligned through close interrelationships and mutual feedback, it is argued, we achieve the best possibility for appropriate, timely and effective action.

Table 11.1 attempts to show how these perspectives were, in effect, 'owned' by different stakeholders in the action inquiry group element of the PSLS and, consequentially, how tensions arose between them as each addressed different concerns. Each stakeholder had particular tensions to manage and, as director of action inquiry groups, I felt that my role was to seek to understand and minimize the tensions experienced by the Cabinet Office secretariat and the facilitators. The means at my disposal were the regular meta-set meetings with facilitators and periodic progress reports to the secretariat (always made in person) on the basis of information supplied by the facilitators about what and how their groups were doing. I did not come under any pressure to breach the confidentiality of action inquiry group proceedings and, in the absence of 'tangible products' such as reports and presentations by the groups, found that reassurance about the benefits the participants were themselves reporting helped to bridge the gap between us. I suspect that similar tensions will inevitably arise in any sort of large-scale action learning process. If the tensions

Table 11.1 Different perspectives on action inquiry groups

Stakeholders	PSLS Secretariat Cabinet Office	Director of action inquiry groups	Action inquiry group facilitators	Individual PSLS participants
Perspective	Visioning	Strategizing	Performing	Assessing
	Long-term impact of PSLS as a whole on public service leadership	Medium- to long-term impact and sustainability of action inquiry group process	Medium- to short-term exercise of facilitator role to sustain life of the group	Short- to medium-term impact of learning in the group on my work and life
Question	How do we know action inquiry groups are 'working well' and represent good value for money for sectoral sponsors?	How can I satisfy the client that we are doing good work whilst keeping the space open for the very different needs of each group?	How can I meet the specific needs of my group which may not look much like the original plan whilst 'playing the game'?	How can this group meet my needs well enough to justify the time I have to take out of my busy life to be here?
Pull towards	Control	Co-ordinate	Facilitate	Relate
	Tangible products that can be shown to others to prove the value of PSLS	Coherent stories of what groups are doing in relation to the aims of PSLS	Activities that promote reflection and improve the practice of participants	Friendships that help me cope with the demands and pressures of life and work
Tensions	Holding the space between the sectoral sponsors and the deliverers	Holding the space between the secretariat and action inquiry group facilitators	Holding the space between director of action inquiry and participants	Holding the space between 'system world' and 'lifeworld'

cannot be 'designed out', then it becomes essential to 'design in' processes, such as those mentioned above, for handling them over the duration of the programme.

So what benefits were achieved?

Given the significant differences between our original intentions and what happened in practice an obvious question to ask is what benefits, if any, did the action inquiry group process provide?

First let us turn to an independent evaluation of the PSLS commissioned by the Cabinet Office and conducted by external consultants (Foster and Turner, 2003). Their methodology included interviews and focus group sessions with participants, their line managers and organizational sponsors, plus a questionnaire for quantitative and qualitative responses. The evaluation was conducted in the period July–October 2003, when cohort 1 had been in the scheme for two years, cohort 2 for one year and cohort 3 had just started. The evaluation report concluded:

> Participants, their line managers and others who sponsor them on PSLS like and value the scheme. There are no significant variances of view about the scheme between participants from the different sectors … PSLS is helping the majority of participants to improve their leadership skills and behaviours and three elements of it – foundation events, network learning events and action inquiry groups are – generally working well, in terms of the way they are delivered, levels of participation and in meeting their objectives. The scheme is having a positive impact on participants' development in particular in:
>
> - increasing self-awareness
> - increasing confidence
> - broadening perspectives in decision making
> - encouraging a consultative approach; and
> - developing partnership working.

Participants' sponsors have observed positive changes in their behaviour in all these areas.

Specifically in relation to the action inquiry groups, the 53 participants who responded to the questionnaire (20 per cent response rate) indicated that cohorts 1 and 2 valued their participation in the groups more highly than, and cohort 3 as highly as, other elements of the PSLS programme. On a scale of 1 (not at all useful) to 6 (very useful), cohort 1 rated action inquiry groups at 4.6, cohort 2 at 4.9 and cohort 3 (three months into the scheme) at 3.6. The full results are shown in Table 11.2.

Overall this represents a high level of participant satisfaction, though the evaluation also revealed that some groups were less influential and beneficial than others and that this was largely attributed to the participant's view of the quality of facilitation they received.

Useful as it is to get an independent evaluation of the scheme, the report does not help us get close to the participants' actual experience of the action inquiry groups. For this, we can turn to the appreciative evaluation exercise conducted with cohorts 1 and 2 in 2003 and 2004. Participants were introduced to the concept of appreciative inquiry (Hammond, 1998; Cooperrider

Table 11.2 Usefulness of action inquiry groups

	Cohort 1	Cohort 2	Cohort 3	All cohorts
Action inquiry groups	4.6	4.9	3.6	4.37
Whole PSLS programme	3.4	4.44	3.65	3.83

et al., 2000) and then asked to interview each other in pairs with the following guidance:

1   Recall a time as a member of your action inquiry group when you experienced learning that was significant for you in some way. Tell me about that time. What was that learning and how was it significant?
2   Recall a time when you felt that your action inquiry group was working really well together. Tell me about that time. How did you contribute to achieving that environment? What did others do?

Following this, they were invited to write any observations about their experience of action inquiry groups that came to mind. In the following section I will quote verbatim from the many pages of text generated by this process to attempt to give you something of the flavour of their experiences. This kind of connotative data is very rich and offers valuable insights. It does not purport to be definitive, objective or comprehensive and I shall not attempt to analyse it beyond offering a few subjective categories to give it some tentative form.

Valuing the experience

Through the action inquiry group I have been challenged and challenged others to consolidate and validate learning. This includes learning brought from the work environment, the network learning events, our individual speakers or even lessons, incidents from our personal lives. The action inquiry group has been for me the most significant element of the programme.

I would feel bereft of something very important to me if I no longer had contact with these people. Work is a key part of my identity, doing it well matters. I know I need to develop myself in order to do the best job I can and I trust my friends and colleagues in the action inquiry group to allow me to test out the things that cause me fear.

Learning environment

In particular the sense of mutual support and discovery engendered within the action inquiry group always sends me back to my work with renewed enthusiasm and a sense of purpose. The ability to explore difficult issues in a safe and challenging environment is invaluable.

The action inquiry group has developed into a communicative and supportive group that has no expectations or pressures on anyone. The progress of individuals and the frustrations have been openly shared and this has enabled empathy, whilst providing an impetus to move on.

I felt that as a group we listened actively and were prepared to challenge the views expressed (where appropriate) with frank and candid questioning. This enriched the learning experience for all of us.

Personal learning

I can seek feedback more easily and accept criticism in a constructive way. I have met a lot of interesting people. I realize that all problems don't need to be solved right away. I have realized every person has strengths and I should look for those.

I have learned that vulnerability, deep feeling and fear of failure are natural issues for all of us when we step forward into a leadership role. Efforts to appear always in control, to have nerves of steel, to always know the answer, aren't helpful in dealing with the people I manage or lead.

Impact on work

In particular, I opened up in this group to issues in my workplace about bullying which I had not even previously admitted to myself were happening. As a result I became empowered to deal with a work relationship I might have just walked away from.

I learned after the action inquiry group in {name withheld} that it is important to me to find some objective space in which I can 'offload' both concerns and ideas I have about my place of work. I find that it helps me to feel less stressed and also to explore ideas that might be frowned upon in my less objective work environment.

Building over time

The action inquiry group has had to take time to build common purpose and only now that we have matured as a group, are we really beginning to share and reflect and support each other in a positive way.

At the beginning, there was a sense of needing to 'do' something – actively inquire about something objective and quantifiable – but we matured, relaxed and began to appreciate the less tangible, more qualitative aspects of our discussions and how we would translate this learning in our own situations.

Networking and relationships

The mix of different people and the sectors they come from makes for good quality discussion. It is within this that learning takes place for me, because my beliefs and understandings are constantly challenged.

I see a high level of emotional intelligence in my action inquiry group, where individuals react to the needs and emotions of participants in a supportive and intelligent fashion. Even between meetings where contact would help, it is given without having to ask. I have never before worked with a group of leaders who have been confident enough to share vulnerability without any show of competition.

Confidence and empowerment

I have become more confident. I was worried about whether I would be up to it intellectually. I needn't have worried. A lot of the issues I face are common to everyone.

The action inquiry group has given me confidence to seek help, try out new things and listen to others. I feel I have gained depth and compassion to my leadership. I am more aware of my weaknesses – giving me something new to strive for.

Increased awareness

This has given me the opportunity to reflect on the different cultures and relationship issues and approaches to management in a variety of public service organizations, which has helped me to understand the way my own organization works, and how I relate to colleagues and managers more fully.

It makes you take an honest look at yourself and how you deal with situations, as others in the group can only give a perspective based on the information you share with them.

If I were to choose one quotation that seems to encapsulate the qualities of the action inquiry group experience for so many participants, it would be the following:

My action inquiry group is important to me in many ways ... The key thing is that it is a safe environment where you don't have to play a role – i.e. wife, boss, senior manager, friend, or colleague. You are literally 'laid bare'. There is no need for being brave, or trying to look clever. You can exhibit all your frailties. An important part of the learning has been that we are all frail, but even more interesting is that actually our problems and issues seem to be common: the difficult boss, being consumed with work, [or] really properly scared of being 'found out'. It's silly because we still all hold on to some belief that we are the only ones to have these problems [and that] everyone else is more capable than [we are].

Reflections on the process

It seems that despite (or perhaps because of) the divergence of the action inquiry groups from the original intention of systematic collaborative inquiry into public service leadership, they provided distinctive benefits for many, though by no means all, participants. Reading the quotations above, what stands out is the participants' desire to reconcile their sense of self as whole persons with the perceived conflicting demands of the organizations and systems within which they work.

This phenomenon is theorized by Habermas (1987) as a boundary crisis between system and lifeworld. My understanding of the importance and relevance of this notion has been greatly influenced by Stephen Kemmis whose brilliant analysis (Kemmis, 2001) I draw upon freely in this section.

> Systems operate through a rational-purposive action – that is, (instrumental means-ends) action oriented towards success. They operate through defi-nition of goals, the definition of criteria against which progress towards achieving the goals can be measured, the setting of targets for what will count as success (maximization of outcomes in relation to goals), and the monitoring of progress towards goals to evaluate and improve system efficiency defined in terms of the ratio of inputs to outcomes achieved. [To operate in this way, the system world] characteristically employs a form of reason, which can be described as functional rationality.
>
> (Kemmis, 2001: 94)

However, this form of logic is quite different from the dynamics underlying the concerns of the lifeworld (culture, social order and individual identity) which 'are "made possible" by three enduring and interacting sets of processes – cultural reproduction, social integration and socialization' (Kemmis, 2001: 94). Not only are the dynamics of the system and the lifeworld of a different order, but Habermas goes on to argue that, in modern industrialized and post-industrialized societies, they have become 'uncoupled' in the sense that:

> systems appear to be 'objects' (reified) to the people who inhabit them, as if (but only as if) they functioned according to their own rules and procedures, in a disinterested manner indifferent to the unique personalities and interests of the individuals inhabiting them, and thus, in a manner which appears to be indifferent to the dynamics of cultural reproduction, social integration and socialization necessary for the development and reproduction of lifeworlds.
>
> (Kemmis, 2001: 97)

Furthermore, Habermas asserts that not only have the system and the life-world become uncoupled, but that the logic and rationality of the former has 'colonized' the latter as:

individuals and groups increasingly define themselves and their aspirations in systems terms – in particular, so that their 'privatized' hopes for self-actualization and self-determination are primarily located ... in the roles of consumer and client ... This is 'colonization' in the sense that the impera-tives of the economic and political-legal systems dislodge the internal communicative action which underpins the formation and reproduction of lifeworlds, providing in its place an external framework of language, under-standings, values and norms based on systems and their functions.

(Kemmis, 2000: 97)

If we accept this argument then the fascination of action inquiry group participants with trying to reconcile their sense of self outside work with their roles as public service leaders becomes eminently understandable. It might not be too much to claim that, when operating at their best, the groups constituted 'communicative spaces' in which participants were able: 'to explore and address the interconnections and tensions between the system and lifeworld aspects of a setting as they are lived out in practice' (Kemmis, 2000: 98).

This seems to mirror quite closely the qualities of the action inquiry group process described by participants in the appreciative evaluation exercise above. I hypothesize that the very looseness of the design allowed the spontaneous creation of communicative spaces for the breach between system and lifeworld experienced by participants to be addressed and, to some extent, healed. For some participants at least, this proved to be an enormously valuable and enriching experience and, I surmise, contributed to the kinds of positive behavioural changes identified by line managers and sponsors in the external evaluation report.

We might also reflect that our encouragement of participants to think of themselves as transformational leaders (as opposed to transactional managers), with a concomitant focus on their values, worldviews and ways of interacting with people, might have raised their awareness of the need to bring system and lifeworld together. Such a change, argue Bill Torbert and others, reflects the need to move from 'expert' and 'achiever' to 'individualist' and 'strategist' modalities (Fisher and Rooke, 2000; Torbert, 2004). The latter demand a more complete personal commitment to leadership roles and making the transition requires a complex and sometimes painful shift from conventional ways of thinking and being, which have enabled participants to operate successfully within their given frames of reference, to post-conventional ways of thinking and being that will enable them to see beyond and challenge their given frames of reference.

As Dr Clare Rigg, a close colleague and action inquiry group facilitator recently said (personal communication, 24 March 2005), transformational leadership 'asks that people bring their spirit as well as their mind to work and it demands emotional labour. So no wonder there are tensions and ambivalences, and no wonder that participants value the communicative spaces.'

Of course, not everyone benefited in the same way or to the same degree from the action inquiry group process. A minority 'voted with their feet' and either did not attend the groups regularly or left the PSLS altogether. It is quite possible that not all participants were ready for this form of developmental opportunity. Palus and Drath (1995) identify a range of internal (personal traits and states) and external (environmental and socio-cultural) factors that influence a person's readiness to engage with developmental processes. There is no need to go into detail here, merely to recognize the implication of their argument that without extensive psychometric screening or pre-selection of candidates for leadership development programmes such as the PSLS, it is highly unlikely that any one design would meet the needs of all participants. This leaves designers and deliverers of such programmes with a dilemma: whether to try to please everyone by reducing the scope of their intervention to the mundane and non-threatening, or to offer worthwhile developmental challenges and opportunities that will be taken up enthusiastically by some and rejected out of hand by others.

The PSLS action inquiry groups were conceived as an inclusive form that could somehow meet the needs of all participants. They evolved into a more intense and demanding process that offered much to those who were ready for the challenge, but ultimately excluded those who were not willing or able to stay the course. Speaking from my position as director of the action inquiry groups and as someone with an overriding passion for human learning and development, I think that is a pretty good bargain but recognize that it adds to the inherent tensions among the various stakeholders in the process.

Conclusion

In the absence of a single elegant conclusion, I will close with a few thoughts about some of my key learning from directing the PSLS action inquiry groups over the past four years and how my perception of this role has developed.

First, I wonder if the groups' predisposition towards first-person inquiry (and away from second- and third-person inquiry) could have been anticipated and met with a different initial design for the inquiry groups. Would a thorough analysis of participants' 360 degree feedback have suggested a different starting point? Possibly, but given the size and heterogeneity of the cohorts it is unlikely that an obvious answer would have emerged. It seems to me more a question of articulating to sponsors, facilitators and participants a 'good enough' set of initial expectations about the purpose, methods and outcomes of the groups to make a start, and of building in processes (such as the facilitators' meta-set) to ensure that the design can evolve quickly enough to meet the actual needs of the groups as they emerge over time.

Second, I have learned not to be too precious about any particular methodology. A 'rose by any other name', action inquiry is simply one way of describing and labelling a set of educational values, intentions and practices. It is crucial to remember that any educational process must be in the service of the participants. It is far less important for the original aims and objectives of the design (the map) to be successfully implemented than it is to respond to the real and emergent needs of the participants (the territory). I learned that my job as director of the action inquiry groups was primarily to create and hold opportunities for this to happen.

Third, this has required personal strength, the support of colleagues and effective processes of communication amongst the various stakeholders to manage the inherent uncertainty and tensions. From my perspective, this includes active ongoing supervision and support of the team of facilitators as well as regular dialogue with the Cabinet Office secretariat responsible for commissioning and overseeing the scheme.

Fourth, I have become aware of some of the pressures of 'scaling up' and commercializing inquiry processes. Elsewhere (Mead, 2002; Chapter 9 in this book) I have written about the work and attention to detail required to convene and facilitate a single action inquiry group in the police service. In that instance, my role was voluntary and unpaid and much more time-consuming than an economically viable commercial arrangement would have permitted. When it finishes, the PSLS will have had a total of 21 action inquiry groups over a five-year period, provided under a commercial contract. Attempting to mainstream such a complex process without compromising the quality by resorting to over-simplification or commodification has been a huge challenge, crucial to which has been the identification and development over time of a highly skilled and experienced team of facilitators.

Finally, I have become even less persuaded that the learning of action inquiry groups (or any other kind of action learning group, come to that) always needs to be manifested in some kind of 'tangible product' such as a report or other organizational initiative. Certainly, that is one way of working – and Kakabadse and Kakabadse (2003) demonstrate its value in the context of using a collaborative inquiry process to develop change management capabilities among senior civil servants – but it is not the only way of working. As Professor Peter Reason concludes in a recent paper on 'Choice and quality in action research practice' (Reason, 2006: 10):

> The formation of communicative space is in itself a form of action. It may well be that the most important thing we can choose to do in certain situations is to help open, develop, maintain [and] encourage new and better forms of communication and dialogue.

Or, as a member of the outgoing cohort 2 said, when feeding back to a senior member of the Cabinet Office secretariat her experiences of the learning she and her action inquiry group colleagues had experienced during their three years on the scheme, '*We* are the products of the Public Service Leaders Scheme.'

Note

1 'World café' refers to conversations between groups of from 12 to 1,200 people engaged around the following principles: creating hospitable space, exploring questions that matter, connecting diverse people and perspectives. See Brown (2000) and Brown *et al.* (2001). 'Open space technology' is a way of enabling all kinds of people with groups of between five and 2,000+ in any kind of organization to create inspired meetings and events. Working in one-day workshops, three-day conferences or the regular weekly staff meeting, participants create and manage their own agenda of parallel working sessions around a central theme of strategic importance, such as 'What is the strategy, group, organization or community that all stakeholders can support and work together to create?' See Harrison (1997). The main purpose of an 'organizational or city raid' is to visit another organization to find out what they do, how and why. See http://www.slfscotland.com/OrganisationalRaids/OrganisationalRaids.htm (accessed 15 March 2006).

12 Partnership action learning[*]

Martin Willis

Introduction

This chapter explores the experiences of four partnership action learning sets which I facilitated as part of the Department of Health-funded Social Care Leadership Development Initiative (SCLDI). For the first three years, SCLDI funded some 50 time-limited action learning sets for individual top managers, or whole senior management teams, in English local authority social services departments (SSDs). From 2002, SCLDI started to invite SSDs to work together with their partner organizations. Initially, these partnership learning sets brought together senior management teams from SSDs and Primary Care Trusts (PCTs). They subsequently focused on authorities that were piloting the development of Children's Trusts with partnerships involving social care, education, health and other stakeholders. SCLDI defined the aims of these partnership sets as 'to work together in protected space on the fundamentals of effective partnership work and the delivery of services that are well joined-up in terms of values, leadership, shared knowledge and trust' (Peryer, 2002: 3).

These sets presented specific challenges to me as the facilitator. I was aware of Mahoney's cautionary words about in-house action learning sets for local authority senior management teams, questioning whether the dynamics of internal politics inhibits learning. He concluded that 'for Chief Officers and particularly Chief Executives it is more sensible for them to work outside the organization in a stranger group' quoting one chief executive who spoke of the importance of 'trust and confidentiality' in the learning set process, suggesting that 'anonymity is a strength which is vital' (Mahoney, 1997: 74). Moreover, I felt that working with whole partnership management teams would inevitably create tensions between individual and organizational learning in relation to both task and process. Given that the members were actively working together outside the learning set, I questioned whether it would be possible, or even desirable, to separate the exploration of learning from decision-making within the meetings. How would the members deal with issues of hierarchy, power, responsibility and accountability which existed both within and between the management teams? Would members be prepared to address difficult personal dilemmas revealing their doubts and limitations in front of colleagues?

However, I also knew from previous experience that such learning sets could provide real opportunities for participants to step outside the day-to-day process of their management practice to reflect on current issues with the very people that they are working with to resolve complex inter-organizational problems. Reassuringly, a number of the participants also expressed their intentions of using the learning sets in this way in a written questionnaire before the first meeting:

'Time out to consider opportunities and challenges facing us at the moment and shared thinking about ideas and issues.'

'Debate and discussion in an atmosphere where hierarchical structures are not a part seems to me one of the most productive methods of learning. Within the workplace it seems that many initiatives falter due to crises which tend to destabilize or throw things off course. Here we have an opportunity to do this in a situation which should be untouched by day-to-day matters.'

'Positive negotiation of conflicting agendas – need to better understand the competing agendas and the parameters partners are required to work in.'

'I need to understand what I need to do better/differently. Maybe some (honest) feedback from partners would be useful?'

This chapter will consider the context and individual journeys of these four learning sets before reflecting on how these dilemmas have affected participants' learning and my choices about style and methods of facilitation.

Context

The emphasis on partnership working in UK social care policy and practice long predates the Labour government's modernization agenda (Department of Health, 1997, 2000). In children's services, a series of high-profile inquiries into the death of children resulted in successive recommendations for improved working relationships between social care, health, education, housing, police and voluntary organizations (Department of Health and Social Security, 1974; Blom-Cooper, 1985, 1987; Sedley, 1987; Laming, 2003). In adult social care, joint financing of social and health care initiatives, particularly aimed at moving people from large long-stay hospitals to community-based homes, was initiated in the 1970s along with a range of joint consultative and planning arrangements. Government white papers and policy guidance have consistently reinforced the partnership imperative in work with both children and adults (Department of Health and Social Security, 1988; Department of Health, 1989, 1998, 2001).

However, since 1997, the emphasis on partnership working has shifted from exhortation and discretionary guidance to legal, structural and financial drivers. Significant amongst these has been the provision in the Health Act 1999 for social care and health to pool budgets, establish joint commissioning and integrate services. In addition, the government has used financial incentives and penalties to stimulate partnership working, particularly with regard to reducing what has become known as bed-blocking by people in hospital awaiting discharge. Structurally, the government has encouraged the creation of Care Trusts and Children's Trusts to integrate health and social care for adults and social care, health, education and other stakeholders for children's services respectively. More recently, the Children Act 2004 established a duty of partnership working and a Director of Children's Services in every local authority in England with responsibility for both education and social care.

This is not to say that government policy has consistently prioritized partnership working over other policy directives. In large measure the accountability arrangements for the key agencies of social care, education, health and the police have remained separate and potentially contradictory. For example, the government performance assessment, inspection and financial accountability frameworks for social care, education, health and the police have not been joined up. As a result, despite the best of intentions, partnership working can become viewed as a luxury.

The significance of strategic leadership in partnership working has emerged more recently in research and policy (Glendinning *et al.*, 2002; Peck *et al.*, 2002; Chief Secretary to the Treasury, 2003; Secretary of State for Health, 2005). However, leadership and management training has also been predominantly developed and undertaken within organizational silos, with government departments sponsoring distinct leadership programmes for health, schools, police and social care. These partnership learning sets thus represented a relatively unique opportunity to explore leadership across organizational boundaries within the context of separate and sometimes conflicting accountability frameworks.

Aims and membership of the partnership learning sets

Once authorities had volunteered to take part in the programme, I met with two or three senior managers to discuss the overall aims of each set and the membership. The aims had a number of common themes which can be analysed using the framework developed by Wistow *et al.* (1998) (Table 12.1). The concept of leadership is not specifically mentioned in this framework and was not included in any of the senior managers' development aims. Indeed, whilst relationship issues were mentioned, there was little emphasis on the skills that managers might need to develop to enable effective partnership working.

The four learning sets were established with an expectation that they would meet six times over a six- to nine-month period, with the option of two of these sessions being combined into an overnight 24-hour event. Table 12.2 sets out details of the membership and the key themes for each set. With a membership of between 13 and 16 participants, I needed to consider how to ensure space for

Table 12.1 Analysis of overall aims of partnership learning set

Principles for facilitating strategic inter-agency collaboration (Wistow et al., *1998)*	*Examples of aims agreed by senior managers*
Shared vision Specifying what is to be achieved in terms of user-centred goals; clarifying the purpose of collaboration as a mechanism for achieving such goals; mobilizing commitment around goals, outcomes and mechanisms.	To explore how children and young people can be put at the centre of partnership developments to create services that children and families want. To explore what a shared commitment really means in practice. Establishing trust in colleagues as individuals.
Clarify roles/responsibilities Specifying and agreeing 'who does what' and designing organizational arrangements by which roles and responsibilities are to be fulfilled.	Mutual understanding of roles, responsibilities, professional practices and priorities. Learning about each other's organization and roles – culture, what people do and decision-making processes.
Appropriate incentives and rewards Promoting organizational behaviour consistent with agreed goals and responsibilities, and harnessing organizational self-interest to collective goals.	Working out ways of engaging with front-line staff, linking strategy and operations. Involving a balance of professional front-line, middle management and senior staff. Making this a reality for staff in all agencies involved – getting people out of silos to sign up to the concept.
Accountability Monitoring achievements in relation to the stated vision; holding individuals and agencies to account for the fulfilment of roles and responsibilities which have been pre-determined; providing feedback and review.	Sharing and analysing progress on development projects. Tackling difficult issues that are sometimes avoided. Strengths and limitations of partnership working – improving understanding about health and social care constraints which limit effective working.

personal reflection as well as plenary discussions. The membership varied from being drawn from two senior management teams to a cross-section of senior, middle and front-line managers from eight organizations. Set C was the only one of the four which did not have chief officer membership from social services and the PCT. A further variation occurred in Set D with learning from the first phase shared at a workshop for 100 managers from partner organizations and a second phase involving two meetings of a core group and two of a wider group of more than 50 people over a total period of two years.

In terms of personal characteristics, all participants in the core groupings were white and none of the sets was specifically challenged on how they worked

Table 12.2 Membership and learning set themes

Set	Membership	Number of participants	Theme
A	Full senior management teams from a local authority borough council SSD and PCT	13	Partnership working for both adult and children's services
B	Senior, middle and front-line managers from a county council children's social services and education, PCT, police, acute hospital, GP, head teacher and local authority councillor	16	Development of child protection partnership working in a geographical part of the county
C	Senior managers from a local authority borough council children's social services and education, PCT, Connexions and a voluntary sector representative	14	Potential Children's Trust partnership
D (Phase 1)	Full senior management teams from a local authority borough council SSD, PCT, Health Professional and Executive Committee Chair and senior education and housing managers	15	Partnership working for both adult and children's services
D (Phase 2)	Core group of senior managers from SSD, education, PCT and Connexions	16	Potential Children's Trust partnership and transfer of learning between senior, middle and front-line managers
	Wider group of managers from police, schools, Youth Offending Team, Child and Adolescent Mental Health Service and Sure Start	50+	

with and for black and minority ethnic colleagues and users. It was equally true that gender dynamics were not central to the sets' considerations in a way that might have emerged with a more exclusive focus on individual rather than organizational and partnership learning.

Almost all of the individual participants completed a questionnaire before the first meeting which asked them to identify organizational and personal learning outcomes. The majority of the replies mirrored the development agendas of their senior managers. Only three specifically focused on aspects of leadership, all with somewhat negative connotations:

'There are many good examples of excellent work, but I wonder whether they are really down to individuals (often front-line and/or middle managers) ... rather than to the influence or leadership of strategic management groups.'

'How do we improve clarity over the leadership arrangements ... because this is currently vague, several of us are "interfering" to try to get things done, but that can backfire and be seen as standing on toes.'

'How can I be an effective leader supporting my staff when they feel frustrated by the partnership agenda?'

A few other learning set members stated their learning needs in personal terms, citing issues of confidence in their ability to manage in a multi-agency context, positive negotiation of conflicting agendas, communication skills and reflection and thinking creatively. One highlighted their personal struggle in partnership working:

I found this the most difficult section to complete. I generally consider my ability to work in partnership a personal strength and find it frustrating that others don't. But probably within this statement lies my greatest learning need! So what else do I need to learn to get my contribution right?

However, overall it was striking that, both organizationally and individually, members emphasized task and process issues rather than personal learning. Leadership capacity did not figure highly on their overtly stated agendas.

Starting the journeys

Given these tensions and this expressed emphasis on task and process rather than personal learning, I provided each participant with an explanation of the learning set process with the aim of distinguishing this from their regular partnership meetings or a course or training event:

A learning set provides the opportunity for participants to share and reflect upon their management experience in order to develop personal and organizational knowledge and skill. It is a chance to stand back from day to day pressures and to explore the bigger picture of how the well-being of individuals and communities can be improved. An effective learning set needs the following key ingredients: clarity amongst participants about what they want to get out of it – both individually and collectively; initial commitment of participants to give high priority to attending all sessions; establishment of trust so that issues can be shared openly and honestly; and the use of a variety of methods to facilitate learning whilst not being a course or training event.

I also determined the agenda for the first meetings which started with a consideration of the collated and anonymous summary of participants' responses to the individual questionnaire, followed by a discussion and agreement on the overall aims and methods of the learning set. As part of the questionnaire, participants had been individually asked what ground rules were needed to make this learning set effective for them, and their responses, with some minor amendments, formed the group's learning agreement. I was seeking to ensure that participants' individual concerns were addressed in the learning agreement. The alternative of constructing this through group discussion at the first meeting may have caused participants to be reticent about expressing what they thought would be viewed as controversial or challenging concerns. The resulting learning agreements included predictable statements about the need for openness, honesty, commitment, attendance and respect, but also some more individual contributions which aimed to address the tensions outlined above:

- 'Agreement on not harbouring longer term resentment if criticism or negative views are shared in the set.'
- 'Difficult to achieve but attempt to suspend hierarchies for the duration of the learning set.'
- 'Thinking here about occupational honesty and courage – what it is like in the real world of service delivery rather than what we might like it to be.'

The issue of confidentiality was raised in all of the learning agreements, with statements about 'Chatham House rules' and 'absolute confidentiality'. I encouraged the groups to explore this further, as the aim of these sets was that learning and ideas should be translated appropriately into practice between and beyond meetings. To address this, one participant suggested that there should be 'no rubbishing each other during the set or thereafter', and another group decided that they would agree what could be shared outside the session and what aspects it would be inappropriate to share. Clearly a balance had to be struck between ensuring a degree of safety to enable open discussion of difficult personal and organizational issues and a total commitment to confidentiality which would have undermined the purpose of the sets. With some notable exceptions, most participants probably chose to err on the side of caution in their choices about what to say, and what not to say, during the course of the meetings. One method that I used to manage this process was to provide opportunities for participants to work in pairs and small groups, as well as in plenary sessions, to enable them to choose what they explored with whom.

For the rest of the first session I asked the sets to work in multi-organizational sub-groups to map the strengths and limitations of their experience of partnership working over the past three years. Whilst the sets chose different subjects for these sub-groups, the discussion was largely task-focused and concluded with a plenary agreement about the thematic focus for future sessions. To begin a consideration of process issues, I also introduced a period for individual reflection on learning at the close of each session, and an opportunity to reflect on developments in partnership working between the set meetings at the start of each subsequent session. These reflections were recorded by me and circulated to all participants as an ongoing record of learning. Following this first meeting, each set undertook a different journey in relation to both content and process.

The different journeys

Set A: Formality, crisis and change

Set A brought together two senior management teams that had a wealth of experience of partnership working. At the first meeting, they chose to focus on three user group areas of joint working over the next three sessions. As a result the discussion was very task-orientated, reviewing current developments and considering future agendas and action plans. These three sessions were predominantly extensions of their existing meetings both in content and process. In an attempt to enable them to understand their way of doing things from a different perspective, I used a fish bowl technique in the second session in which each team discussed their vision and outcomes for services for older people whilst being observed by members of the other team. However, for the next two sessions the set members decided to start with presentations from key managers followed by plenary discussion. A significant feature of these sessions was the degree to which members stayed in their hierarchical relationships, though a few chose to share more personal and critical comments with me during breaks.

Where learning sets are working with existing management teams which have already established patterns of culture and behaviour, it is inevitably challenging for them to stand back and reflect on their individual and organizational interactive dynamics. As one member commented in the final review, 'some of the sessions have skirted around the fundamental underlying issues and problems'. Another said 'I think we have prepared the groundwork for allowing us to deal with some of the difficult/sensitive issues. I don't think we would have been able to have the kind of explicit discussion we are now having without the learning set.'

The fifth meeting was cancelled at short notice as a result of a serious budgetary crisis within one of the partner organizations, which had led them to withdraw a commitment to joint funding of an aspect of service delivery. I decided to recommend that I facilitated a meeting of four of the more senior members of the set. This meeting saw a significant shift in understanding about the different financial and star rating drivers on the two organizations and a realization that their shared sense of direction was not as robust as they thought. Added to this was a recognition of the cultural differences between the SSD and the PCT, such as their approaches to decision-making which contributed to a belief that people do not always say exactly what they mean. The learning from this session was shared with the full management teams at the final meeting, providing an opportunity for the partners to develop a deeper understanding of their different approaches to risks and to surface joint issues which might otherwise have remained hidden. They also decided to continue the process of reflection on their partnership working by building in reviews at the end of their joint monthly meetings and a more thorough overall review after six months. As one member said, 'Maybe we needed to spend longer getting to know each other and understanding the cultural differences rather than leaping into the challenging arena of service redesign.' The pressure to achieve demonstrable results through partnership working can cause organizations to neglect the fundamental steps of relationship-building. This learning set appeared to enable these senior managers to recognize the importance of the process of leadership and organizational development and not just getting things done.

Set B: The power of process mapping

In contrast, Set B brought together people who, although they mostly knew each other, were not in an established partnership relationship with agreed strategies, structures and regular meetings. The membership was also different in being drawn from a wider range of organizations and from strategic, middle and front-line managers. It had a narrower task definition focusing on child protection partnership working within one geographical area. This enabled a more detailed examination of current practice using a process mapping technique (Accounts Commission, 2000). Participants created large visual process analyses which revealed considerable gaps in knowledge about different organizational decision-making principles and practices.

In subsequent meetings, the set progressively moved towards strategic action planning, which meant that the partnership task tended to dominate any discussion of the process of developing leadership and organizational capacity. However, issues of culture and communications were addressed and participants commented on creative aspects of their learning. Important learning was achieved about each other's roles and responsibilities following the realization of how little people knew about what the others did and other agencies' policies, working practices and constraints. The opportunity to reflect was also highlighted in participants' comments.

> 'Greater understanding and impetus for positive inter-agency working. A real blueprint for an integrated team pilot and a commitment to make it happen.'

> 'My way of thinking about education and social services is quite different.'

> 'Reflection is not a technique I have used before and I am impressed by how personal reflection informs other people's.'

> 'Process mapping exercise proved invaluable in creating and maintaining learning set's purpose and scope.'

At an early stage in the process, the reflections on developments between sessions revealed a damaging communications failure between two of the partners which had resulted in the press publishing criticisms of one of the organizations which were made at another's open meeting. This provided a valuable opportunity to consider issues of communication and trust with the learning that partnership means considering the implications of your actions on others and not assuming that a lack of any response signals agreement. It further reinforces the analysis from Set A that critical learning can occur as a result of crises in partnership working as long as there is a mechanism to reflect and not just react. As one organizational group commented, such work is 'time consuming and hard and needs motivation'.

Set C: Managing without strategic leadership

Set C grew out of the central government policy initiative of encouraging Children's Trusts to pilot the development of joined-up children's services at local level. Whilst the membership reflected a range of local organizations concerned with children's services, learning was at times frustrated by key participants from education not attending (one as a consequence of moving jobs) and lacked senior officer participation. As with Set A, my attempt to shift the culture of the way the group worked at the second meeting by using a group interactive flipchart method was followed by sessions in which they chose plenary discussions. However, this did enable them to address their concerns about a lack of chief officer commitment in the final session by inviting four senior officers from the local authority, social services, education and the PCT to hear a presentation on their achievements and learning and to discuss future priorities. In earlier meetings, uncertainties about the commitment of strategic leaders had resulted in a lot of discussion about roles, membership of key decision-making bodies and who had power to progress actions. This was especially evident when the group was presented with the possibility of taking the lead in developing children's centres and expressed reluctance to take this forward:

> 'Lots of baggage still about ownership and control that we need to work out.'

> 'Board needs to be clear about when we need to make a decision and what decision we have to make.'

> 'Need to be clear about individual role in implementing decisions and how we see those through to their conclusion.'

Participants' evaluative comments at the end of the process expressed ambivalence as to the usefulness of the learning set:

> 'I am not convinced that we have still learnt how to tackle the big issues effectively.'

'The realization that a small shift can unblock a major problem. So the focus for me is concentrating on what I can change.'

'I have more awareness of the work of other areas and awareness of some of the "power" struggles that are around.'

'It was a valuable opportunity to clarify my work priorities and explain some of these to my colleagues.'

'Allowed dedicated time for in depth discussions on a number of topics that have brought out issues that needed to be resolved.'

'We have still managed to avoid dealing with the difficult issues . . . allowing ourselves to avoid difficult issues and retreating to the safety of operational detail and minutiae.'

'There has been a working ethos but the group has not often addressed the real underlying tensions implicit in departmental differences. Because we are all frightened of conflict?'

The set struggled with how to translate the enthusiasm and commitment on the ground to partnership working for the benefit of children and young people into strategic planning and decisions. Towards the end of the process the participants began to shift their thinking from an overriding concern with structures, roles, responsibilities and processes to thinking about outcomes for children and young people. As one participant expressed, perhaps it was necessary to resolve issues about internal management before the group could start addressing this more critical area.

Set D: Cascading learning down and up

As with all the above examples, the progress of Set D was influenced by both national and local partnership agendas. This set had two phases over a two-year period, both of which involved processes to share learning between a core group of senior managers and a larger group of middle and front-line managers. As such this set represents a different model of action learning aimed both at cascading learning from senior manager sets to other staff and also to listening to the issues which partner agency staff felt that senior managers should be addressing.

The commitment of the directors and chief executives from the partner organizations was evident throughout, especially in maintaining the process without the facilitator between the phases and ensuring that the learning was shared with the wider groups of stakeholders. Thus this learning set was not seen as an isolated opportunity for reflection and partnership-building but part of a longer-term process of creating a learning partnership, akin to the concept of a learning organization (Argyris and Schön, 1978; Senge, 1993). Senge sets out five basic disciplines which he suggests are required to enable everyone in an organization to learn: systems thinking, personal mastery, mental modes, building shared vision and team learning. These disciplines were tangibly evident throughout the process: for example, in the commitment to long-term learning beyond the lifetime of the learning set and the willingness to listen to staff views about how specific behaviours of strategic leaders reinforce or undermine effective partnership. Participants' comments in their individual and team learning reviews also serve to illustrate these five disciplines:

> 'Partnership working is everyone's business and needs to happen at all levels.'

> 'Still a lot of work to do to exploit the real benefits.'

> 'Agreeing style/medium to air differences and agree ways forward.'

> 'Shared vision built on trust, respect and willingness to change.'

> 'Individual and team fear factor of being self-exposing overcome and shared through the set.'

A further notable feature of this learning set was that discussion focused more on culture, synergies, tensions and learning rather than tasks, structures, roles and responsibilities. In addition, members were enthusiastic about the use of fish bowl and other group-work techniques. In terms of situational leadership theory (Hersey and Blanchard, 1977), the partnership had relatively low task-related development needs and a higher preparedness to focus on relationship behaviour. On reflection I recognize how this opened opportunities for me as facilitator to be more focused on participative and less on selling approaches.

Individual, organizational and systemic development

The final point in the previous section underlines the tension in partnership action learning sets between the processes of individual and organizational learning and the task dimensions of policy development, prioritization, decision-making and action planning. I aimed to ensure that the former was not overwhelmed by the latter by starting and finishing with time to reflect on developments between sessions and identifying personal and organizational learning. Where this worked well, the strength of this approach was that participants were able to explore both double-loop learning (Argyris and Schön, 1978) linking individual and organizational development and second-order learning (Bateson, 1973) by an ongoing iterative process of analysis, learning, action and reflection. This required participants to separate thinking from doing, the former involving a suspension of hierarchies within the group to enable challenge and risk-taking, the latter recognizing that action needed to take place in an organizational context with externally driven policies, constraints and performance imperatives.

Several participants commented on the opportunity provided by these learning sets to stand back from day-to-day pressures and think creatively with colleagues. A key determinant of how this was achieved concerned the role of directors and chief executives and how they exercised their leadership. In one group, their physical absence throughout most of the process tended to stultify progress, being cited by participants as a reason why they felt disempowered from developing their thinking and learning. This process was also evident in other groups when the power of external leaders such as local authority chief executives and health consultants was used as a means to argue that participants would be thwarted in progressing the learning outside the sessions by the lack of commitment from or sabotage by others.

The role of directors and chief executives within the group was also significant as to whether their behaviour and contributions legitimized the exploration of thinking and learning or sought to control it within the existing culturally accepted norms of team interaction. This created both inter- and intra-team tensions exemplified by fears of speaking out of turn and revealing internal differences to partner agencies. Where such tensions existed, sessions became substantially business meetings which, whilst productive in sharing policy thinking in an atmosphere unpressurized by lengthy agendas and immediate decision-making, were relatively lacking in risk-taking or personal exploration of learning.

By their very nature, all of these learning sets were concerned with systemic thinking. This ranged from developing understanding of values, priorities, roles and responsibilities between senior management teams from partner organizations to learning about how to engage and empower staff at all levels across whole systems to benefit individual users and communities. One group approached this by including senior, middle and front-line managers from a range of different practice settings in the learning set. Another chose to focus one of its sessions on how to ensure two-way communication between strategic and operational staff and a third by alternating set meetings of strategic managers with wider meetings of key stakeholders. Systemic thinking was also evident in the fact that each of the learning sets chose topics for their sessions which were directly concerned with aspects of partnership working rather than individual issues or competencies. Individual learning thus became a product of organizational and systemic learning, although, as revealed by some of the participants' comments, was mainly implicit rather than explicit. Whether this is a serious limitation of the structure of these partnership learning sets or creates effective double-loop learning is a matter for further research. Some reassurance can be gained from the comment of one participant who felt that individually they and others had 'grown here, mutually influencing the success of growing away from here in day-to-day relationships'.

Facilitating the journeys

This section will examine four key choices which I made in my role as facilitator of these learning sets. The first concerns the balance between my interventions and group self-determination and self-direction. A number of participants commented on this aspect of my role in their final review of learning:

'The facilitation was essential. Martin's non-directive style was (I think) designed to get us taking responsibility for ourselves.'

'Facilitation – balance between leading and allowing the group to lead.'

'I liked the approach. It may have worked better had there been more direction at times but of course this would not have exposed the weaknesses and strengths in the way it did.'

'Style of facilitation has been excellent – allowing appropriately free ranging discussion but equally keeping us on track.'

Such comments illustrate the dilemmas involved. In some aspects my role was directive: for example, in constructing and circulating a programme agenda for each session and setting out methods of working. On occasion, I also chose to act as an independent chair for the more business-orientated discussions, suggesting frameworks for action planning. Overall, I took responsibility for deciding how the learning sets worked whilst enabling the groups to agree the content or topic for their discussions. I encouraged advice or feedback from individuals or the whole group, both formally and informally, throughout the process. In responding to this, there were times when my preference for interactive group work was overridden by the set's desire to stay in the more familiar, and therefore safer, mode of plenary discussion. Whilst this might have been experienced as 'good (subtle) leadership and steering' as one participant commented, it may also have stifled initiative by providing too much comfort and by avoiding potentially energizing conflicts between individual group members or between the group and me. Thus the facilitator can both open and close doors on the journey. One of the sets benefited from my absence from one session due to illness which 'demonstrated it was able to work without a facilitator'. This group put this learning into practice by continuing to meet after the initial sessions, inviting me on occasions when it felt there was a particular need for external facilitation.

The second choice concerns my use of specific action learning techniques. In other contexts, my starting point has usually been individual and personal agendas. Because of the organizational and systemic agendas involved in these partnership learning sets, my chosen techniques derived more from group-work theory. For example, fish bowl exercises[1] allowed participants to share and observe partner team dynamics with revealing observations about differences in leadership styles and cultures. Process mapping[2] and time chart progress mapping[3] enabled a cross-cutting and systemic analysis of decision-making over time. Structured group-work frameworks[4] ensured consistency of analysis and reporting of learning. However, all of this was set in the context of reflective practice, which for some participants was a new and rewarding technique which they intended to continue outside the learning set experience.

Third, the number of participants in each group was larger than that commonly associated with learning sets. This caused some difficulties as identified by one member who said that 'sometimes the group seemed too large for all opinions to be heard'. In most sessions, I chose to address this by creating opportunities for group-work on roles, case study areas of responsibility and cross-organizational relationships. This was aimed at achieving a balance between in-depth personal exploration and plenary group development. Much of the small group work was recorded and subsequently provided for all participants so that learning could be shared. Of course, further learning could develop outside of the formal sessions, particularly for those groups who chose to include a 24-hour session in their programme. Opinion, though, was divided about the value of such extended meetings, with one person saying that it was 'very effective, allowing for a more relaxed discussion and planning', and another from the same group saying that they were 'not sure the 24-hour event generated as much as it might, it was quite tiring'. Four participants from another set, which initially chose not to have a 24-hour session, commented at the end that one or two might have been valuable in 'breaking down barriers and an opportunity to get to know the individuals behind the roles'.

Finally, I believe that significant learning opportunities can arise in partnership working through exploration of tensions or the grit in relationships. Thus I was keen to encourage members to reflect on conflicts that had occurred outside the learning set meetings, such as the communication issues in Set B, and to bring external tensions into the sessions, such as inviting chief officers to the final meeting in Set C. However, it is a question of judgement when and how to do this as the group needs sufficient trust both in each other and the facilitator to ensure that this is productive and not destructive. Yet how is such trust to be established except through the taking and exploration of risks?

Conclusions and summary of learning points

These four learning sets were part of a five-year national initiative managed by a steering group which held regular meetings with all of the facilitators. At their final meeting, which reviewed the experience of more than 30 partnership learning sets, I asked the other facilitators to summarize their own learning about effective work in developing partnerships (SCLDI, 2004). Their thoughts echoed many of the points highlighted in this chapter and can be grouped under four headings.

Values, vision and outcomes

The first group of responses emphasized that partnership working is a means to an end and not an end in itself, with a need to 'communicate, listen and develop shared understanding' and to 'achieve clarity about what will change for users, and how partners will know'. Action learning sets can provide a powerful forum for enabling partner organizations to explore the extent to which they have a shared vision about user and community outcomes. The exposing of contrary external drivers and inter-organizational tensions that occurred in these sets led to an explicit recognition that aspects of this vision can be organizationally different yet complementary. The mirroring of partnership working offered insights into how, by retaining this emphasis on user outcomes, partners can hold on to their overall shared vision and avoid becoming engulfed by the tensions. Effective leadership involves seeing both the wood and the trees.

Leadership-in-partnership

The other facilitators stressed 'leadership-in-partnership not leadership for partnership' and the 'commitment and integrity of leaders who will say no as well as yes'. This chapter has demonstrated how learning sets can provide opportunities for strategic directors and chief executives to participate in challenging interactions with partnership colleagues that go beyond hierarchical organizational power relationships. This is of critical importance to learning that leadership-in-partnership involves both sharing power to gain influence and giving clear messages about the boundaries for discussion and decision-making.

Building relationships

Comments from the facilitators included 'don't underestimate the need for people just to get to know each other and their organizations face-to-face' and the need to 'create space to ask difficult questions and space for different conversations'. The must-do, can-do performance culture can drive partnerships to work towards task achievement before they have established the basic building blocks of sound inter-group relationships. These sets created space for senior managers to step back from day-to-day pressures and begin the process of developing a better understanding of individuals' roles and responsibilities and differences in organizational culture. The learning set process was in sharp contrast to the norms of communication through formal meetings and emails.

Recognizing and legitimizing difference

The final category was expressed in terms of the need to 'differentiate in order to join together' and 'create routes and incentives for reluctant partners to engage'. Partnership working requires mutual respect and this includes a recognition that deciding when to work separately is as important as deciding when to work together. If these learning sets provided an opportunity to examine legitimate differences and the limitations as well as the possibilities for effective partnership working, the potential benefits for service users will have been greatly enhanced.

Notes

* This paper arises from an action-learning programme entitled the 'Social Care Leadership Development Initiative' commissioned by the UK government's Department of Health. The views of the author do not necessarily represent those of the commissioning body or the organizations involved in the steering group and each learning set.
1 The fish bowl technique used here involved a group of participants discussing a topic whilst being observed by their colleagues who were then asked to comment on what they had learnt from the interaction. The roles were then reversed.
2 A useful explanation of process mapping is available from Accounts Commission (2000).
3 Time chart progress mapping involved groups of participants producing a pictorial representation of significant events over the past three to five years, including their judgements about the highs and lows of progress towards effective partnership working.
4 In structured groupwork, participants worked on agreed tasks with systematic processes of analysis, prioritization and conclusion.

13 Action learning in inter-organizational sets

David Coghlan and Paul Coughlan

Opportunities for operational improvement arise within the public service in many ways. Some arise in the context of individual departments facing changing client demands, increased transparency, new technologies or leaner resources. Other opportunities arise in the context of groups of departments interacting with each other but in ways that may be inefficient and may require a high degree of responsive capability in delivering benefits to clients. Yet further opportunities arise in the context of increased outsourcing of services previously provided by the public service. Here, the contractual nature of the relationship allows the establishment of measurable targets but may constrain the exchange of learning based on collective experience. In each context, the opportunities for improvement provide opportunities for learning. If such learning can be captured and internalized, then there is the prospect of an overall improvement in operational practice and performance.

Much of the literature on action learning focuses on managers developing their capacity to learn and transform their own organizations. Given the new context within which organizations operate and relate to one another in a more collaborative manner, action learning can also perform a role in contributing to inter-organizational learning and change (Coughlan and Coghlan, 2004). This chapter explores the application of action learning in both contexts and is structured as follows: first the components of action learning are introduced. Then the application of action learning in a non-contractual inter-organizational setting is outlined and illustrated with a case drawn from the public service. This section is followed by an exploration of action learning in an inter-organizational setting where contractual relationships exist between the participants. The chapter concludes with a reflection on the differences between the contexts and the applicability of action learning in each.

Action learning is an approach to the development of people in organizations which takes the task as the vehicle for learning (Pedler, 1996). It reverses the traditional learning process where one learns something first and then applies it. In action learning the starting point is the action. Revans (1998) distinguishes between puzzles and problems. Puzzles are those difficulties for which a correct solution exists, such as reducing costs, and which are amenable to specialist and expert advice. Problems are difficulties where no single solution can possibly exist because different people advocate different courses of action in accordance with their own value system, past experience and intended outcomes. Revans (1998) outlines the assumptions underpinning action learning. Learning is cradled in the task. Formal instruction is not sufficient. Problems require insightful questions. Learning involves doing. Learning is voluntary. Urgent problems or enticing opportunities provide the spur for learning. Learning is measured by the results of the action. Processes such as action and feedback, asking fresh questions, learning from and with each person in a learning set, the contribution of peers, and creating a multiplier effect are central to action learning.

Components of action learning

The practice of action learning is demonstrated through many different approaches (Pedler *et al.*, 2005). Two core elements are consistently in evidence:

- participants work on real organizational problems that do not appear to have clear solutions; and
- participants meet on equal terms to report to one another and to discuss their problem and progress (Marsick and O'Neil, 1999).

Marquardt (2004) presents a useful expansion of these core elements. In his development of the practice, action learning has six distinct interactive components:

A problem – whereby complex organizational issues which touch on different parts of the organization and which are not amenable to expert solutions are selected and worked on.

The group – comprises a typical number of six to eight members who care about the problem, know something about it and have the power to implement solutions.

The questioning and reflective process – whereby the learning formula ($L = P + Q$) is enacted. Marquardt advocates a ground rule for the action learning group to the effect that only asking questions, rather than making statements, is allowed. Asking questions first enables clarification of the nature of the problem and exploration of possible solutions and courses of action. Asking brings out what is not known as well as what is known.

The commitment to taking action – Action learning is based on the premise that no real learning takes place unless and until action is taken. Implementation, rather than recommendations to others, is central.

The commitment to learning – Action learning aims at going beyond merely solving immediate problems. An increase in the knowledge and capacity to better adapt to change is more important.

The facilitator – Action learning groups benefit from having a facilitator, that is, one who plays a variety of roles for the group as coordinator, catalyst, observer, climate setter, communication enabler and learning coach among many (McGill and Beaty, 1995; Casey, 1997). While much of what is generally considered as group facilitation, i.e. chairing meetings, enabling communication through clarification, summarizing, etc. is inherent in this role, a critical additional element is that of enabling learning to take place. Hence, not only do the facilitators facilitate the processes of learning set meetings, they also work at enabling learning to take place and to be articulated. It is well argued that the characteristics and skills of the action learning coach are more in the areas of group facilitation and learning coach than the specific expertise related to the task (McGill and Beaty, 1995; Casey, 1997). Such content expertise may create an 'expert' role for the facilitator and inhibit the self-directed learning of the members of the learning set.

Two contexts for action learning in inter-organizational settings

There are many contexts in which action learning can be used in inter-organizational settings. Two are of interest here. The first context is where members of separate organizations come together voluntarily to form an action learning set, in which each member then explores a problem in his/her organization. The set may be comprised of individuals or pairs from separate organizations. The relationship between the separate organizations is non-contractual, and therefore inter-organizational action learning is driven by voluntarily exploiting the opportunity to interact. In sum, the setting is inter-organizational and the projects are intra-organizational.

The second context is where the relationship between the organizations is contractual. Here, inter-organizational action learning is driven by the imperatives of the operational area of activity linking the organizations, such as the supply chain or the service delivery system. In this setting, the participating organizations are systemically linked by contractual arrangements and obligations. For the organizational members who participate in this inter-organizational action learning set, participation has a compulsory tone to it. In addition, the action learning set meets against a background of a history of pre-existing relations between the organizations and with an explicit basis of power inequality. In sum, both the setting and the projects are inter-organizational.

In the next two sections, we present case reports on action learning initiatives in the two inter-organizational contexts identified, non-contractual and contractual. The components of action learning transfer readily to these inter-organizational settings. The action learning set comprises members of the same or separate organizations who come together to confront a problem. The learning set engages in the questioning and reflective process, with commitments to action and to learning and with the help of a learning coach or facilitator.

Inter-organizational action learning in a non-contractual setting

In the first setting, inter-organizational action learning took place in separate organizations between which the relationship was non-contractual. We present the case of MapMake (a fictitious name), a government agency which was the sole producer of geographical information services and which was beginning to face international competition for contracts (Coughlan *et al.*, 2002). Correspondingly, its product/service identity was being redefined – from being a producer of maps to being a provider of information for customers. It was widely recognized within the organization that such product/service changes were fundamental to survival. The Single European Act had meant that competition would continue to grow. The free mobility of goods, services and labour within the European Community, combined with the doctrine of a 'level playing field' for all competitors, was an increasing threat to the organization.

The setting in which the action learning took place was a structured European Union-funded research programme called National Action Learning Programme (NALP), in which two members of five organizations formed an action learning set around the topic of world-class operations (Coghlan and Coughlan, 2002; Coughlan *et al.*, 2002). Four of the participating organizations were from the private sector with MapMake from the public sector. The setting, therefore, was non-contractual, as the participating organizations had no formal or competitive relationship with one another. Yet all of the problems emerging within the set were subjected to a common, interactive questioning and reflective process. The commitments to action and to learning were intra-organizational, and focused on the move to world-class operations.

We explore MapMake as a case of inter-organizational action learning in a non-contractual setting along two dimensions, the inter-organizational and the intra-organizational.

The inter-organizational dimension

How was the inter-organizational dimension organized and structured? Seven actions defined the NALP approach in which the MapMake case was set (Coughlan and Coghlan, 2004):

1.   Each company in the set completed and received feedback from a detailed self-assessment instrument matched to the world class manufacturing theme (Hodgetts *et al.*, 1994). The matching of the instrument to the theme or issue was key, as was the rapid provision of customized, comparative feedback. Each self-assessment instrument was supported by a computer-facilitated report generation and feedback system.

2.   Each organization within the set made a monthly presentation to the set on the progress (or lack of it) against the change agenda it was working on. The organizations' representatives experienced considerable pressure to show that they were achieving measurable performance in relation to their stated goals.

3.   Each organization received feedback on its change initiatives from peer companies in the set.

4.   When requested by the set, academics, business managers and consultants addressed the particular issues the set was actually confronting through lectures, case studies and presentations.

5.   The set received a tailored set of reading material.

6.   Action learning coaches provided one-to-one coaching to the organizations' representatives and facilitated the raising of issues which were more personal than business-oriented, and which might be seen as not sufficiently related to business issues to raise in the monthly meetings of the set.

7.   Site visits and business consulting, as distinct from the coaching by the learning coaches, facilitated a focus on the emerging business issues.

This structure provided a framework for the inter-organizational dimension and facilitated open interaction within the set.

The intra-organizational dimension

How was the intra-organizational dimension organized and structured? The aim of the organization was to maintain the current position as the leaders in the field of geo-spatial and topographic data linking mapping, information and technology. The growth of geographical information services was expected to have a significant impact on MapMake and the data it supplied. Further, any change of status or location had the potential to create great benefit but also conflict for the organization. How these challenges were managed would determine future prospects as either a dynamic force in the geographical information industry or as a manager of a mapping database.

MapMake carried out a number of customer satisfaction surveys to determine the issues that customers felt to be important. A number of user groups were set up with principal customers to identify areas of potential innovation for the mutual benefit of both parties. Response to these issues was necessary if the organization was to survive. For example, the change from a paper to a digital environment had raised many unforeseen issues in recent years. For example, data that were quite adequate for paper maps needed a number of improvements before they were suitable for digital use. In addition, data fitness, consistency and accessibility via the Internet would determine how present and potential customers perceived the firm. There was a growing awareness of how competition and technological forces were impacting on the industry, and the organization was determined to maintain position as a leader within the marketplace.

MapMake addressed these issues in a number of ways:

* A new improved map sales office was opened at headquarters. This was to remain open during lunch hours. A dedicated area for answering customer queries and taking orders over the phone was set up.

- A number of agencies were set up throughout the country with the aim of bringing the product to the customer and creating greater awareness of the firm's maps and services.
- Some dedicated client managers were appointed to cater for larger customers.
- A working group involving main customers within the local authorities was set up to examine practices.
- A joint venture with sister organizations in Great Britain and Northern Ireland was established with the aim of standardizing products.
- Consultants were engaged to look at problems and offer a solution arising from data translation between different work platforms.
- A large-scale data specification was produced with the aim of creating a common standard of product.
- New product processes, which incorporated elements of ISO9000, were introduced into the work flow-line for graphics. The same procedure was extended to flying and plotting, while a similar type of process and specification was being examined for small-scale products.
- A webmaster was appointed to manage the linkage with the Internet.
- An intranet was installed to facilitate communication and expedite the transfer of data between offices.
- There was a determination to maintain position as industry leaders in the area of new technology.

MapMake recognized the importance of communication and staff buy-in throughout this process. This recognition led to a large increase in the areas of communication within the organization. For example, a staff climate survey highlighted areas of staff dissatisfaction concerning communications, morale, training and organizational bureaucracy. Attempts were made to address these issues through the following initiatives:

- Senior management attended a purpose-developed management develop-ment programme. This programme was perceived to be a very useful exercise as it exposed the managers to current theories and practices, especially in the private commercial sector.
- Staff fora, overseen by trained facilitators, were held, in which all members were encouraged to offer their opinions and suggestions.
- The systematic use of a team-based approach to new projects was begun. Concurrently, a fundamental change in work practice was introduced through a new computerized method of field data capture. Staff who would actually use this technology were involved with the software engineers in the development process.

A communications group was set up with responsibility for examining shortfalls in communications and recommend improvements. This group led to a resurrection of social activities within the organization as well as to other useful inputs.

Senior management recognized the importance of devolved responsibility to these local offices. Regular meetings between the managers of the regional offices and headquarters were initiated. While those involved were still finding their way in the management of these meetings, there was consensus that these meetings facilitated the management and coordination of various contracts, resulted in improved coordination between the different offices, and tabled for discussion difficulties arising in the various regions.

MapMake raised a number of issues through participation in NALP. At the outset, some staff members had thought that participation was aimed at staff satisfaction rather than organizational innovations in general. They seemed to expect, unrealistically, that NALP would be a panacea for all that they perceived to be wrong within the organization. In contrast, participation high-lighted the importance of champions of change, especially at senior manage-ment level. It also underlined the importance of staff empowerment in the production process.

An examination of the results of feedback reports generated during the programme provided valuable insights. An initial reaction to the improvements profiled was that 'we must be doing something right'. Many of the positive changes outlined were confirmed – there had been a dramatic improvement in all areas of communication and management style and policies. However, these improvements were balanced by a realization that there remained ample room for further innovation.

Reflection

The MapMake case deals with a network of public and private sector organizations faced with the task of sharing experience, thinking together about strategic development and taking action to change organizational practice on a permanent and self-sustaining basis. It illustrates, in particular, how senior managers of a public sector organization, faced with substantive and substantial change in their competitive environment and identity, utilized action learning as a vehicle for organizational renewal and learning. Participation by the MapMake senior managers in the action learning set with the private sector managers concerned about the same kinds of issue in their own organizations enabled vibrant interaction within the set and learning for all the participants. The members of the set developed an interest in and care for what was taking place in the other organizations and provided support and challenge to one another as they created a community of co-learners in the set (Dromgoole and Gorman, 2000). This peer-based, cyclical and organic approach to organizational renewal and learning was evidently successful, more so than through a top-down approach implied in the term 'disseminating best practice'. The hard practical task was not that of taking the good idea, making it relevant and making it happen, but of interpreting the particular context and experience, judiciously making decisions to change and reflecting on the experience of trying to make that change. This task was aided by the engagement with a learning set where members of different organizations who shared a similar problem and, with commitments to action and to learning, engaged in a questioning and reflective process beneficial to their respective organizations.

Inter-organizational action learning in a contractual setting

In the second setting, inter-organizational learning takes place in separate organizations linked systemically by contractual arrangements and obligations. Accordingly, for organizational members who participate in such an inter-organizational action learning set, participation has a compulsory tone to it and the action learning set may meet against a background of pre-existing relations and explicit power inequality. Opportunities for inter-organizational action learning emerge from the interdependent task within the supply chain or the service delivery system.

We now present the case of ControlLimit (a fictitious name), a private sector Dutch company, specializing in 'motion control' systems for the automotive, truck, marine, medical and agriculture markets. The case describes an inter-organizational action learning programme in which ControlLimit engaged with three key suppliers. This private sector case provides an example of inter-organizational action learning in a contractual setting that can be extrapolated to the emerging outsourcing arrangements in the public sector. As with MapMake earlier, we explore the case along two dimensions, but here the dimensions are different. Both are in an inter-organizational context, but at different levels: at the level of the whole learning set, and at the level of the specific collaborative improvement initiative.

The whole learning set dimension

How was the whole learning set dimension organized and structured? ControlLimit selected three suppliers to participate in the action learning project. Each represented a different kind of relationship and delivered different kinds of components. This meant that information and communication could pass freely throughout the whole learning set without running the risk of giving or losing sensitive information to competitors. The underlying reason for ControlLimit selecting these suppliers was that they perceived them to be highly involved in collaboration and to be dedicated partners that fully supported ControlLimit in assembling and delivering the components. Over a period of 18 months, ControlLimit and the suppliers started five collaborative improvement (CoI) initiatives in the areas of quality, change order management and manufacturing. The CoI initiatives were multi-disciplinary and required the involvement of different functional departments from all the companies, such as purchasing, engineering, sales, quality and production.

The action learning set met 15 times in the 18-month period. During these meetings (or workshops), at least two representatives from ControlLimit and one representative from each of the suppliers were present and participated actively in open group discussions. The workshops were used to monitor each improvement initiative and to facilitate a reflective process. The workshops aimed at engaging companies in collaborative improvement activities involving processes of diagnosing, fact-finding, implementation and evaluation of improvement actions. In each workshop, explicit attention was given to the progress and process of each improvement initiative, during a number of phases within each meeting:

- collaborative improvement action planning and evaluation
- presentation and reflection plenary on the process and progress of the project
- practical, reflective and challenging discussion on the issues arising in the improvement activities.

The results of the improvement initiatives were presented and discussed in plenary to evaluate and to reflect on the process and progress in order to identify experiences, observations and learning moments.

A reflective document was used to facilitate a reflection on the process and progress of improvement projects between the companies in order to learn from their experiences, observations and reflections. Evaluation and reflection were not naturally an integral part of the improvement process, and therefore the participating people/companies would have skipped the evaluation/ reflection process and been driven by the priority of daily activities after an improvement project. The reflective document and process of action learning emphasized the importance of a structured questioning and reflective process. Using this document people/companies within the learning set began to see the importance and benefits of evaluation and reflection.

The specific improvement initiative dimension

How was the specific improvement initiative dimension organized and structured? One of the five initiatives involved ControlLimit and a supplier concerning a quality problem with one of the supplier's components. The component had caused severe problems in the final products of ControlLimit due to component failure during product operation. The inter-organizational project team comprised people from purchasing, sales, engineering and quality.

It was recognized that the supplier was not able to technically optimize their processes to prevent the malfunctioning of the component. Therefore, the team engaged in a systematic process of problem-solving in order to retrieve additional information and suggestions. This process was open and constructive, trying to find the underlying causes and how they could be solved. An improvement plan was developed, assigning different tasks and responsibilities to team members with due dates. Regular face-to-face meetings were used to share information, to discuss the process and progress of the initiative, to reflect on and evaluate the achievements, and to synthesize learning. These meetings maintained the momentum of the initiative, created an atmosphere for direct communication and honesty, and increased the awareness of the benefits of collaborative improvement and learning. As the process unfolded over time, a researcher facilitated the entire CoI process.

The outcomes of the project and the learning achieved were:

- new material composition of the component, reducing cost and increasing quality for ControlLimit and reducing internal scrap rate for the supplier by 33 per cent;
- increased awareness of the need for information sharing and communication as part of the CoI process;
- recognition that openness, trust, goal sharing and mutual understanding were required to allow actual collaboration and to translate efforts in CoI into effective results.

Reflection

The commitment of ControlLimit and the three suppliers was to take the necessary strategic and operational steps to engage in collaborative improvement initiatives. The premise underlying this commitment was that no real improvement or learning would take place unless and until action was taken. The commitment to action was reflected in a schedule of meetings (or workshops) to support and to facilitate the questioning and reflective process. During the workshops, explicit focus was given to learning through presentations and discussions in plenary of the collaborative improvement initiatives which facilitated the diffusion of knowledge, experiences and lessons.

This case study is particularly significant for the public sector, although it is about the private sector. It illustrates that good practice in the private sector typically involves managing a relationship across the contractual divide. Managing quality up and down the supply chain is not a new idea in the private sector, and yet this case illustrates the enormous effort taken to achieve that objective. Here, adopting a peer-directed problem-solving approach, with the emphasis on reflection and learning, ensured that not only did the company and their suppliers solve the problem but also improved their capacity to solve problems together in the future. They built up the social capital which comes through networking and understanding other key players in the supply chain. This case is relevant to the public sector faced with working through contract, and signals that contracting can work better if it is also linked to collaboration.

Summary and conclusions

This chapter has reflected on inter-organizational action learning in three stages. First, the chapter presented the components of action learning, as proposed by

Marquardt (2004) and transferred them to the inter-organizational setting. Second, the chapter explored the first of two inter-organizational contexts in which action learning can be used – non-contractual, where members of separate organizations come together to form an action learning set, and in which each member then explores a problem in his/her own organization. The setting is inter-organizational and the projects are intra-organizational. Third, the chapter explored the second of two inter-organizational contexts in which action learning can be used – contractual. In this context, the participating organizations are systemically linked by the contractual structures of the production operation or service delivery system, and the inter-organizational action learning is driven by the task, such as the improvement of the supply chain or the service delivery system. Accordingly, in this setting, for organizational members who participate in an inter-organizational action learning set, participation has a compulsory tone to it and the action learning set meets against a background of a history of pre-existing relations between the organizations and with an explicit basis of power inequality.

Action learning is a distinctive approach in organizations that begins from experience. It reverses the traditional learning process where one learns something first and then applies it and it has a healthy disrespect for expertise. Accordingly, in action learning, facilitators or learning coaches do not act as experts who direct participants in a particular direction or who impart their knowledge. Rather, they facilitate the processes of learning set meetings and work at enabling learning to take place and to be articulated. The roles played by the facilitators in these two cases accorded with the action learning coaching roles outlined above in order to enable the development of the self-directed learning of the members of the learning set.

The two cases presented in this chapter illustrate the two different inter-organizational settings in which action learning was central. Both cases can be extrapolated to the public sector setting where, increasingly, agencies are coordinating their efforts and also developing contractual relationships with external service providers. In these settings, there is a need to coordinate efforts between collaborating parties to increase their responsive capabilities to deliver benefits to clients, especially where the quality of care cannot be compromised or scarce resources cannot be squandered.

Section V

Conclusion

14 Action learning in the public service system

Issues, tensions and a future agenda

Clare Rigg

Chapters 5–13 in this book present accounts of different ways in which action learning is currently being deployed in leadership and organization development in public service organizations. They provide a rich collection of examples of action learning applied to a range of themes that draw from across different public services. The collection is particularly unique in focusing on developing organizational capacity and on the wider public service system, as well as on individual development, with examples from both intra- and inter-agency contexts.

When first considering this book we had various questions as to why and how action learning was being used as part of public service capacity-building, and in particular what action learning offers that not only develops the individual but also tackles other capacity issues within organizations and across the wider system, such as partnership-building, networking, working with diversity, and collective problem-solving. In this final chapter these are questions to which I aim to draw together insights illuminated by the previous chapters. In breaking new ground on organization and systemic development, they provoke new questions, not least around the role of the facilitator which, I will argue, challenges the traditional minimalist and process-focused role. This chapter will end with comment on future agenda issues for action learning in this wider public service context.

Uses of action learning

We were initially interested, when different programmes and initiatives claimed to use action learning, as to what they meant and whether they meant the same, similar or very different things. The chapters in this book provide further substantiation for Pedler *et al.*'s finding that action learning is interpreted in various ways. In design they all incorporated most of what Pedler *et al.* (2005: 10) refer to as Revans' classical principles (RCP):

- the requirement for action as the basis for learning
- working with problems that have no right answers
- action learners work in sets of peers to support and challenge each other

- the search for fresh questions and 'q' (questioning insight) takes primacy over access to expert knowledge or 'p'.

In some instances the principle that problems are given and aimed at organizational as well as personal development was evident: for example, the chapters by Blackler and Kennedy, Willis, and Fox, Rigg and Willis, whereas in many chapters problems emanated from the individuals and were worked on individually rather than collectively. In most chapters, a further principle was evident: that of the intention of profound personal development resulting from reflection upon action. However, there were other examples where this was not the starting intention (even if it happened incidentally), as in the chapters by Fox, Rigg and Willis and Coghlan and Coughlan. In all chapters, by virtue of how they were commissioned from the facilitator, the action learning sets inevitably had a facilitator. In all cases the role was conceived in traditional action learning terms as helping the participants with engaging in the process of learning through reflecting on action and in working effectively as a group. However, in several accounts the facilitator also contributed content expertise, as I discuss further below. Composition of action learning sets was also varied. Revans' notion of 'comrades in adversity' is generally interpreted as meaning peers facing common problems who can learn from each other. And indeed grouping people with very similar contexts was an explicit priority in several chapters, notably those by Richards, Lyons and Rigg, Blackler and Kennedy and Fox, Rigg and Willis. However, in other chapters a diversity of roles was essential to exploring problems, so as to enhance either intra-organizational learning (e.g. Yapp's chapter) or inter-organizational learning (e.g. Willis; Coghlan and Coughlan).

Overall, therefore, the chapters provide an illustration of a shared ethos that constitutes action learning with variation in some of the principles incorporated. The next section explores what the chapters offer our understanding of how action learning has impact at individual, organizational and systemic levels.

Individual impacts

In Chapter 3 Marquadt and Waddill demonstrated how the potency of the action learning process can be understood in terms of a variety of theories of learning, suggesting that when examined through the lens of each adult learning theory, action learning addresses the full range of adult learning needs. In addition to these insights, several chapters illustrate the potency of action learning in terms of what it offers individuals in the challenging context of change, improvement and modernization that characterizes public service leadership roles. Many chapters, notably Blackler and Kennedy, Lyons and Rigg, Richards on probation leaders, Mead on the Public Service Leaders Scheme (PSLS), and Fox, Rigg and Willis, illuminate the complexity and turmoil of organizational life and just how pressurized people can be. Mead's use of the notion of communicative space, and Blackler and Kennedy's suggestion of facilitator as container, give us other valuable explanations of how and why action learning can be so potent for individuals.

I would also argue that the very processes of action learning helps develop leadership skills: processes such as taking responsibility for self-direction, developing skills in questioning and learning to act in the context of uncertainty and turmoil. Also, because it is not simply about cognitive learning, but also about working with emotion and helping participants learn how to cope, action learning helps participants develop an emotional intelligence that is invaluable for relating to and leading others.

Understanding organization impact

The potency of action learning in terms of organizational development is that processes within the set not only provide opportunities for learning about the organization, but also for enacting change within the organization through working on these behaviours within the set. The action learning set can be understood in many ways as a microcosm of the organization. In Chapter 7 Blackler and Kennedy describe this as parallel processes, which provide insights into organizational life. In Chapter 8 Yapp echoes this perspective, arguing that the most powerful learning lies in moments of discomfort within a group which make action learning sets almost unique opportunities to push through this barrier, to address underlying group issues, and in doing so to address wider organizational issues. Blackler and Kennedy draw from activity theory to link individual recognition of tensions within their practices to organization change as they begin to reconfigure their activity systems by developing new objects of activity and new approaches in practice.

In Chapter 4 I theorized how insights from organization dynamics, combined with social constructionist thinking, enable us to conceive of organizations in processual terms as a community of meaning sustained and perpetuated by patterns of communication and interaction, which are shaped by members' power relations and emotions. Action learning as an approach which engages participants in social interaction and also facilitates action within the social network that constitutes an organization or wider system, creates a dynamic whereby organization members literally bring new ways of organizing into being through new communicative acts: experimental interactions, new ways of thinking, talking and interrelating. Conceiving of 'an' organization in this way easily extends to conceptualizing a wide public service system – a more complex social network.

Action in the system

Cross-organizational action learning sets offer a rich opportunity to develop skills appropriate for working in partnerships, networks and across the contractual divide. Yapp concluded:

it is difficult to think of, or even imagine, a job in public service management that does not require an individual to work collaboratively with many others, often in very complex circumstances. If we are honest with ourselves, we know how very hard this can be, and how unfortunate, even in the best of organizations, the consequences of failing can be for services and communities. Technical proficiency can only take us so far. And, of course, it is not only services and vulnerable people in our communities that are affected. Managers impact directly on their staff, and vice versa, and have a huge role in creating the culture and practice in, and between, organizations as a whole.

In Chapter 12 Willis described the multi-agency sets he worked with as by their very nature concerned with systemic thinking. This ranged from developing the understanding of values, priorities, roles and responsibilities between senior management teams from partner organizations to learning about how to engage and empower staff at all levels across whole systems to benefit individual users and communities. Coghlan and Coughlan indicated that investment in collaborative problem-solving across the contractual divide has wider systemic impacts in that participants built up the social capital which comes through networking and understanding other key players in the supply chain.

It is the difference within cross-organizational action learning sets that renders them such a rich source of learning and potential for systemic development, and in several chapters the diversity of role amongst set members was essential to exploring problems across the public service system. In a sense participants were not only learning from each other, as in traditionally conceived action learning, but also about each other. In intra-organizational (e.g. Yapp's chapter) and inter-organizational action learning (e.g. Willis, and Coghlan and Coughlan) forging relationships across the contractual divide or across a public policy system is the very purpose of action learning. And yet there is a conundrum presented by that very diversity. Revans' notion of 'comrades in adversity' is commonly understood to imply peers facing common problems who can learn from each. This diversity stretches, and I would argue challenges, the notion of 'comrades in adversity'. In doing so it has implications for the facilitation involved: for holding the process together. The facilitator role and learning the craft of facilitation is a theme we now turn to.

Facilitating – the role in the context of the public service system

Revans (1998) was very wary of action learning groups becoming dependent on facilitators, feeling that their presence could hinder the group's growth. One of the orthodoxies of traditional action learning is that 'the process will out', meaning that dynamics within the action learning set will work themselves through, the implication being that this will happen despite or regardless of the facilitator. Looking at the experience within these chapters I want to argue that facilitation is actually more significant than this. Several authors refer to specific moments which can be described as tipping points in the sense of being times at which, if the facilitator makes the right intervention, something in the group releases; but missing the moment or saying the wrong thing could push the group into reverse, as Carol Yapp suggests in her account. Timing, I would argue, is therefore an essential element of the facilitator's mastery.

I also want to suggest that the dynamic of balancing expertise and process facilitation is more complex than traditionally conceived of, and that, if the organization/systemic impact is to be maximized, the facilitator has a wider role than if the focus is primarily on the individuals within a specific action learning set. In Chapter 3 Marquardt and Waddill advocate that: 'The action learning coach must have the wisdom and self-restraint to let the participants learn for themselves and from each other.' They go on to say:

> In the action learning set, the learning coach acts as facilitator when she enables the group members to make sense of their learning by helping the participants both with the process (asking questions, reframing, providing feedback) and by challenging assumptions. The coach's actions are collaborative and provocative of thought rather than directive.

They indicate how facilitation in this way is consistent with constructivist learning theory: 'Constructivists ... interpret the role of the instructor as one who "facilitates and negotiates meaning with the learner"' (Merriam and Caffarella, 1999).

Probably no author in this book would disagree that they tried to work with these principles, and some stated this as an explicit intent despite their subject expertise: for example, Michael Lyons, as a three-times local authority chief executive working with new chief executives, and Carol Yapp as an insider-facilitator with prior knowledge of the organization members she worked with. However, I want to make two challenges to the traditional process-only focus of facilitation: first, to argue the value of bilingualism and, second, to problematize the distinction between facilitation, coaching and mentoring within action learning.

Bilingualism

Several chapters suggest that in the context of a complex public service system, in which the intended use of action learning is to enhance organization or systemic capacity, there is value in shifting the balance between process and expert facilitation, in the sense that facilitators speak both a public policy language as well as that of learning and development. In this context, facilitators are not simply building up knowledge about the participants and groups they work with. They are in a unique position to generate knowledge about the wider organization or wider system they are working with. For example, in the turnaround action learning sets (Fox, Rigg and Willis, Chapter 10), this position was deliberately created, with facilitators also acting as researchers on the process of organization turnaround. In Richards' work with probation managers she was valued by the participants because of her wider policy knowledge and her resultant ability to help them interpret what was happening to them and their service. In other organization development programmes we have run as external consultants, the action learning set facilitators collate insights culled from their respective groups to provide feedback on corporate issues, such as repeating patterns, blocks to change, organizational messiness or dysfunction. As such, the intention of action learning is both individual and social, and the facilitators are regarded as both developers and knowledge creators.

Bilingual facilitation challenges the traditional Revans principle of minimalist facilitator, focused primarily on the process, but our argument is that it is a lost organization development opportunity not to draw on facilitators' organizational and wider public service knowledge, and to conceive of them only as supporting the action learning set members. In fact, in a client–consultant context where action learning is commissioned by, for instance, a chief executive, the client wants the facilitators' growing organizational knowledge, in addition to their work with specific groups of organization members.

Implications for commissioning

An extension of our argument is that generic facilitators, in not being bilingual, would not offer as much to action learning developments. This has implications for commissioning leadership and organization development.

Most of the facilitators in this book are engaged both in the practice and studying of learning and development and, in most cases, also in researching and consulting on public policy. As such they are bilingual as facilitators of development, and are also academics, engaged simultaneously in creating knowledge and in facilitating other people's knowledge construction. Herein lies another tension, in terms of how much the knowledge creation of academic institutions is given validity. There is frequently a pull by clients and participants just to be concerned with action, and to eschew anything that hints of academia. The point I am emphasizing here is that one of the themes from several chapters in this book is the value bilingualism can bring to public service action learning, which is not necessarily recognized as valuable by commissioners of development.

Facilitation, coaching and mentoring

Chapters 5, 7 and 11 highlight a particularly interesting issue in relation to the comparison between facilitation, and coaching and mentoring. (We are not suggesting that coaching and mentoring are the same, but we will talk of them together, as forms of one-to-one intervention, in contrast to the one-to-several relationship between the facilitator and an action learning set.) These chapters all describe action learning in combination with some form of one-to-one coaching or mentoring, although not necessarily with the same individual acting as facilitator and coach or mentor.

Michael Lyons refers to a 'hybrid model' by which he means 'an array of tools ... at my disposal; mentoring, coaching as well as facilitation'. The context of his account, comprising new local authority chief executives meeting just three times a year, was one where he was what could be described as a 'master craftsman' given his experience. His reflection on one dysfunctional action learning set was that he believed the group process would have been helped had he deployed coaching or mentoring with one member whose individual support needs were particularly high and which detracted from the group functioning to everyone's benefit. Our analysis, drawing on Rigg's heuristic model in Chapter 4, is that the action learning set in this time-pressurized context could not attend equally to both performative and emancipatory outcomes. There was a degree of personal communicative space that supported individual emancipatory goals, but the intent of participants in engaging in the action learning was also on performative outcomes, particularly their own capability in their new roles. In this sense the set would only function if there was balanced space for both, as in the case of the other two sets Michael Lyons described. His conclusion is that coaching/mentoring interventions, outside the action learning set space, could have addressed the individual's needs and saved the group: what he described as hybridity in combining action learning with one-to-one intervention. Perhaps this combination of one-to-one with set facilitation is a way of dealing with the tension between expert and process when the facilitator is a Michael Lyons, a 'master craftsman' in relation to the participants: a way of having space to use the expertise without compromising the group process.

In Blackler and Kennedy's account of designing a programme with experienced health service chief executives, participants engaged in a mix of learning events, receiving personal one-to-one consultations, working with colleagues in small groups and as the full group, on a variety of pressing problems, and reflecting on the processes involved. This again could be described as a hybrid model, where the small group alone was not seen as offering as much development as when it was in combination with other forms of coaching-style intervention. In this instance there were again pressures of time on how quickly the group could become a mature source of support and challenge, and there was also an intention (in terms of the heuristic model in Chapter 4) to combine individual and social (organizational) transformations with emancipatory and performative intentions. As Blackler and Kennedy describe it, the combination together was designed to support new perspectives 'on personal issues and career matters, organizational problems, institutional tensions and leadership roles'.

The third example offering comparison between facilitation and coaching/ mentoring is Geoff Mead's account of the PSLS (Chapter 11). Here a personal development adviser providing one-to-one guidance and challenge was an integral element of the programme alongside the action inquiry groups and large group events (network learning events). He describes how the action inquiry groups were constituted as 'communicative spaces' in which participants were able to try to reconcile their sense of self outside work with their roles as public service leaders. The one-to-one consultations tended to remain more focused on performative outcomes. The inquiry groups were facilitated to promote sharing, inquiry and reflection, and met around six times a year for up to three years, so they had more opportunity than in the previous two examples to build relations of trust and challenge. We speculate that this continuity, rather than the one-to-one consultations, was significant in enabling the groups to provide for this individual emancipatory intent.

The conclusion from these three examples is that they do not actually suggest that action learning facilitation is the same as coaching or mentoring. It is not that some of the skills of questioning or challenge are not common, but primarily that the focus of the facilitator is on the social interaction process, and on helping the group members to support, challenge, coach and exchange with each other. These three chapters are useful because they illustrate ways in which one-to-one consultation can be offered in combination with action learning sets, but without clouding the facilitation role within the set. This is a departure from traditional action learning, but I argue that part of the future agenda for employing action learning to public service development, particularly when there are severe time pressures on participants and time-limited funding from clients, may be to combine one-to-one intervention with action learning groups in an integrated programme.

Learning the craft of facilitation

Facilitators in these chapters played multiple roles: at times as the facilitator of the process; at times as a source of subject expertise; and sometimes constructed as, and allowing themselves to be constructed as, a mentor to participants. Facilitating is a craft, with multiple moments of judgement and choices to be made. There are also manifold opportunities for facilitators to learn from experience, and like their participants to gain insight from experimentation and reflection.

Also like participants, facilitators are people too. They bring their own anxieties, impulses to control and responses to uncertainty, which influence the process of action learning as much as dynamics between the group participants. For example, Sue Richards' chapter on probation sets and Martin Willis's on health/social care both illustrate clearly how solutions and creativity emerge from fluidity. How the facilitator responds to this fluidity, whether they are sufficiently confident and open to let it go, or whether they feel compelled to rein it back in a direction they have more control over, is therefore deeply influential on the action learning process. But how do you learn to do this? Most chapters in this book describe facilitators working alone, yet concluding that they would have valued support or supervision from peers or more experienced others. In two instances, Mead on the PSLS and that described by Fox, Rigg and Willis, facilitators gained from collaborating and sharing with each other. This highlights the value of what Mead describes as a meta-set – an action learning set of facilitators – as an integral part of a programme.

Context and intent of action learning

In this section I want to comment on an issue raised earlier: the focus or intent of action learning and the constraints imposed by different stakeholders, the context of commissioned action learning and the implications of hierarchy. In terms of intent, the heuristic model in Chapter 4 summarizes two spectrums: one that prioritizes the relative importance given to individual compared to social (organization or wider system) outcomes. A second spectrum illustrates the relative priority given to pursuing performative goals, aiming to improve practice of some kind, compared to emancipatory outcomes, in the sense of provoking transformations in perspective, stimulating new self-insights, or increasing awareness of power, otherness and powerlessness in the social context of the public policy system.

Mead's chapter on the PSLS is particularly helpful in clarifying how different stakeholders in a development programme can come with varying and conflicting intentions. Table 11.1, 'Different perspectives on action inquiry groups', illuminates this clearly. This raises two questions. The first concerns how feasible it is to work at the extremes of the model – say, only focused on achieving organization performance improvements or only emphasizing individual emancipatory outcomes. The second concerns how to hold and communicate the tensions between stakeholders.

On the first question, several chapters problematize attempts to work at the level of organization performance without also, or first, undertaking individual work. Michael Lyons' account of new local authority chief executives, Carol Yapp's experience with a local government management team, Geoff Mead's account of the PSLS, as well as Fox, Rigg and Willis's description of action learning sets as part of organization turnaround from poor performance, all found that focus on organization performance was resisted by participants until some individual focus was given, or, in Reason and Bradbury's terms (2001), first-person work was undertaken. Fox *et al.* concluded that holding space for individual concerns and issues was valuable, even where the design prioritizes organization outcomes. Mead on the PSLS concluded that the participants resisted the original client pull to focus on systemic performance outcomes because the action inquiry groups constituted 'communicative spaces' in which participants were able to try to reconcile their sense of self outside work with their roles as public service leaders: 'to explore and address the interconnections and tensions between the system and lifeworld aspects of a setting as they are lived out in practice'.

An interesting question raised by Carol Yapp's chapter is whether organization/systemic improvement – for example, in partnership working – could ever be cultivated 'out there', if it cannot be created 'in here' in terms of individual behaviours and understandings within the group. Coghlan and Coughlan's account of a supply chain also illustrates effective collaboration between an individual and a social focus, asking, 'how do we do it ourselves?'

Several chapters illustrate clear contextual constraints on the choice of intent. This can be driven by the agenda of a client, as we see in Mead's analysis of the PSLS, or by individual preferences, as with Lyons and Rigg, where the new chief executives prioritized work on their own individual performance, and with the managers in the chapter by Fox, Rigg and Willis whose primary intent, once they had had a little space for individual concerns, was to see improvements in their organizations. Two chapters, Mead on developing police leaders and Coghlan and Coughlan, highlight the role of hierarchy as a constraint. Mead illuminates the challenges of working with the collaborative principles of action learning within a hierarchical organization where the culture is unfamiliar with them. In Coghlan and Coughlan's chapter inter-organizational learning takes place in separate organizations linked systemically by contractual arrangements and obligations. Accordingly, for organizational members who participate in such an inter-organizational action learning set, participation has a compulsory tone to it and the action learning set may meet against a background of pre-existing relations and explicit power inequality.

The conclusion has to be that use of action learning must be crafted to the politics, interests and priorities within a particular context. In the public service context, where increasing sums are being invested in leadership and organization capacity-building, there are implications of the creation of non-participating client-owned action learning that is also different from the traditional Revans style of participant-owned and -directed action learning (Revans, 1982). It places a different pressure on the facilitator who is pulled in the direction of both the participants' best interests and the client's brief. And it challenges the programme co-ordinator to be alert to potential client–participant tensions. Opportunities for inter-organizational action learning up and down the supply chain is not a new idea in the private sector, but Coghlan and Coughlan illustrate the enormous effort taken to achieve that objective. The chapters raise questions worthy of further exploration, including whether action learning can ever be effective if starting with the intent of organization/systemic performance outcomes inquiry without giving space for individual emancipatory inquiry; under what circumstances the sole emphasis on organization outcomes can be successful; and whether this is simply tactical in a particular client context, or whether the optimum is multi-level working.

Concluding thoughts: the potential of action learning in a public service context

Below is a summary of the core themes covered in this chapter with cross-reference to the chapters where they are addressed.

Core theme	*Chapter*
Individual development	3, 4, 5, 6, 7
Organizational development	7, 8, 9, 10
Systemic change	11, 12, 13
Facilitator role	3, 5, 8
Facilitator bilingualism	6, 10
Facilitating compared with coaching and mentoring	5, 7, 11
Learning the craft of facilitation	6, 10, 11, 12
Commissioning and clients	10, 11
Implications of hierarchy	9, 13
Intended outcomes of action learning	4, 5, 8, 10, 11, 13
Learning the craft of leadership	5, 7
Public service contracting	13

The final area I want to comment on from the chapters is the potential of action learning within some of the characteristics of the public service context. The context, as has been described, is complex, uncertain and dynamic. Public services are systemic, interconnected and not necessarily delivered by the public sector. Players are increasingly private and third (voluntary and community) sector as well. Learning public leadership cannot be distilled down to simply acquiring a pre-defined body of knowledge or competencies. Lyons and Rigg's chapter, for example, gives insight into the extent to which learning to lead as a chief executive is learning a craft rather than a technical task. Personal values are highly significant in driving the individual. The chapter shows clearly how at the most senior levels public leadership is exercised through the relations between elected political and managerial leadership. It further shows how, at times, relations between these roles enters territory that is unspoken, that almost dares not speak its name, when the chief executive faces choices that must be engaged with if a service or organization is to be led, but which ought to be the realm of political leadership. Judging how and when to stir political leaders into action and when to step back into the technical specification of their respective roles is craft knowledge that cannot be learned on a traditional input-led public management programme. Inquiry, experimentation, the opportunity to share with peers, and even the support of a master/apprentice relationship as in Lyons' example, are the potency that action learning offers in learning the craft of public leadership.

The Coghlan and Coughlan chapter has particularly important messages for public service contracting, which are becoming more pertinent as we move further towards seeing a public service system delivered by combinations of public, private and third sector organizations. Their chapter illustrates that good practice in the private sector typically involves managing a relationship across the contractual divide: that is, between organizations linked system-ically by contractual arrangements and obligations. Opportunities for inter-organizational action learning emerge from interdependent tasks within the supply chain or the service delivery system. Coghlan and Coughlan illustrate the enormous effort taken to achieve that objective through a peer-led problem-solving approach, with the emphasis on reflection and learning, but importantly they highlight how engaging in action learning enhanced partici-pants future capacity to work in this way and solve problems together in the future. A lesson for public management is that this implies contracting arrangements built on relationships, not on a supermarket model of pur-chasing. It further implies recognition of knowledge asymmetry in the contractual divide, whereby a supplier may well have more expertise in their specific service or product area. In such a context improvement and learning are endangered by contracting that fails to recognize clients' knowledge limi-tations and too tightly specifies processes and inputs. The implication is that learning to work with contractual partners can be enhanced through action learning.

Finally I want to argue that action learning has much to offer the next generation of public service leaders. The future needs transformational as well as transactional leadership, not simply management in a command-and-control way. We also have a new generation of people acculturated to engaging the self rather than simply obeying orders. Action learning is in tune with people learning through activity, becoming more aware of how their values drive them, and becoming more reflective and accepting that as the world constantly changes leadership also has to continuously look for improvement.

This book has presented many examples of how individual learning and development can be translated into changed organization or systemic practice. It has drawn from organization and learning theory to analyse how this can be understood, and why action learning as a social learning process has such potential to facilitate systemic development. The implication is more shared leadership development – opportunities to learn, talk and think that are shared across public sector organizations if not also by the private sector as well. The key implication for leadership development is that taking a relational per-spective on organizing implies that leaders fundamentally need to become better inter-relators. Relating the context of public leadership back to the heuristic model in Chapter 4, the complexity for individuals in the public sector needs 'both-and' intentions: both performative learning to improve practice, address problems and enhance capacity; and emancipatory learning in the sense of provoking transformations in perspective, stimulating new self-insights, and increasing awareness of power, of otherness and powerlessness in the social context of the public policy system. Action learning, as a broad church of approaches with shared principles, has the unique potential to meet this challenge.

References

Accounts Commission (2000) *The Map to Success: Using Process Mapping to Improve Performance*. Edinburgh: Audit Scotland.

Alimo-Metcalfe, B. (1998) *Effective Leadership*. London: Improvement and Development Agency.

Alimo-Metcalfe, B. and Nyfield, G. (2002) 'Leadership and organizational effectiveness', in I. Robertson *et al.*, *The Role of Individual Performance in Organizational Effectiveness*. London: Wiley.

Argyris, C. (1991) 'Teaching smart people how to learn', *Harvard Business Review* 69(3): 99–109.

Argyris, C. and Schön, D. (1978) *Organizational Learning: A Theory of Action Perspective*. Harlow: Addison-Wesley.

Argyris, C., Putnam, R. and Schön, D. (1985) *Action Science*. San Francisco, CA: Jossey-Bass.

Armstrong, D. (2005) *Organization in the Mind: Psychoanalysis, Group Relations and Organizational Consultancy*. London: Karnac Books.

Atkins, H., Kellner, K. and Linklater, J. (1996) 'Employing the workplace within', in *Organization 2000: Psychodynamic Perspectives*, International Society for the Psychoanalytical Study of Organizations Symposium, New York.

Australian Flexible Learning Framework, 2001, available at http://www2.training village.gr/download/editorial_comm/rapporteurs/2001-053.doc (accessed 7 March 2006)

Bandura, A. (1986) *Social Foundations of Thought and Action: A Social Cognitive Theory*. Englewood Cliffs, NJ: Prentice Hall.

Bannan-Ritland, B. (2003) 'An action learning framework for teaching instructional design', *Performance Improvement Quarterly* 14(2): 37–52.

Bate, P. *et al.* (2004) *Towards a Million Change Agents*, NHS Modernisation Agenda.

Bateson, G. (1973) *Steps Towards an Ecology of the Mind*. London: Paladin.

Bazerman, C. (2001) 'Anxiety in action: Sullivan's interpersonal psychiatry as a supplement to Vygotskian psychology', *Mind, Culture and Activity* 8(2): 174–86.

BBC/IHM Survey (2002) *NHS Managers Keep Quiet Rather Than Tell It As It Is*. London: Institute of Healthcare Management (results broadcast on the BBC Radio 4 *Today* programme on Monday, 7 October).

Belenky, M. F., Clinchy, B. M., Golderger, N. R. and Tarube, J. M. (1986) *Women's Ways of Knowing: The Development of Self, Voice and Mind*. New York: Basic Books.

Bennis, W. (1989) *Why Leaders Can't Lead*. San Francisco, CA: Jossey-Bass.

Bion, W. (1961) *Experiences in Groups*. London: Tavistock.

Blackler, F. (1993) 'Knowledge and the theory of organizations: organizations as activity systems and the reframing of management', special issue of *Journal of Management Studies* 30: S863–4.

Blackler, F., Crump, N. and McDonald, S. (1999) 'Managing experts and competing through collaboration, an activity theoretical analysis', *Organization: The Interdisciplinary Journal of Organization, Theory and Society* 6(1): 5–31.

Blackler, F., Crump, N. and McDonald, S. (2000) 'Organizing processes in complex activity networks', *Organization: The Interdisciplinary Journal of Organization, Theory and Society* 7(2): 277–300.

Blom-Cooper, L. (Chair) (1985) *A Child in Trust,* Report of the panel of inquiry into the circumstances surrounding the death of Jasmine Beckford. Harrow: Kingswood Press.

Blom-Cooper, L. (Chair) (1987) *A Child in Mind: Protection of Children in a Responsible Society,* Report of the commission of inquiry into the circumstances surrounding the death of Kimberley Carlile. London: London Borough of Greenwich.

Bonnet, M., Harris, M., Huxham, C. and Loveridge, R. (2001) 'Mapping action research practices', European Group for Organizational Studies Conference, Lyons, France.

Boshyk, Y. (2002) *Action Learning Worldwide: Experiences of Leadership and Organizational Development.* Basingstoke: Palgrave.

Bowlby, J. (1973) *Attachment and Loss*, vol. 2: *Separation, Anxiety and Anger.* London: Pelican Books.

Bowlby, J. (1988) *A Secure Base: Parent–Child Attachment and Healthy Human Development.* New York: Basic Books.

Boyne, G. A. (2003) 'Sources of public service improvement: a critical review and research agenda', *Journal of Public Administration Research and Theory* 13: 367–94.

Boyne, G. A. and Enticott, G. (2004) 'Are the "poor" different? An empirical analysis of the internal characteristics of local authorities in the five CPA groups', *Public Money and Management* 24(1): 11–18.

Boyne, G. A., Martin, S. and Walker, R. (2004) 'Explicit reforms, implicit theories and public service improvement', *Public Management Review* 6: 189–210.

Bramley, P. (1991) *Evaluating Training Effectiveness.* London: McGraw-Hill.

Briscoe, J. P. and Hall, D. T. (1999) 'Grooming and picking leaders using competency frameworks: do they work? An alternative approach and guidelines for practice', *Orgnizational Dynamics* 28(2): 37–52.

Brookfield, Stephen (1994) 'Tales from the dark side: a phenomenology of adult critical reflection', *International Journal of Lifelong Education* 13(3): 203–16.

Brooks, A. and Watkins, K. E. (1994) *The Emerging Power of Action Inquiry Technologies.* San Francisco, CA: Jossey-Bass.

Brown, J. (2000) *The Birth of the World Café*, available at www.theworldcafe.com (accessed 15 March 2006).

Brown, J., Isaacs, D. and the World Café Pioneers (2001) 'The world café: living knowledge through conversations that matter', in *The Systems Thinker.* Cambridge, MA: Pegasus Communications.

Brown, J. S. and Duguid, P. (1991) 'Organizational learning and communities of practice: toward a unified view of working, learning, and innovation', *Organization Science* 2(1): 40–57.

Bruner, J. (1965) *In Defense of Verbal Learning. Readings in the Psychology of Cognition.* New York: Holt, Rinehardt and Winston.

Canada School of Public Service (2005), available at http://www.myschool-monecole.gc.ca/main_e.html (accessed 10 January 2005).

Carter, L., Giber, D., Goldsmith, M. and Bennis, W. (eds) (2000) *Best Practices in Leadership Development Handbook: Case Studies, Instruments, Training*. San Francisco, CA: Jossey-Bass.

Casey, D. (1997) 'The role of the set adviser', in M. Pedler (ed.), *Action Learning in Practice*, 3rd edn. Gower: Aldershot, pp. 209–20.

CEML (Council for Excellence in Management and Leadership) (2002a) *Managers and Leaders: Raising our Game*. London: CEML.

CEML (2002b) *The Contribution of the UK Business Schools to Developing Managers and Leaders*. London: CEML.

Charters, A. N. and Hilton, R. J. (eds) (1989) *Landmarks in International Adult Education: A Comparative Analysis*. London: Routledge.

Chesterman, D. and Horne, M. (2002) *Local Authority: How to Develop Leadership for Better Public Services*. London: Demos.

Chia, R. (1996) *Organizational Analysis as Deconstructive Practice*. Berlin: De Gruyter.

Chief Secretary to the Treasury (2003) *Every Child Matters*, Cm 5860. Norwich: TSO.

Clarke, M. G. and Stewart, J. D. (1997) 'Handling the wicked issues', working paper, Institute of Local Government Studies, University of Birmingham.

Claxton, G. (1997) *Hare Brain, Tortoise Mind*. London: Fourth Estate.

Clegg, S. R. and Hardy, C. (eds) (1999) *Studying Organizations*. London: Sage.

Coghlan, D. and Brannick, T. (2001) *Doing Action Research in Your Own Organization*. London: Sage.

Coghlan, D. and Coughlan, P. (2002) 'Developing organizational learning capabilities through inter-organizational action learning', in M. A. Rahim, R. T. Golembiewski and K. MacKenzie (eds), *Current Topics in Management*, vol. 7. New Brunswick, NJ: Transaction, pp. 33–46.

Cole, A. (2000) 'Sacked, fired with anger: chief executives tell all', *Health Service Journal*, 8 June, pp. 24–7.

Cole, A. (2001) 'Staying power: what does it take to survive as a chief executive?' *Health Service Journal*, 3 May, pp. 24–7.

Cole, A. (2002) 'Chief executives: further to fall', *Health Service Journal*, 20 June, pp. 18–21.

Cole, M., John-Steiner, V., Scribner, S. and Souberman, E. (eds) (1978) *Vygotsky: Mind in Society. The Development of Higher Psychological Processes*. Cambridge, MA: Harvard University Press.

Conger, J. and Benjamin, B. (1999) *Building Leaders: How Successful Companies Develop the Next Generation*. San Francisco, CA: Jossey-Bass.

Cooperrider, D. L. (1995) 'Introduction to appreciative inquiry', in W. French and C. Bell (eds), *Organization Development*, 5th edn. London: Prentice Hall.

Cooperrider, D. L., Sorensen Jr, P. F., Whitney, D. and Yaeger, T. F. (eds) (2000) *Appreciative Inquiry: Rethinking Human Organization toward a Positive Theory of Change*. Champaign, IL: Stipes Publishing.

Coughlan, P. and Coghlan, D. (2004) 'Action learning: towards a framework in inter-organizational settings', *Action Learning: Research and Practice* 1(1): 43–61.

Coughlan, P., Dromgoole, T., Duff, D. and Harbison, A. (2001) 'Continuous improvement through collaborative action learning', *International Journal of Technology Management* 22(4): 285–302.

Coughlan, P., Coghlan, D., Dromgoole, T., Duff, D., Caffrey, R., Lynch, K., Rose, P.,

Stack, P., McGill, A. and Sheridan, P. (2002) 'Effecting operational improvement through inter-organizational action learning', *Integrated Manufacturing Systems* 12(3): 131–40.

Cunningham, I. (1994) *The Wisdom of Strategic Learning: The Self Managed Learning Solution*. London: McGraw-Hill.

Currie, G. (1999) 'Resistance around a management development programme: negotiated order in a Hospital Trust', *Management Learning* 30(1): 43–61.

Czarniawska, B. (1998) *A Narrative Approach to Organization Studies*. London: Sage.

Davies, L. and Kraus, P. (2003) 'Individual learning from exceptional events', in M. Lee, *HRD in a Complex World*. London: Routledge, pp. 179–92.

Defence Leadership Centre (2005), available at https://da.mod.uk/DLC/Leadership %20Thinking/Definitions/document_view (accessed 1 August 2005).

Department for Education and Skills/Department for Trade and Industry (2002) *Government Response to the Report of the Council for Excellence and Management in Leadership* London: DfES/DTI.

Department for Transport, Local Government and the Regions (2002) *Strong Local Leadership – Quality Public Services*, Local Government White Paper. London: DTLR.

Department of Health (1989) *Caring for People. Community Care in the Next Decade and Beyond*, Cm 849. London: HMSO.

Department of Health (1997) *Modernising Social Services*. London: Department of Health.

Department of Health (1998) *Partnership in Action: A Discussion Document*. London: Department of Health.

Department of Health (2000) *The NHS Plan*. London: Department of Health.

Department of Health (2001) *Building Capacity and Partnership in Care: An Agreement between the Statutory and the Independent Social Care, Health Care and Housing Sectors*. London: Department of Health.

Department of Health and Social Security (1974) *Report of Inquiry into the Care and Supervision Provided in Relation to Maria Colwell*. London: HMSO.

Department of Health and Social Security (1988) *Working Together: A Guide to Arrangements for Inter-Agency Co-operation for the Protection of Children*. London: HMSO.

Deutschman, A. (1991) 'The trouble with MBAs', *Fortune* 124(3): 67–73.

Dewey, J. (1916) *Democracy and Education*. New York: The Free Press.

Dewey, J. (1933) *How We Think*. New York: D. C. Heath.

Dilworth, R. L. (1998) 'Action learning in a nutshell', *Performance Improvement Quarterly* 11(1): 28–43.

Dilworth, R. L. and Willis, V. J. (2003) *Action Learning: Images and Pathways*. Malabar, FL: Krieger.

DiMaggio, Paul J. and Powell, Walter (eds) (1991) *The New Institutionalism in Organizational Analysis*. Chicago: University of Chicago Press.

Dotlich, D. and Noel, J. (1998) *Action Learning: How the World's Top Companies are Re-creating their Leaders and Themselves*. San Francisco, CA: Jossey-Bass.

Dromgoole, T. and Gorman, L. (2000) 'Developing and implementing strategy through learning networks', in P. Flood, T. Dromgoole, S. Carroll and L. Gorman (eds), *Managing Strategy Implementation*. Oxford: Blackwell, pp. 196–209.

Easterby-Smith, M., Johns, A. and Burgoyne, J. (1997) 'Evaluating action learning', in M. Pedler, *Action Learning in Practice*. London: Gower, pp. 347–54.

Eaton, L. (2001) 'Let's leave God out of it, Milburn tells managers', *Health Service Journal*, 5 July, p. 10.

Edmonstone, J. and Western, J. (2002) 'Leadership development in healthcare: what do we know?' *Journal of Management in Medicine* 16(1): 34–47.

Engeström, Y. (1987) *Learning by Expanding. An Activity Theoretical Approach to Developmental Research.* Helsinki: Orienta-Konsultit.

Engeström, Y. (1996) 'The tensions of judging: handling cases of driving under the influence of alcohol in Finland and California', in Y. Engeström and D. Middleton (eds), *Cognition and Communication at Work.* Cambridge: Cambridge University Press.

Engeström, Y., Miettinen, R. and Punamaki, R. (eds) (1999) *Perspectives on Activity Theory.* Cambridge: Cambridge University Press.

Ferlie, E., Ashburner, L., Fitzgerald, L. and Pettigrew, A. (1996) *The New Public Management in Action.* Oxford: Oxford University Press.

Fisher, D. and Rooke, D. (2000) *Personal and Organizational Transformations through Action Inquiry.* Boston: Edge/Work Press.

Fletcher, D. E. (1997) *Organisational Networking. Strategic Change and the Family Business.* Unpublished Ph.D. thesis, Nottingham Trent University.

Fletcher, D. E. (2002) 'A network perspective of cultural organising and "professional management" in the small, family business', *Journal of Small Business and Enterprise Development* 9(4): 400–15.

Foster, E. and Turner, J. (2003) *Evaluation of the Public Service Leaders Scheme.* London: Cabinet Office, available at http://www.publicserviceleadersscheme.gov. uk/documents/doc/PSLSEvaluationReport.doc (accessed 5 March 2006).

Freire, P. (1973) *Education for Critical Consciousness.* New York: Seabury Press.

Freire, P. and Shor, I. (1987) *A Pedagogy for Liberation: Dialogues on Transforming Education.* London: Macmillan.

Gilkey, R. (1999) *The Twenty First Century Healthcare Leader.* San Francisco, CA: Jossey-Bass.

Glendinning, C., Hudson, B., Hardy, B. and Young, R. (2002) *National Evaluation of Notifications for Use of the Section 31 Partnership Flexibilities in The Health Act 1999: Final Project Report.* Leeds: Nuffield Institute for Health; Manchester: National Primary Care Research and Development Centre.

Gold, J. (2002) *Towards Management and Leadership in Professions.* London: CEML.

Grant, D., Keenoy, T. and Oswick, C. (1998) *Discourse and Organization.* London: Sage.

Greener, I. (2003) 'Performance in the National Health Service: the insistence of measurement and confusion of content', *Public Performance and Management Review* 26(3): 237–50.

Gregory, M. (1994) 'Accrediting work-based learning: action learning – a model for empowerment', *Journal of Management Development* 13(4): 41.

Habermas, J. (1987) 'Lifeworld and system: a critique of functionalist reason', *Theory of Communicative Action* 2: 381–3.

Ham, C. (1999) *Health Policy in Britain.* London: Macmillan.

Hammond, S. A. (1998) *The Thin Book of Appreciative Inquiry.* Plano, TX: Thin Book Publishing Company.

Hardy, C., Lawrence, T. B. and Phillips, N. (1998) 'Talk and action: conversations and narrative in interorganizational collaboration', in D. Grant *et al.*, *Discourse and Organization.* London: Sage, pp. 65–83.

Harrison, A. and Dixon, J. (2000) *The NHS: Facing the Future.* London: King's Fund.

Harrison, O. (1997) *Open Space Technology: A User's Guide*, available at http://www. openspaceworld.org/news/world-story (accessed 15 March 2006).

Harrison, R. (1983) 'Strategies for a new age', *Human Resource Management* 22(3): 209–35.

Hartman, S. and Crow, S. (2002) 'Executive development in healthcare during times of turbulence: top management perceptions and recommendations', *Journal of Management in Medicine* 16(5): 359–70.

Hatton, N. and Smith, D. (1995) 'Reflection in teacher education: towards definition and implementation', *Teacher and Teacher Education* 11(1): 33–49.

Hawkins, P. and Chesterman, D. (2004) *Developing Leadership Capacity in Local Government: The Contribution of SOLACE and its Scheme of Continuous Learning.* London: SOLACE.

Henderson, G. M. (2002) 'Transformative learning as a condition for transformational change in organizations', *Human Resource Development Review* 1(2): 186–214.

Hergenhahn, B. R. (1988) *An Introduction to Theories of Learning.* Englewood Cliffs, NJ: Prentice Hall.

Heron, J. (1992) *Feeling and Personhood.* London: Sage.

Heron, J. (1996) *Co-operative Inquiry.* London: Sage.

Hersey, P. and Blanchard, K. (1977) *Management Organizational Behaviour: Utilising Human Resources.* Englewood Cliffs, NJ: Prentice Hall.

Hinshelwood, R. and Skogstad, W. (2000) *Observing Organizations: Anxiety, Defence and Culture in Health Care.* London: Routledge.

Hirschman, A. (1970) *Exit, Voice and Loyalty.* Cambridge, MA: Harvard University Press.

Hodgetts, R. M., Lee, S. M. and Luthans, F. (1994) 'New paradigm organizations – from total quality to learning to world-class', *Organizational Dynamics* 22(3): 5–19.

hooks, b. (1993) 'bell hooks speaking about Paulo Freire – the man, his work', in P. McLaren and P. Leonard, *Paulo Freire: A Critical Encounter.* New York: Routledge.

hooks, b. (1994) *Teaching to Transgress: Education as the Practice of Freedom.* New York: Routledge.

Hughes, M., Skelcher, C., Jas, P., Whiteman, P. and Turner, D. (2004) *Learning from the Experience of Recovery: Paths to Recovery: 2nd Annual Report.* London: Office of the Deputy Prime Minister.

Hunter, D. (1996) 'The changing roles of health care personnel in health and health care management', *Social Science and Medicine* 43(5): 799–908.

Ireland Trainers Network (2003), available at http://www.trainingvillage.gr/etv/projects_networks/LLL/prj_view.asp?TheUID=106 (accessed 10 November 2004).

James, K. (2001) *Leadership and Management Excellence: Corporate Development Strategies.* London: Council for Excellence in Management and Leadership.

Jervis, P. and Richards, S. (1997) 'Public management: raising the game', *Public Money and Management* 17(2): 9–16.

Kakabadse, N. K. and Kakabadse, A. (2003) 'Developing reflexive practitioners through collaborative inquiry: a case study of the UK civil service', *International Review of Administrative Sciences* 69(3): 365–83.

Katz, D. and Kahn, R. L. (1978) *The Social Psychology of Organizations.* New York: Wiley.

Keller, C. and Keller, J. (1993) 'Thinking and acting with iron', in S. Chaiklin and J. Lave (eds), *Understanding Practice: Perspective on Activity and Context.* Cambridge: Cambridge University Press.

Kemmis, S. (2001) 'Exploring the relevance of critical theory for action research: emancipatory action research in the footsteps of Jurgen Habermas', in P. Reason and H. Bradbury (eds), *Handbook of Action Research*. London: Sage, pp. 91–102.

Kirkpatrick, D. (1975) 'Techniques for evaluating programs', Parts 1, 2, 3 and 4 in *Evaluating Training Programs*. American Society for Training and Development.

Klein, R. (2001) *The New Politics of the NHS*. London: Longman.

Knorr Cetina, K. (1997) 'Sociality with objects. Social relations in postsocial knowledge societies', *Theory, Culture and Society* 14(4): 1–30.

Knorr Cetina, K. and Bruegger, U. (2000) 'The market as an object of attachment: exploring postsocial relations in financial markets', *Canadian Journal of Sociology* 25(2): 141–68.

Knowles, M. S. (1970) *The Modern Practice of Adult Education: Andragogy vs. Pedagogy*. New York: Association Press.

Knowles, M. S. (1984) *Andragogy in Action*. San Francisco, CA: Jossey-Bass.

Knowles, M. S., Holton, E. F. I. and Swanson, R. A. (1998) *The Adult Learner*, 5th edn. Woburn, NA: Butterworth-Heinemann.

Kolb, D. A. (1984) *Experiential Learning*. Englewood Cliffs, NJ: Prentice Hall.

Korzybski, A. (1941) *Science and Sanity: An Introduction to Non-Aristotelian Systems and General Semantics*. New York: International Non-Aristotelian Library.

Laming, H. (Chair) (2003) *The Victoria Climbié Inquiry*. London: Department of Health.

Lather, P. (1991) *Getting Smart: Feminist Research and Pedagogy With/in the Postmodern*. New York: Routledge.

Lave, J. and Wenger, E. (1991) *Situated Learning: Legitimate Peripheral Participation*. Cambridge: Cambridge University Press.

Leadbeater, Charles (1997) *The Rise of the Social Entrepreneur*. London: Demos.

Leaders UK (2005), available at http://www.leadersuk.org (accessed 5 March 2006).

Leadership Development Commission (LDC) (2004) *Towards a Leadership Strategy for Local Government*. London: Improvement and Development Agency and Employers' Organization.

Lee, M. (2003) 'The complex roots of HRD', in M. Lee, *HRD in a Complex World*. London: Routledge.

Lenderman, H., Lastar, F. and Lenderman, R. (2004) *Performance-Based Degrees Earned at Work*. Oxford: Prestoungrange University Press.

Lewis, A. (1994) 'Action learning in Prudential Assurance', *Management Bibliographies and Reviews* 20(6/7).

Lindeman, E. C. (1926) *The Meaning of Adult Education*. New York: New Republic.

Lyons, M. (2003/4) 'Do we need better public service managers or better managers for public services?' *Articulate* No. 2, University of Birmingham School of Public Policy.

McGill, I. and Beaty, L. (1995) *Action Learning*, 2nd edn. London: Kogan Page.

McKenna, J. (1992) 'Learning in adulthood', *Journal of Consumer Affairs* 26(1): 207.

MacLure, M. (1996) 'Telling transitions; boundary work in narratives of becoming an action researcher', *British Educational Research Journal* 6(1).

Mahoney, R. (1997) 'Using action learning to enhance managerial performance', in J. Cook, D. Staniforth and J. Stewart (eds) (1997) *The Learning Organization in the Public Services*. Aldershot: Gower.

Marquardt, M. J. (1998) 'Using action learning with multicultural groups', *Performance Improvement Quarterly* 11(1): 112–27.

Marquardt, M. J. (1999) *Action Learning in Action: Transforming Problems and People for World-Class Organizational Learning*. Palo Alto, CA: Davies-Black.

Marquardt, M. J. (2000) 'Action learning and leadership', *The Learning Organization* 7(5): 233–40.

Marquardt, M. J. (2003) 'Developing global leaders via action learning programs: a case study at Boeing', *Thai Journal of Public Administration* 3(3): 133–57.

Marquardt, M. J. (2004) *Optimizing the Power of Action Learning*. Palo Alto, CA: Davies-Black.

Marquardt, M. J. and Berger, N. O. (2000) *Global Leaders for the 21st Century*. Albany, NY: State University of New York Press.

Marsick, V. J. (1992) 'Experiential-based executive learning outside the classroom', *Journal of Management Development* 9(5): 50–60.

Marsick, V. J. and O'Neil, J. (1999) 'The many faces of action learning', *Management Learning* 30(2): 159–76.

Marsick, V. J., Cederholm, L., Turner, E. and Pearson, T. (1992) 'Action-reflection learning', *Training and Development* 46(8): 63–6.

Mead, G. (1988) 'Organization culture', *Federal Bureau of Investigation Management Quarterly* 8(4): 1–5.

Mead, G. (1990) 'The challenge of police leadership: the contribution of the special course', *Management Education and Development* 21(5): 406–14.

Mead, G. (1995) 'Millennium management for a new age police service', *Policing Today* 1(5): 4–7.

Mead, G. (2002) 'Developing ourselves as police leaders: how can we inquire collaboratively in a hierarchical organization?', *Systemic Practice and Action Research* 15(3): 191–206.

Mellahi, K., Jackson, P. and Sparks, L. (2002) 'An exploratory study into failure in successful organizations: the case of Marks and Spencer', *British Journal of Management* 13: 15–29.

Menzies, I. (1959) 'A case-study in the functioning of social systems as a defence against anxiety: a report on a study of the nursing service of a general hospital', *Human Relations* 13: 95–121.

Merriam, S. B. and Caffarella, R. S. (1999) *Learning in Adulthood*, 2nd edn. San Francisco, CA: Jossey-Bass.

Meyerson, D. E. and Scully, M. A. (1995) 'Tempered radicalism and the politics of ambivalence and courage', *Organization Science* 6(5): 585–600.

Mezirow, J. (1991) *Transformative Dimensions of Adult Learning*. San Francisco, CA: Jossey-Bass.

Mintzberg, H. (1993) *Structure in Fives: Designing Effective Organizations*. London: Prentice Hall.

Mintzberg, H. (1994) *The Rise and Fall of Strategic Planning*. London: Prentice Hall.

Morgan, Gareth (1990) 'Paradigm diversity in organizational research', in John Hassard and Denis Pym (eds) *The Theory and Philosophy of Organizations*. London: Routledge.

Mumford, A. (1991) 'Learning in action', *Personnel Management* 23(7): 34–40.

Mumford, A. (1995) 'Managers developing others through action learning', *Industrial and Commercial Training* 27(2): 19.

Murphy, K. and Cifuentes, L. (2001) 'Using web tools, collaborating, and learning online', *Distance Education* 22(2): 285–305.

National College for School Leadership (2005), available at (www.ncsl.org.uk/the_college/college-publications-ldf-framework.cfm) (accessed 1 August 2005).

National Health Service Institute for Innovation and Improvement (2005), available at http://www.institute.nhs.uk/ (accessed 1 August 2005).

Nelson, H. (1994) 'The necessity of being "undisciplined" and "out-of-control": design action and systems thinking', *Performance Improvement Quarterly* special issue 7(3).

Newman, J. E. (2001) *Modernising Governance: New Labour, Policy and Society*. London: Sage.

NHS Modernization Agency (2004), available at http://www.modern.nhs.uk/home/default.asp?site_id=58&id=1115 (accessed 19 November 2004).

Omolade, B. (1987) 'A black feminist pedagogy', *Women's Studies Quarterly* 15(3–4).

O'Neil, J. A. (1999) *The Role of the Learning Advisor in Action Learning, Adult Education and Continuing Education*. New York: Columbia University Teachers College.

Ormond, J. (1999) *Human Learning*. Upper Saddle River, NJ: Prentice Hall.

Palus, C. A. and Drath, W. H. (1995) *Evolving Leaders: A Model for Promoting Leadership Development in Programs*. Greensboro, NC: Center for Creative Leadership.

Papadopoulos, R. (1999) 'Storied community as secure base: response to the paper by Nancy Caro Hollander "Exile: Paradoxes of loss and creativity"', *British Journal of Psychotherapy* 15(3): 322–32.

Peck, E., Gulliver, P. and Towell, D. (2002) *Modernising Partnerships: An Evaluation of Somerset's Innovations in the Commissioning and Organization of Mental Health Services*. London: IAHSP, King's College.

Pedler, M. (1981) 'Developing the learning community', in T. Boydell and M. Pedler (eds), *Management Self-Development: Concepts and Practices*. Farnborough: Gower, pp. 68–84.

Pedler, M. (1996) *Action Learning for Managers*. London: Lemos and Crane.

Pedler, M. (ed.) (1997) *Action Learning in Practice*. London: Gower.

Pedler, M., Burgoyne, J. and Brook, C. (2005) 'What has action learning learned to become?' *Action Learning: Research and Practice* 2(1): 49–68.

Performance Improvement Unit (2001) *Strengthening Leadership in the Public Sector*. Cabinet Office Strategy Unit, available at http://www.number-10.gov.uk/su/leadership/default.htm (accessed 5 March 2006).

Perren, L. and Burgoyne, J. (2002) *Management and Leadership Abilities: An Analysis of Texts, Testimonies and Practice*. London: CEML.

Peryer, D. (2002) *Social Care Leadership Development Initiative: Social Services Top Managers Programme 2002–03*. London: SCLDI.

Pettigrew, A., Ferlie, E. and McKee, L. (1992) *Shaping Strategic Change*. London: Sage.

Police Leadership Centre (2005), available at http://www.centrex.police.uk/nplc (accessed 1 August 2005).

Power, M. (1994) *The Audit Explosion*. London: Demos.

Raelin, J. (1999) 'Preface', *Management Learning* 30: 115–25.

Raelin, J. (2000) *Work-Based Learning: The New Frontier of Management Development*. Upper Saddle River, NJ: Prentice Hall.

Raudenbush, L., Marquardt, M. and Walls, T. (2003) 'Growing leaders at the US Department of Agriculture: a case study of leadership development using action learning', Proceedings of the Conference of the Academy of Human Resources Development, Minneapolis.

Reason, P. (ed.) (1988) *Human Inquiry in Action*. London: Sage.

Reason, P. (ed.) (1994) *Participation in Human Inquiry*. London: Sage.

Reason, P. (2006) 'Choice and quality in action research practice', forthcoming in *Journal of Management Inquiry*.

Reason, P. and Bradbury, H. (2001) *Handbook of Action Research*. London: Sage.

Reason, P. and Heron, J. (1999) *A Layperson's Guide to Co-operative Inquiry: What is Co-operative Inquiry?*, available at http://www.bath.ac.uk/carpp/layguide.htm (accessed 7 March 2006).

Reason, P. and Rowan, J. (eds) (1981) *Human Inquiry*. Chichester: Wiley.

Reed, Michael I. (1992) *The Sociology of Organizations*. Hemel Hempstead: Harvester Wheatsheaf.

Revans, R. W. (1980) *Action Learning: New Techniques for Management*. London: Blond and Briggs.

Revans, R. W. (1982) *Action Learning: Its Origins and Growth*. Bromley: Chartwell-Bratt.

Revans, R. W. (1983) *The ABC of Action Learning*. Bromley: Chartwell-Bratt.

Revans, R. W. (1988) *The Golden Jubilee of Action Learning: A Collection of Papers Written during 1988*. Manchester: Manchester Action Learning Exchange.

Revans, R. (1997) 'Action learning: its origins and application', in M. Pedler (ed.), *What is Action Learning?* London: Gower.

Revans, R. W. (1998) *The ABC of Action Learning*. London: Lemos and Crane.

Reynolds, M. (1998) 'Critical reflection and management education: rehabilitating less hierarchical approaches', *Journal of Management Education* 23(5): 537–53.

Reynolds, M. and Trehan, K. (2001) 'Classroom as real world: propositions for a pedagogy of difference', *Gender and Education* 15: 357–72.

Reynolds, M. and Trehan, K. (2003) 'Learning from difference?' *Management Learning* 34(2): 163–80.

Richards, S. (2001) *Four Types of Joined Up Government and the Problem of Accountability*. London: National Audit Office.

Rigg, C. (2005) 'Becoming critical – can critical management learning develop critical managers?', in C. Elliott and S. Turnbull (eds), *Critical HRD*. London: Routledge.

Rigg, C. and Dalziel, R. (2005) 'What space for constructionist evaluation in a consultancy context?', in Sixth International Conference on HRD Research and Practice Across Europe – 'Human Resource Development: Addressing the Value', Leeds, 25–27 May.

Rigg, C. and Trehan, K. (1999) 'Black women raise challenges for critical action learning', *Gender and Education* 11(3): 265–80.

Rigg, C. and Trehan, K. (2004) 'Reflections on working with critical action learning', *Action Learning* 1(2): 149–65.

Rogers, C. and Freiberg, H. J. (1994) *Freedom to Learn*. New York: Macmillan College Publishing Company.

Rossett, A. (1999) 'Action learning in action: transforming problems and people for world-class organizational learning', *Personnel Psychology* 52(4): 1100.

Rotter, J. B. (1992) 'Cognates of personal control: locus of control, self-efficacy, and explanatory style: comment', *Applied and Preventive Psychology* 1(2): 127–9.

Salopek, J. J. (1999) 'Action learning in action: transforming problems and people for world-class organizational learning', *Training and Development Journal* 53(4): 58.

Schön, D. (1983) *The Reflective Practitioner*. New York: Basic Books.

Social Care Leadership Development Initiative (SCLDI) (2004) 'Some Key Requirements for Effective Work on Partnership', notes from the SCLDI Review Meeting, November 2004.

Searles, H. (1955) 'The informational value of the supervisor's emotional experience', *Psychiatry* 18: 135–46.

Secretary of State for Health (2005) *Independence, Well-Being and Choice: Our Vision for the Future of Social Care for Adults in England*, Cm 6499. Norwich: TSO.

Sedley, S. (Chair) (1987) *Whose Child?* The report of the panel appointed to inquire into the death of Tyra Henry. London: London Borough of Lambeth.

Senge, P. (1993) *The Fifth Discipline: The Art and Practice of the Learning Organization*. London: Century Business.

Skinner, B. F. (1976) *About Behaviorism*. New York: Vintage.

Social Exclusion Unit (SEU) (2000) *Report of Policy Action Team 16: Learning Lessons*. London: SEU.

Storm, H. (1972) *Seven Arrows*. New York: Ballantine Books.

Strong, P. and Robinson, J. (1990) *The NHS under New Management*. Milton Keynes: Open University Press.

Sullivan, H. and Skelcher, C. (2002) *Working Across Boundaries*. London: Macmillan.

Swanson, R. A. and Holton, E. (2001) *Foundations of Human Resource Development*. San Francisco, CA: Berrett-Koehler.

Timmins, N. (1999) *The Five Giants: A Biography of the Welfare State*. London: Fontana Press.

Torbert, B. (2004) *Action Inquiry: The Secret of Timely and Transforming Leadership*. San Francisco, CA: Berret Koehler.

Torbert, W. R. (1991) *The Power of Balance*. Newbury Park, CA: Sage.

Torbert, W. R. (1999) 'The distinctive questions developmental action inquiry asks', *Management Learning* 30: 189–206.

Torbert, W. R. (2001) 'The practice of action inquiry', in R. Reason and H. Bradbury (eds), *Handbook of Action Research*. London: Sage, pp. 250–60.

Training Village (2003), available at http://www.trainingvillage.gr/etv/Projects_Networks/ttnet/publications/Topic_view.asp?theID=40andcatid=13andacronym=dk (accessed 7 March 2006).

Van Wart, M. (2003) 'Public-sector leadership theory: an assessment', *Public Administration Review* 63(2): 214–28.

Vasilyuk, E. (1991) *The Psychology of Experiencing: The Resolution of Life's Critical Situations*. Hemel Hempstead: Harvester Wheatsheaf.

Vince, R. (1996) 'Experiential management education as the practice of change', in R. French and C. Grey, *Rethinking Management Education*. London: Sage.

Vince, R. (2004a) 'Action learning and organizational learning: power, politics and emotions in organizations', *Action Learning* 1(1): 63–78.

Vince, R. (2004b) *Rethinking Strategic Learning*. London: Routledge.

Waddill, D. (2005) 'Action e-learning: the impact of action learning on the effectiveness of a management-level web-based instruction course', paper presented at the AHRD 2005 International Research Conference, Estes Park, Colorado.

Waddill, D. and Marquardt, M. J. (2003) 'Adult learning orientations and action learning', *Human Resource Development Review* 2(4): 406–29.

Walshe, K. and Smith, J. (2001) 'NHS reorganization: cause and effect', *Health Service Journal*, 11 October, pp. 20–3.

Weick, K. (1979) *The Social Psychology of Organizing*, 2nd edn. London: Addison-Wesley.

Weick, K. E. (1995) *Sensemaking in Organizations*. Thousand Oaks, CA: Sage.

Weil, S. W. and McGill, I. (1989) *Making Sense of Experiential Learning*. Milton Keynes: Open University Press.

Weiland, G. F. and Leigh, H. (eds) (1971) *Changing Hospitals*. London: Tavistock.

Weinstein, K. (1994) 'Experiences of action learning: a dialogue with participants', *Management Bibliographies and Reviews* 20(6/7).

Weinstein, K. (1995) *Action Learning: A Journey in Discovery and Development*. London: HarperCollins.

Wenger, E. C., McDermott, R. and Snyder, W. M. (2002) *Cultivating Communities of Practice*. Boston, MA: Harvard Business School Press.

Wertsch, J. (1979) *The Concept of Activity in Soviet Psychology*. Armonck, NY: M. E. Sharpe.

Whitehead, J. (1993) *The Growth of Educational Knowledge: Creating Your Own Living Educational Theories*. Bournemouth: Hyde Publications.

Wistow, G., Hardy, B., Henwood, N. and Hudson, B. (1998) *Inter-agency Collaboration: Final Report*, update issue 6. University of Leeds, Nuffield Institute for Health.

Woodilla, J. (1998) 'Workplace conversations: the text of organizing', in D. Grant *et al.* (eds) *Discourse and Organization*. London: Sage.

World Bank (2005), available at http://lnweb18.worldbank.org/ESSD/sdvext.nsf/60ByDocName/SocialDevelopment (accessed 7 March 2006).

Yolles, M. and Iles, P. (2003) in M. Lee, *HRD in a Complex World*. London: Routledge.

Yorks, L., O'Neil, J. and Marsick, V. J. (1999) *Action Learning: Successful Strategies for Individual, Team, and Organizational Development*. San Francisco, CA: Berrett-Koehler.

Index

References to tables and figures are in **bold**.

(0)1264 343070

Gratis

‹LER
:ter
NOLOGY DEPT

IN CASE OF QUERY PLEASE QUOTE.

Account Number	M010113878 R
Document Number	5000566Y SR
Document Date	15SEP06
Document Type	Gratis
Payment to be Received By	Payment due 15-SEP-06

VAT No. GB365462636

LETTER 2ND CLASS

Total Quantity -   1

CLR H

	Price	Disc%	Net Value	Desp Value	Tax	Total Value
G & RI	70.00					

Gratis - Payment not required

		Total Net Value	Total Desp Val	Tax Total	TOTAL

Terms and Conditions of Supply are available on request

eceipt of Invoice

10113878   **Invoice Number - 5000566Y SR**   **Amount GBP**

TERCARD / VISA / AMEX or SWITCH)   ISSUE NO

not required

nt £   Signature

10 5BE   an **informa** business

Taylor & Francis
Taylor & Francis Group
P O Box 6329 , Basingstoke , RG24 8DR

For a full list of Taylor & Francis imprints please visit o
www.tandf.co.uk
Customer Service Contacts: UK Trade - 01264 342926 , Internat
Direct Sales - 01264 343071 , Fax: 01264 343005
Account Contacts: 01256 813000 , Fax : 01256 354663

INVOICE TO

DELIVER TO M01011387

University of Lancaster
ORG WORK & TECHNOLOGY DEPT
Management School
Bailrigg
LANCASTER
LA1 4YX

Prof. FRA
University
ORG WOF
Managem
Bailrigg
LANCAST
LA1 4YX

72QL5C
Shipper -

Line	Order Reference	Product ID	QTY	Title / Author Details
1	T SUTTON	9780415372701 0415372704	1	COMPLIMENTARY COPIES - FREE ACTION LEARNING LEADERSHIP P

Order Lines - 1	Net Weight - 0.643	Total Quantity - 1
OP JOM Batch 55799 /011	Document Type - GRC	Entered Date 15SEP06
Despatch Method - LETTER 2ND CLASS		Site - Andover - T&F

All claims for shortages and damages must be made within 14 da

PAYMENT METHODS (Please ensure you quote your account number.)   **Account N**

CREDIT or CHARGE

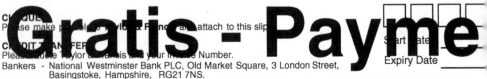

CHEQUE
Please make payable to Taylor & Francis and attach to this slip
CREDIT TRANSFER
Please quote Taylor & Francis and your Invoice Number.
Bankers - National Westminster Bank PLC, Old Market Square, 3 London Street,
Basingstoke, Hampshire, RG21 7NS.
STERLING Sort Code: 60-02-49 , Account Number: 80772048, IBAN number : GB88 NWBK 6002 4980 7720 48

Start Date
Expiry Date

Please send your payment to - Taylor & Francis, P O Box 6329, Basingstoke, Hampshire, RG24 8DR, UK.
All Orders,Claims and Returns should be addressed to - Thomson Publishing Services, Cheriton House, North Way, An